Edition:
4 3 2 1
2015 2014 2013 2012

HAYMON tb **127**

Haymon Taschenbuch, Innsbruck-Wien 2012
www.haymonverlag.at/haymontb

ISBN 978-3-85218-927-7

Graphical presentation of cover and text:
hoeretzeder grafische gestaltung, Scheffau/Tirol
Cover picture: IMAGNO/Austrian Archives
(Newspaper wood engraving based on an 1890 drawing by Theo Zasche)
Author photo: Amalthea
English translation: Jeffrey McCabe

Printed on eco-friendly,
chlorine- and acid-free paper.

Martina Winkelhofer

The Everyday Life of the Emperor

Francis Joseph and his Imperial Court

Translated from the German
by Jeffrey McCabe

Martina Winkelhofer

The Everyday Life of the Emperor

Table of contents

Foreword

This book aims to tell a tale from history: the history of a community bound together by fate, comprising approximately 1,500 to 2,000 people ranging from His Majesty by the Grace of God all the way down to the lowliest servant, which was unique in European tradition. During my work in the archives, which form the basis of all historic research, the question of 'how' was the unflagging point of departure and remained the guideline throughout the writing: How did people actually live inside the walls of the Viennese court? What was expected of them? How was the overall enterprise organised and managed (which nowadays would be considered a corporation)? How was this oldest of all European courts financed?

Today, no one knows much of anything about the court under Emperor Francis Joseph, its structure, its daily agendas and processes, or about the human beings who lived and worked with the emperor and were the closest witnesses of the longest reigning emperor in the history of Austria. It sometimes seems as if there were nothing which could still be told about the smallest city inside the capital of the empire and imperial residence of Vienna. No memoirs were left behind, neither by members of the imperial family, nor by employees; there exist no photographs portraying daily life at court. And most of all, the oral tradition of handing down knowledge and experiences – the only thing which made it possible to run a court to begin with – completely disappeared after 1918. Centuries of familiarity with the processes and organisation of a court, passed down from generation to generation, sank together with the monarchy itself into oblivion. Those people who were born into the court or learned their trade or profession under its aegis would have been able to tell elaborate tales, but were never asked; and in the 21st century, they are long dead.

At the Vienna Archives, however, the historical memory of the court and its inhabitants yet dwells, its heart still beats. Distributed through more than three and a half thousand cartons, not only the entire history of the imperial court under Francis Joseph slumbers, from the files of the chancellery to the protocols of the ceremonies, but also the stories of the human beings who form part of the overall complex. Each single file, as dry as it might appear at first glance, the greater part of them opened by the author for the first time since the monarchy came to an end, tells its own little story: about highly proper court officials who recorded the file to begin with; about the wheels of court administration; about the problems of communication; about awards and warnings from higher echelons. Yet the files also include touching personal details, revealing the worries and problems of people in a long past epoch: requests and petitions to the emperor for help in emergencies, hopes and concerns in providing for children at court, ambitions to be promoted or make a career at court. Even the downfall of the court, the dissolution of a 600-year old institution and the termination of an unspoken yet omnipresent pact between the ruler and his household community was recorded in minute detail and displays upon examination how those people who lived in the immediate vicinity of the emperor experienced the change of governmental systems.

Significant source materials bearing witness to the era have also survived in a variety of private archives. In stark contrast to the prosaic, dry files of court, views of court life from an utterly personal perspective through the eyes of those who worked and lived with and around the emperor, often in positions of high authority, are provided from such sources.

Only by combining and connecting the court sources of the administration and the personal memoirs of contemporaries of the emperor does it become possible to put together a comprehensive, multi-faceted and complete picture of life at the imperial court.

A closer look at the court also brings to light hidden aspects of the historic personality of Emperor Francis Joseph, providing a number of surprising discoveries. How did the emperor deal with the weakest links of the human chain at court? What was his view of the cultural responsibilities of the court? What did he expect of the uppermost ranks of court society, the elite? How did he navigate the court household through the turbulent and volatile periods of a regency which lasted 68 years?

A scientific, historic investigation of the relationship between emperor and court unveils a completely different picture of Emperor Francis Joseph, far different from the uncontested clichées depicting a stubborn and rigid ruler. It reveals how Francis Joseph reacted to political and social cataclysms, what novel strategies a ruler had to devise to navigate the transition of Austria from an absolutist state to a constitutional one, what instruments of power were torn from his hands and what techniques he devised to replace them; as well as the difficulties which arose when a ruler who embodied tradition and continuity was suddenly thrust into a new era in political, social and personal ways.

Last but not least, this history of the court of Emperor Francis Joseph, written just under one hundred years after the end of the monarchy, also provides the launch of a re-evaluation of Austria's longest serving ruler himself.

Vienna, October 2008

I
A Day in the Life of the Old Emperor

Emperor Francis Joseph was awakened by his First Valet every morning at 3:30 am. Following his morning prayers, a rubber bathtub was dragged into the room and His Majesty's First Bath Attendant – tauntingly called 'Washcloth' by the courtiers – began his daily period of service. His undemanding duties consisted of soaping up the emperor and rinsing him off. His task was made more difficult by the fact that he invariably came to work inebriated. Often reprimanded by his superior, Washcloth invariably protested that he was the victim of his early hour of service. He had to start the day so early that he couldn't get out of bed; so he simply didn't go to bed, and stayed up all night at a local inn. And in order to keep awake until 3:30, he treated himself to a glass or two of wine. That was the sole cause for his staggering to work each day, redolent with alcohol, to perform his duties.

The emperor was always lenient with Washcloth. Occasionally, Francis Joseph remarked that the bath attendant really did reek of alcohol, but was always reluctant to fire him. It was not until Washcloth one time appeared for work so drunk that he couldn't even stand up straight, and had to hold himself upright by grabbing onto the neck and shoulders of the soaped-up emperor with all his strength to keep from toppling over, thereby nearly overturning emperor and bathtub alike, that the limits of patience were exceeded. The bath attendant had to be relieved of his arduous duties. However, he was not dismissed, merely transferred to a different court job which did not entail getting up so early in the morning.

The story of Emperor Francis Joseph and his bath attendant is symptomatic of the relations between the emperor and those in his employ at court. Francis Joseph was indulgent, he shied away from harsh penalties and above all refused to dismiss servants, much to the despair of his leading officials. He lived utterly in the aura and unspoken terms of patriarchal traditions of providing for those beneath him, seeing himself as father of his court servants.

They were his children whom he had to take care of. They were not to be dismissed, even if they performed their duties poorly.

After his bath, valet Eugen Ketterl helped the emperor put on his uniform. Then followed breakfast: the identical breakfast served to officials and servants was brought to him at his desk. Apart from coffee and milk, he had breakfast rolls, butter and ham. And in the meantime, the court slowly lumbered to life. By 5:00 am at latest, a buzz of activity filled the halls of the court of Vienna. The first coaches delivered firewood, groceries and stationery needs for the officials. The wood carriers wheezed beneath the burdens of their bundles, trudging up and down every staircase of the Hofburg to supply each living and working section with the requisite fuel to last through the day. The cleaning staff ran back and forth across the inner yard carrying buckets full of water to commence the daily cleaning labours. In the court kitchen, more than 500 breakfasts were prepared, since only those servants who began their period of duty at 4:30 am had already had breakfast. The huge ovens in the court kitchen were fired up and the kitchen staff began to wash, scrub and slice the ingredients for the day's pre-planned menu. As on every other day, hundreds of breakfasts, lunches and suppers had to be prepared. Throngs of livery servants, doormen and chamber servants scampered across the inner courtyards to their respective places of work, while night watchmen and supervisory staff retired to their rooms after a long night of service to finally rest their weary heads.

By 7:30 am, the entire court was awake and humming. The court officials started their shift. They bade their wives farewell, left their court apartments impeccably dressed in the official uniforms of which they were so proud, clearly distinguishing each official from simple servants, and went to the court chancellery and office chambers. Another day of studying files, reports and correspondence began anew.

When the officials took their place at their desks, the emperor already had three and a half hours of work behind him. Francis Joseph began his work with the first labourers who appeared at court and didn't terminate it until the last shift of servants had retired to their quarters. In the interim, life at court ran like a strictly regulated precision clock, day in and day out. It was a mechanism which employed more than 1,500 people, each with his or her own specific working place and list of tasks, trimmed to each individual yet intertwined in many ways. Not even large-scale ceremonial events like court balls or state visits could disturb or impede the perfect operations. The microcosm of the court was based, after all, on 600 years of experience.

Visitors walking through the courtyards of the imperial residence nowadays feel an aura of cool serenity. The windows are closed and one assumes that there is not much going on behind the walls, with the possible exception of the gala rooms of state. The attic abodes appear to have been unlived in for a century. Nothing about this tranquil, stately silence at the Hofburg recalls the bustling little city within the city of Vienna which once thrived. In Emperor Francis Joseph's day, the court radiated the hustle and bustle of a beehive. The residence was crammed to the roof with people. Whoever worked at court also lived there. All the living units in the vast tracts, from the cellar rooms to the attic lodgings, were occupied. Depending on one's societal rank, court ladies, officials and servants residing in the countless apartments spent not only their working days but also their entire lives at court. People were born here, worked here, served their emperor here and died here. For generations of employees, court was not only the lustrous center of the Habsburg Empire, it was also space to live in, one's home and place of origin. A majority of the officials and servants lived with their entire family in the innumerable apartments; sometimes married couples and their children lived no more than a few hundred meters distant from the imperial family, all of them under the selfsame roof. A greater degree of social intermingling could not be found anywhere in the empire.

The Hofburg was a bubbling, animated bit of territory and not at all cut off from the real world, even back then. The gates of the court gardens were not ever locked. On the contrary, they opened the way to passages and paths through the imperial grounds. Every child knew which windows the emperor worked behind, and behind which windows he slept. Whoever walked through the palace grounds during the day invariably encountered an immense buzz of activity. Officials ran back and forth from one office to another with files under their arms. Livery servants rushed about, carrying buckets of water or trays across the yards. Coaches stopped and started. Delivery wagons drove up, blocking the way, prompting enraged, fist-shaking responses of passers-by and valet coaches alike. The entire spectrum of society came and went, day after day. The prime minister and his cabinet drove up once weekly, the imperial suppliers of goods came daily. Aristocratic gentlemen cantered on horseback across the palace grounds each day on their way to the racing grounds in Prater. The nannies of the rich citizens pushed their prams through the court gardens. The maidservants and hired hands of neighbouring palaces bore their groceries from the Naschmarkt or fish market stalls across the grounds on their way back to their employers.

In the epicentre of all this humming activity beat the heart of the empire. Emperor Francis Joseph personally held the reins of an empire comprising 50 million people in his hands. The court was not only his own representational stage setting, for official state receptions of new ambassadors or affairs of state in the gala halls of the Hofburg, it was also his living quarters and home. Regardless whether the emperor was in residence at the Hofburg, at Schönbrunn Palace or in Budapest, the imperial court was wherever he was. The miniature universe of the imperial court was simply unimaginable without the person of Francis Joseph. And yet, the emperor could not form, could not hold together that court without the human beings who were the backbone of its operations. Francis Joseph and his officials and servants were bonded inexorably to one another: they lived together, they interspersed and intermingled, and although they hailed from vastly different social backgrounds, they remained intimately tied to each other. The autonomy of the court was demonstrated not least by the loyalty of its members. Its officials were servants of the emperor, not of the state, even though *de jure* the emperor held sway over this court only as head of state. Every right and every guarantee of a safe and secure life for employees at court stemmed solely from the person of Francis Joseph. He alone guaranteed compliance with the centuries-old privileges of court officials. As long as the emperor remained in place, the work and security of every person employed there was assured.

After he finished breakfast, Emperor Francis Joseph rang for his adjutant, Count Heinrich Hoyos, who sat poised for action at his desk in the charge office adjacent to the imperial apartments, impeccably outfitted in full uniform as of 3:00 am each and every day. It was his habit to lay his head in his folded hands and try desperately to get a bit of sleep until the moment when he was called. As soon as the imperial bell rang, he sprang still half asleep to his feet, quickly combed his hair, grabbed his briefcase and rushed to the emperor. Adjutants began their shift when even the emperor himself was still sound asleep. As honourable as the position was, it was unspeakably hard for most of them to begin their working day that early. In the darkness of night, they stumbled to their offices, bumping into no one except sleepy-eyed doormen and guards, and waited until their master called for them. The first half-year of service was always the hardest. Count Hoyos, who attended to the emperor in later years, each day wrote a letter to his wife in which he complained of the punishing tiredness and the torture of getting up every single day at 2:30 am and waiting in an ice-cold office, long before the servants assigned to heat the rooms were awake.

It was a tradition that the adjutants, who fluctuated between three and six in number, performed their services for the monarch in cyclical rotation. Those ambitious individuals thought to be suitable for such work were selected from the various branches of military service and presented to the emperor for his final, personal selection. After Francis Joseph decided on four men to fill the position, they entered service for a period of two or three years, more or less at the emperor's side uninterruptedly for that time. The adjutants were not only the constant escorts of the emperor, they were also responsible for the unending flow of files and reports between emperor and war ministry. When the emperor rang, the adjutant on duty brought the dispatch case with the latest papers and reports sent from the war office the evening before to the monarch. The adjutant then picked up the completed papers from Francis Joseph and dispatched them to the ministry.

Thereafter, the adjutant resumed his place at his desk, examined the list of visitors scheduled for that day and waited for the first to arrive. In most cases, the leadoff visitor on the agenda was the imperial doctor who came to talk to his master first thing each morning. Since the emperor enjoyed sound physical health, a short chat usually took the place of an examination.

Following the doctor, the first adjutant general appeared: Count Eduard Paar, who had served his emperor for decades. He was the immediate superior officer of the adjutant escorts, but apart from that was the personal confidential advisor of the emperor. As active general, he still worked for the war office, thus, on paper was not a member of the court; nonetheless he was in integral part of the daily life of the emperor and of his court. Although Count Paar had no readily discernible responsibilities, except for the smooth and precise functioning of the adjutants, the emperor refused to dispense with his daily visits.

Count Paar possessed a serene, well balanced personality. He accompanied the emperor on all his trips, on his daily coach rides and to all festivities. Francis Joseph was the axis of his life, he grew old alongside his emperor and gradually became a fatherly confidante of the younger officers at court. He was one of the very few at court about whom his contemporaries had not a single bad thing to say. He was always calm, lenient in his judgments, radiated a stoic serenity and remained utterly impartial even with the emperor. He was known to go about his business whistling quietly to himself, something generally prohibited in the vicinity of the emperor, but tolerated by Francis Joseph. Such was the emperor's longstanding closeness to Paar that he didn't even take note of it. As a further proof of indulgence, the adjutant general also smoked quite heavily while with the emperor; he was notorious for creating a cloud of smoke on their train trips, often so thick that the servants entering the train compartment couldn't distinguish between the emperor and the adjutant. It disturbed the emperor not a whit. As long as he didn't have to go without the presence of old Paar, neither whistling nor pipe smoking were a problem. Paar's daily visit to the emperor was invariably short. Immediately thereafter, the Chancellor of the Exchequer appeared. Prince Alfred Montenuovo entered the imperial apartment in his uniform dangling with medals and ribbons.

The Chancellor (*Obersthofmeister*) was the pre-eminent personality at court who directed all its operations. He was master of the ceremonies, organising all external entries and appearances of the emperor, and his top ranking manager. He supervised everything, with a power of observation which missed nothing, court expenses, governed the entire staff, was in charge of security at court and was the only person allowed to stand in for the person of the emperor. Only descendants of princely families were permitted to assume this mantle, which gave its bearer the pre-eminent office at court. Every aristocrat in the monarchy had to follow in his wake in the retinue accompanying the emperor. Any lesser ranking dynastic personality would have hopelessly roiled the hierarchical status system, and Emperor Francis Joseph liked nothing less than unnecessarily complicating tried-and-tested systems.

Prince Montenuovo conferred with Francis Joseph only for a short time, since he didn't have to review all the points on the daily agenda at the morning audience. He, and he alone, had the right to enter the imperial apartments unannounced. Whenever he wished to confer with the emperor, he simply appeared before the Doorman of the Chamber, something no one except Francis Joseph's closest family was permitted to do (and even they didn't dare to exercise that privilege except in emergencies). In practice, the emperor's family usually asked Montenuovo whether or not they might come and see the emperor.

Chancellor Montenuovo was the fourth person to perform the duties of that office under Francis Joseph, something attributable to the very long life and reign the emperor enjoyed, since it was an appointment for life. The emperor outlived three earlier chancellors, even though two of them were younger than he was. In the course of a reign lasting 68 years, Francis Joseph outlived most of his court officials. He accustomed himself to new personnel quickly, but the loss of certain of them weighed heavily on him. His first Chancellor, Prince Karl Liechtenstein, had to go into retirement more than 50 years earlier. Liechtenstein was the most fatherly chancellor. He scored no crowning achievements during his period of office, but is considered to have been an important conciliatory figure, striking a balance between the requirements of the menial court servants and the severe rigours of thrift which the court demanded.

His successor, Prince Konstantin zu Hohenlohe-Schillingsfürst, was easily the most notable figure in the office of Lord Chancellor. No one knew just why the emperor chose this small adjutant who had no experience in court and was, apart from that, not even Austrian, but a German aristocrat; it seemed an ironic choice to make a German the top man at court immediately after the Austrian defeat by Prussia. Was the emperor trying to send a political signal? Under pressure from Prussia, Austria had been ousted from the German Confederation after Königgrätz. One of the most boisterous Prussians voting Austria out was Hohenlohe's brother, who was President of Bavaria at the time. Whether the emperor wished to demonstrate that he still considered himself embedded in the traditions of the Holy Roman Empire of the German Nation, in spite of everything, or simply followed his instincts in selecting someone of such extraordinary abilities as Hohenlohe, the new chancellor was a good catch for the imperial court and for the entire era of Emperor Francis Joseph.

Hohenlohe led the court into a brand new era. He modernised it, placed it on a sound financial footing and broke with outdated, anachronistic traditions. Whoever wished to make a career at court under his directorship had to do good work, and a lot of it. Venerable, decorated officials who showed little aptitude and less ardour were sent into retirement or simply skipped over when they were scheduled for promotions. In their place, he hired and advanced simple but well educated and industrious citizens at court. Under Hohenlohe, even farmer's sons were able to work their way into key positions at court, for the first time in history. He combed the aristocratic families he was befriended with, such as Schwarzenberg, Liechtenstein or Wilczek, for young candidates who had enjoyed an outstanding education based on their intrinsic abilities (and whose parents often still worked in the fields) for the court chancellery. He brought a lot of fresh blood to court functions, introducing a meritocracy to replace traditional family connections. In other ways, too, Hohenlohe carried out his programme and his ideals without compromise: his agenda of thrift brooked no excuses, and all the complaints of courtiers, officials and servants which crossed his desk on the way to the emperor left him utterly unmoved. He did not desire to be loved, but rather to turn the ship of state into an economically viable operation.

Hohenlohe was the primary support of the emperor for more than 30 years. Francis Joseph trusted him unhesitatingly. He gave him the sole responsibility for composing the tenders and ultimately, signing the contracts for the great buildings along the new Ringstrasse. He left the most important court appointments in his hands, from the director of the Burgtheater all the way to the head accountant for the imperial family's private fund. Hohenlohe's greatest achievement, overshadowing all the administrative tasks, was after the tragedy of Mayerling: not one word leaked outside the court precincts, no gritty or pathetic stories were fed to the newspapers. Whatever stories were spread about Mayerling while Francis Joseph was still alive did not have their source at court. The emperor lavished favour on Hohenlohe, decorated him repeatedly and was utterly shocked when Hohenlohe's life-threatening heart disease forced him to hand on his duties to his chosen successor.

Chancellor Hohenlohe's grave illness and death which followed shortly after his withdrawal plunged the court into a crisis. It soon became evident just how relentlessly he had held all the reins in his hands. Criticism of corruption soon flowed: in the financial office of court, which was responsible for all the luxurious purchases, cries of waste and mismanagement were presently heard. The First Chef (*Oberstküchenmeister*), Count Wolkenstein, was fired; and the shame which covered him was so great that he hanged himself. Scandal reigned. The fact that a respected court official committed suicide due to accusations of corruption was something that had never happened before. Even among the directors of the imperial theater, morale plummeted rapidly; the General Artistic Director was convicted of criminal assault in a litigated case, the rumours of corruption and nepotism in assigning stage roles were rampant, and many other departments of court life bubbled with dissatisfaction and influence trafficking. The interregnum went on for too long, every department suffered from the loss of Hohenlohe's strong and steady hand.

His successor, Prince Rudolf Liechtenstein, slowly managed to straighten out the corruption, with the assistance of Hohenlohe's trusted appointments, but the heyday of precision and correctness at court was over. The appointment of Liechtenstein was an act of pure friendship on the part of the emperor. "Handsome Rudi" was a favourite of the deceased empress, he was devoted to the imperial family and was considered to be a trusted aide of the emperor himself, particularly because of his cheerful personality. But any understanding of business administration was alien to him; nor did ceremonials arouse his interest in the slightest. Before long, the aristocracy was complaining bitterly. "No, no, Prince Rudolf is anything but a good Chancellor!"

Yet Emperor Francis Joseph even outlived his Rudi, as he was known at court. He was followed by Prince Alfred Montenuovo, his

Chancellor Rudolf Liechtenstein's morning visit to the emperor

grand nephew and the grandson of Marie Louise, former Empress of France. Montenuovo was not as brilliant as Hohenlohe but assertive and impartial. He performed the duties of his office conscientiously, and as a result remained utterly unloved throughout the court. The aristocrats, of whom he himself was rather suspicious, hailing as he did from the Habsburg family, despised his sharp tongued cynicism. Franz Ferdinand, heir to the throne, hated him profoundly. Montenuovo let him feel too blatently that his reign had not yet commenced. Every attempt on the part of Franz Ferdinand to speak his mind at court and to make his personal desires felt was cooly undercut by Montenuovo.

After the Chancellor took his leave from the emperor's side, Francis Joseph prepared himself for his daily audiences. Several times each week, ordinary citizens were permitted to speak their minds to him personally. Most wanted to thank the emperor for an appointment or a distinction awarded them. There was never a surprise, since each and every subject to be raised, regardless whether a petition for assistance or application for a post, was first reviewed and filtered in the ministry and then submitted to the emperor for approval.

Those who were permitted to appear for an audience had to report to the forechambers of the representational salons at the appointed time. The dress code had to be strictly adhered to. Those in the military came in uniform, civil persons appeared in swallow-tailed suits; medals were permitted, gloves were mandatory. The ladies were required to appear in neck-high dresses of restrained colours (decolleté gowns were permissible only at court balls), discreet and unobtrusive jewellery was allowed; and if the court was in mourning this had to be observed by visitors as well. In times of "deep grief" (lasting three months following the death of a high-ranking Archduke), black was compulsory; for "lesser grief" restrained colours were admissible in the weeks following the death, although any lace or feathers on dresses or hats had to be black. Citizens who had no means to purchase swallow-tailed suits or dresses were permitted to appear for their audience in their festive regional garb. No one should be impeded from his or her right to appear at court for financial reasons.

Visitors were prepped on etiquette requirements by an assistant of the chancellor: never speak to the emperor until requested; never turn your back on him. After one's name was announced, one proceeded to a foyer where an adjutant was waiting to check the name on the list against the person before him. The name was then repeated in a loud voice at the entrance, so that the emperor was informed who was poised to appear. Only as of that moment was the person permitted to cross the threshold into the audience salon. Upon entry, ladies were required to make a deep curtsey, men a low bow. Upon prompting by the emperor, one was permitted to stand upright again. The audience itself lasted for maximum three minutes. The emperor stood at his lectern at which the audience book was opened and read aloud to the visitor the arranged purpose of the visit. Thereupon, the emperor reported his considered response with regard to aforesaid purpose, which of course was already known to the visitor. The visitor then thanked the emperor from the depths of his/her heart and edged, backwards, towards

Audience visitors wait until their name is called

the door. In general, the audience was over before the visitor even realized what had happened. That was the only way the emperor could manage several hundred audiences each month. Longer audiences with ministers, parliamentarians, regents or governors were handled in different fashion, usually upon personal invitation by the emperor. They were nearly always held in private.

The emperor informed himself of all the goings on throughout the monarchy through his files and personal conversations with politicians. All reports of former deputies agree on one point: they call attention to the fact that the emperor tolerated only very brief reports, after which he posed elaborate and extremely precise questions. Politicians had to be very well informed about the fields and subject matter for which they were responsible. Francis Joseph asked unexpected and sometimes complex questions and compared the answers he was given to those of other politicians in order to piece together a composite picture. He usually questioned a number of politicians on one and the same theme in order to ferret out any possible contradictions.

When Francis Joseph didn't grant audiences, he devoted his mornings to studying files and reports. Occasionally he summoned Court Counselor Franz von Hawerda-Wehrlandt, general director of his own personal financial assets, from which all the staff members were paid and which were kept strictly separate from those of the court, to appear in his office. The counselor had to report with minute accuracy about the personal assets of the emperor, including share transactions, purchases, revenues from leases, and also report on expenses and allowances for the emperor's daughters and grandchildren. As long as the empress lived, she was the recipient of most of Francis Joseph's private bounty; in the main, this comprised Elisabeth's travel and building expenses, which exceeded the scope of everything else at court. After her death, Francis Joseph granted allowances and special gifts such as savings books especially to his ever larger brood of grandchildren.

Two to three times weekly the emperor received Lord Chamberlain Count Leopold Gudenus (*Oberstkämmerer*), the sixth man to hold this position under Francis Joseph, the emperor already having outlived Gudenus's five predecessors. The chamberlain filled the second highest office at court, ranking directly beneath the Chancellor. Count Gudenus was responsible for the art collections (in today's Kunsthistorisches Museum), the Treasury, the Arsenal, the natural history collections (today's Natural History Museum) and Ambras Castle in Tirol. He was the one who decided upon new purchases of art works. Only when the purchase price was far above the ordinary was special permission from the emperor necessary, something which did not occur often, since Francis Joseph was never happy when asked to spend inordinate amounts of money on anything.

Contrary to the prevalent opinion that Francis Joseph was interested solely in the military, he in fact was deeply interested in the arts, and was particularly receptive to applied art. The official opening of exhibitions and Vienna's big crafts fairs were mandatory items on his agenda. As often as possible, plans to visit such events were written onto his calendar, even if most exhibitions which were not of overriding importance and frequently had to give way in the last minute due to the pressure of events. In order to make visits to at least a few such events possible in his densely packed agenda, Chancellor Hohenlohe made great efforts in late years to map out the route of the emperor's coach ride home so that he could at least make a 10-minute stopover at an exhibition along the way. The museum and painting gallery directors were often informed at the last minute that the emperor desired a fifteen-minute guided tour of the highlights of an exhibition.

Whenever the Lord Marshal (*Obersthofmarschall*), the third highest office at court, met with the emperor more than once every two months, everyone knew that there were internal difficulties in the imperial family again which caused the emperor to call on Count Bela Cziraky to concoct a solution for the latest threatening scandal. As Marshal of the Chamber, the Hungarian Count Cziraky was legal advisor to the imperial family, his office was the exclusive legal management bureau of the Habsburgs. Ordinarily, the Lord Marshal was seldom seen at court, since he was basically responsible for legacies, marriage contracts, relinquishments, certifications or disciplinary matters. But at the turn of the century, as the number of morganatic and cross-class marriages of young archdukes increased, individual members of the Habsburg family opted out of the main trunk of the dynasty and a number of young family members caused European-wide scandals, Cziraky's legal

Most of the emperor's life was spent at his desk

knowledge was in high demand, making his appearance at court a regular occurrence.

The fourth and last of the four highest court officials was the Master of the Stables (*Oberststallmeister*), Prince Ferdinand Kinsky, the court's inordinately handsome dandy. Kinsky, nephew of Lord Chancellor Liechtenstein, received his appointment purely through family patronage, a subject for avid gossip, but was nonetheless a competent expert in his area of responsibility. As Master of the Stables, he was in charge of the Marstall, the imperial stables housing several hundred horses, the Wagenburg, the forage and fodder depot, the vehicle fleet, the Imperial Riding School and the Lipizza and Kladrub horse breeding farms. The staff under his authority was extremely costly, and thus was closely monitored by the chancellor and central financial office at court. Prince Kinsky had to report to this office daily, since the management of the imperial stables required full-time presence at court.

Each day between 11:30 am and noon, a servant brought the emperor his lunch. Francis Joseph always dined alone, and always ate lunch at his desk. It was carried up from the court kitchen, then re-heated on a burner in the foyer of the imperial apartments, and

Final preparations of the emperor's lunch in the foyer

served together with a stack of files and reports. The same general menu was served each day: soup, a piece of meat with one or two side dishes, beer or wine, followed by a classic Viennese dessert.

While the emperor dined, the cooking operations down in the kitchen were stoked up to maximum output. Hundreds of people had to be fed within the time span of two hours. There was neither a cafeteria nor a large dining room at court, so lunch was eaten either at one's place of work or in one of the countless corners and niches of the court hallways and chambers. Officials, taking their example from the emperor, were served their meal at their desks, with insulating metal dome lids; house officers and servants had to fetch their trays from the kitchen themselves and then find a quiet spot on the stairs or an unfrequented corner where they could eat in peace.

Court servants had the option of taking a meal subscription from the court kitchen, meaning they received breakfast, lunch and dinner at the cost of producing it. This was one of the many financial attractions of working at court. They could choose from three categories of meals, the most expensive being the daily menu of the emperor, consisting of soup, main course and dessert. The other two variants were of no lesser quality, simply were less time-consuming in their preparation. Each court employee could select freely the variant he preferred. The officials usually took the "emperor menu", whereas the servants most often selected the less expensive variant for lunch and dinner. The food was simple, but nutritious, and the portions were copious. A visitor at court who selected the basic menu recalls: "*The menu was rather simple, for example, schnitzel with side dishes and a dessert omelette with applesauce, but it was prepared to perfection.*"[4] The portions were so bounteous that the most expensive menus usually were finished by a second person. Many higher officials sent half of their meals to their servants and scores of lower officials shared their lunch with their wives, who in turn shared their half with a servant in their court apartment.[5]

With meal service as generous as that, outlandish abuse was the logical consequence. Many simple servants improved their income by secretly selling their meal tickets. Princess Nora Fugger recalls: "*Half of Vienna freely admitted to living off the court kitchen and wine cellar. The expenses incurred were immeasurable. What to begin with were occasional transgressions slowly evolved to habitual fraudulence over time and came to be considered a privilege to which one was entitled ... Some things changed over the years; but the mischief in the court economy remained until the very end.*"[6]

Following lunch, the emperor was visible at his window each day as he observed the changing of the guard in the courtyard. Apart from the court guards there were also the imperial bodyguards who since time immemorial had been responsible for the safety and the secure escort of the imperial family. Their management was the authority of the Chancellor, as chief of all court guards; however, as an exception they were not paid for out of the emperor's purse, but by the War Ministry, since the guards were militarily trained personnel on active duty. Six different guard regiments were employed at court, four of which were active military sentries to ensure safety and order. The other two, which served as honour guard and security service, were manned by retired officers still capable and suitable. These retired officers received a supplement to their pensions for their service at court.[7]

In the afternoon, the emperor returned to his study of reports and files, occasionally interrupted by single audiences. In late afternoon, he permitted himself a stroll in the Schönbrunn gardens or, in case the daily agenda was not too densely planned, in the park at Laxenburg Palace. On the way to his coach, the emperor often encountered officials and servants who did not form part of his innermost circle. As soon as he left his apartments to cross the courtyard, all the female servants dropped into curtsies while officials and livery servants – and even the firewood carriers – bowed down deeply whenever their paths crossed. For his personal modesty and his sense of duty, which were legendary even during his lifetime, the aging emperor was held in highest esteem by one and all. Everyone at court knew that the one remaining purpose in the emperor's life, after having been struck by so many blows of fate, was the preservation of the dynasty.

From the point of view of his employees, Francis Joseph was the perfect employer. He was polite and benevolent to all those beneath him, utterly free of sarcasm or verbal expressions of disdain. All the tides of criticism hurled against the court as an institution or against certain policymakers or against measures which were taken invariably stopped at the person of the emperor. Everyone who worked in his presence or immediate vicinity rhapsodized about him. His notorious chamber servant Eugen Ketterl records the modest, abundantly courteous manners of the emperor: "*The emperor was always kindhearted to us. He never barked orders, simply requested a given service and invariably expressed thanks, e.g. if someone brought him a glass of water.*"[8] His adjutant, Count Hoyos, was repeatedly astonished about the patience with which he faced and carried out his strenuous ceremonial duties, e.g. on the occasion of the festivities at the imperial anniversary of 1908: "*I am dead tired, my eyes are drooping. His Majesty, however, got out of bed much earlier than I did this morning, listened to reams of speeches, had to speak and perform ritual duties at every juncture, while I was but a spectator. And what patience and love was evident in everything he did! He is nearly 80, he has suffered so many disappointments; I could never have mustered such patience ...*"[9] On another occasion, when officials had to stand in full ornamental uniform for hours in withering sunshine and intense heat, he reports: "*Everyone could have kissed and knelt down before His Majesty! In that heat, he stood in fur and decorated uniform for 3 hours conversing amicably. Archduke Franz said to someone standing next to him: 'I have been to the equator twice, but I was never as hot as today.'*"[10]

When the emperor returned from his stroll, the last files of the day were handed to him by the adjutant on duty, after which preparations were made for the final and most demanding duty of the day. The evenings were free time only in the rarest circumstances. Three times weekly there were offical dinners, so-called 'serial dinners', to which just under 30 people were invited. There were military dinners with high officers and foreign attachés; diplomatic dinners to deepen relationships and connections with foreign states; and dinners for ministers, regional governors, deputies and distinguished personalities of public life as the invited guests. The highest nobility was often invited to these dinners, in revolving fashion in order to avoid anyone being insulted. Ladies were invited only seldom to the serial dinners, most of the guests hailed from the military, economic and aristocratic elite. They were invited not for pleasure, but for political or governmental tasks.

The invitation lists were arranged by the Chancellor and presented for approval to the emperor, who regularly crossed out a name or two and rearranged the seating plan at table. The emperor was informed about every single high ranking foreign visitor and structured his invitations around those individuals. Members of foreign ruling families spending time in Vienna were invited as honoured guests, bourgeois parliamentarians who had been recipients of some distinction were guests, as well as distinguished scientists. The seating plan and the written invitations were the province of the Department of Ceremonies, under the authority of the Chancellor. The dinners always took place in the Alexander apartments of the Hofburg, unless there were more than 30 guests, in which case the Ratsstube was used.

Menu suggestions were presented by the First Chef de Cuisine to the emperor. He studied the recommendations meticulously and crossed out any items he disapproved of with a red pencil, replacing them with one of his choosing. Once the emperor had given final approval, the invitations were written on court stationery at the Office of the Chancellor and delivered to the invitees. Highest ranking personalities and members of foreign dynasties were brought 'oral invitations' by a court coachman. Official dinners commenced at 6:00 pm. By the time the emperor had put the final working task of the day behind him, most court officials and servants had long since retired to their apartments inside the Hofburg.

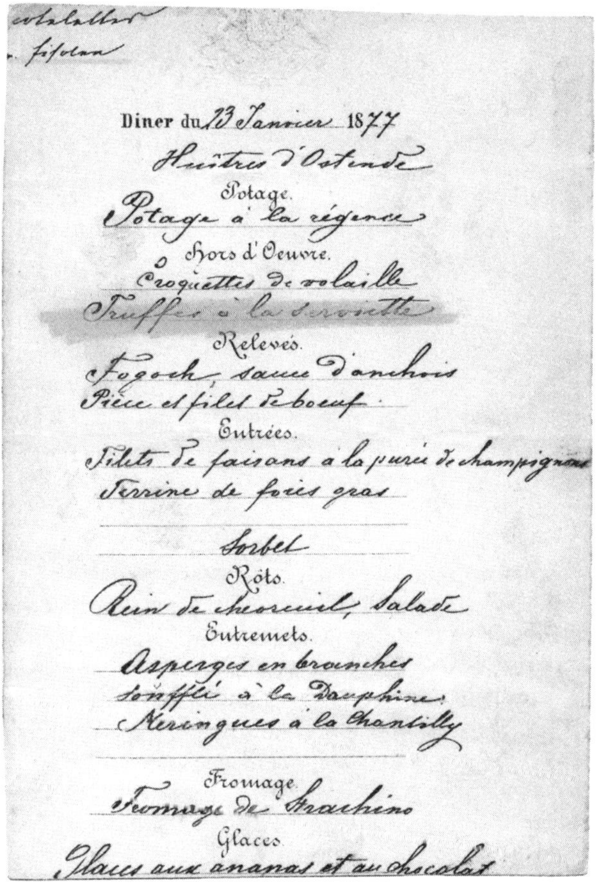

Diner du 13 Janvier 1877

Huîtres d'Ostende

Potage.

Potage à la régence

Hors d'Oeuvre.

Croquettes de volaille

Truffes à la serviette

Relevés.

Fogosch, sauce d'anchois

Pièce et filet de boeuf

Entrées.

Filets de faisans à la purée de champignons

Terrine de foies gras

Sorbet

Rôts.

Rein de chevreuil, Salade

Entremets.

Asperges en branches

Soufflé à la Dauphine

Meringues à la Chantilly

Fromage.

Fromage de Stracchino

Glaces.

Glaces aux ananas et au chocolat

A menu proposal the emperor corrected. At upper left, Emperor Francis Joseph wrote in the dish he preferred.

Emperor Francis Joseph greets his guests.
At his left, Chancellor Rudolf Liechtenstein

They took their supper from the kitchen with them, usually just cold cuts and bread, butter and some vegetable, with wine or beer.

For the emperor, the working day was still not over. After his guests had arrived, the emperor was given notice that all were present. Punctually, the Ceremonial Master lowered his staff three times onto the floor, signalling that the emperor was entering the salon. All the guests stood, in accordance with their rank. The emperor walked in, greeted the guests, and walked to his place at the center of the head table.

If no honoured guests were present, the Chancellor sat across from the emperor. Adjutant General Paar was often present at these dinners, as were some of the highest officials. The meal was served swiftly and adroitly, with next to no clatter. Generally, seven courses were served. Each court dinner began with a clear broth, was followed by oysters, then salad, fish, meat course and, last of all, dessert and cheese. Exquisite wines and champagne were served with the meal. For every two persons, a waiter was designated to wait on them. The emperor was attended by one waiter alone. He was always served first, then all other guests were served simultaneously. Dinner conversation was limited to one's immediate table partner. The gathering dined for 40 – 45 minutes.

The imperial dining table

The many anecdotes which are hawked about the guests leaving the dining room still hungry, since the meal *per force* terminated as soon as the rapidly-eating emperor had finished, are utterly unfounded. The chivalrous emperor would never have permitted the dinner to be officially ended before all guests had been served. Not a single contemporary witness who was personally present at court invitations reports any such thing. Following dinner, a small circle formed in an adjacent salon, where the emperor honoured certain invited guests with a brief personal chat, then withdrew. As a valuable memento and 'farewell gift', the guests were permitted to take home with them the box of the renowned court candies placed next to each guest's dinner plate at the dining table.[11]

For the aged emperor, the serial dinners were extremely strenuous, made even more burdensome by the fact that he got up each morning before 4:00 am. But the dinners also provided the monarch with an opportunity to converse with people whom he rarely encountered, since they were designed to include many persons from the 'outside world'.

When Emperor Francis Joseph retired to his own apartments between 8:00 and 8:30 pm, he skimmed the most important files which the day's last messenger had recently delivered, wrote a few private letters and let his valet get him ready for bed. Each day around 9:00 pm, when the old emperor retired for the night to his spartanic field bed, the nocturnal servants began their shift. The security guards went on duty. Some of the night guardians were posted at the court gates, others made their rounds through the courtyards The salon doormen prepared themselves for a long night. Lantern lighters no longer existed, as they had in Francis Joseph's youth, or rather, only a few, since gas lanterns had replaced them. As Francis Joseph slept, the court sank into a deep silence until the next day when, after seven hours of repose, the emperor and his court awoke at 3:30 am and the day began anew.

II
Taking the Reins: A Young Emperor at an Old Court

The well-ordered, well-functioning court of the aging emperor bore little resemblance to the court at which young Francis Joseph assumed the reins of power on 2 December 1848, stepping onto the political stage for the first time. When he took control, the spirit of the *ancien régime* still prevailed. The emperor himself was raised to power under a completely different definition of what his tasks as supreme ruler would be. Nonetheless, he was the one who would soon have to respond to the challenges of the modern age in ways utterly different from all his predecessors. Francis Joseph would need to deal with the loss of Italy, the autonomy of Hungary, the forfeiting of Austria's leadership in the German Federation, the undreamt of legislative powers of parliament and, last but not least, the personal changes within the dynasty itself.

Decades later, and many personal and political defeats later, Francis Joseph was a ruler who had bowed to the demands of the modern age. As nearly no other ruler could boast, Emperor Francis Joseph possessed phenomenal abilities to adapt. Whatever in his estimate seemed to be unavoidable, regardless if it went deeply against his own principles and attitudes, a mournful look back in time was not his way. Princess Marie Hohenlohe, widow of the most important Chancellor who observed the emperor at close quarters for more than a half century, wrote about the ruler in 1913: *"He suffered too many catastrophes which forcibly transformed him into a modern soul. His childhood and youthful memories must be soundly buried in the coffins of the deep past, as if they belonged to another person, for they were swiftly dissolved under Emperor Franz and endured their baptism of fire under Radetzky."*[12]

To start with, the fact that Emperor Francis Joseph was even able to take up residence in the lodgings and salons of the Vienna Hofburg bordered on the miraculous, since two months before his coronation a fire broke out in the buildings which was able to be put out only through the tireless efforts of the brave Viennese citizens who adored their emperor. On 31 October 1848, the day on which Field Marshall Alfred Windisch-Graetz captured the city, a fire broke out in the court library. Whether or not it was an act of sabotage or simply carelessness was never cleared up. Anton Thiel, counselor of accounting in the court bookkeeping office, later wrote a report about the firefighting actions taken which reveals that the court had neither emergency plans for such emergencies, nor was the court in any way prepared to pitch in together in times of disaster or extreme need. The courtiers watched utterly helplessly as the flames began to spread and failed utterly, lacking leadership by competent superiors, in coordinating the efforts to fight the flames. The numerous curious Viennese who ran to the fire saw empty-headed, incompetent courtiers who never even thought of picking up and using the water sprayers which were lying around everywhere. It was not until a passer-by, who could no longer bear to be witness to such foolishness, set about combating the fire, that the situation could be gradually turned around. According to the report, a simple man shouted to the crowd of onlookers: "*Whoever has any respect for the House of Austria, come with me, we can save the palace.*"[13] The citizen army of assistants took over the action, ordered the courtiers to fetch buckets of water, organised additional passers-by into troops of firefighters and ran endless times to the courtyard and the second floor where the seat of the fire was, upstairs with full buckets, downstairs with empty ones, since there were too few helpers to form a line to pass the buckets. Just where the numberless servants and officials who resided at court were at this juncture, was never able to be explained. The work of the volunteers was made more difficult by the fact that the courtiers who had been ordered by the citizenry to pitch in were "*individuals and classes who were unaccustomed to this kind of work.*"[14] By ten o'clock in the evening, the fire was finally out, thanks to no one but the decisive Viennese populace.

The fire at court showed that the buildings which were taken over by the young Francis Joseph were in no way equipped to face emergency situations of any kind. Lacking organisation plans, lacking individual initiative, most of all, a paralysis of will power and motivation underscored the scathing bite of public opinion and profound prejudice of the people against the privileged court class. For most of the Viennese, employment at court was nothing but a sinecure to reap in profit. Performance didn't count as much as loyalty to the imperial family. The picayune fussiness and complex unwillingness of the imperial agencies were notorious far and wide.

The court of Emperor Francis Joseph's predecessor, Emperor Ferdinand I., was a fossil from the 18th century. Reforms were long overdue. The administration was utterly antiquated, the management inefficient. Not even the Chancellor had an overview of the major offices, processes and responsibilities. The long list of complaints and warnings shows to what degree a sharp, disciplined organisation and watchful leadership were lacking. Under Emperor Franz I (II) (1792–1835), neglect was everywhere apparent in the daily agenda, but during the reign of Emperor Ferdinand (1835–1848), working morale and watchfulness dropped a further notch, descending into utter disrepair. Court officials who either were guilty of gross abuse of the rules or simply didn't do any work at all had to be dismissed. This threw a bad light not only on the dismissed employees, but on their superiors. The most horrendous grievances were not even noticed, and nothing was acted on until the situation became downright intolerable. In particular, dismissals due to lack of supervisory control on the part of superiors could not be blamed on lower level personnel alone; to a far greater extent they had to be blamed on the superiors themselves, who neglected the essential oversight. The modern principle of bearing responsibility for one's actions could not be applied at a patriarchal court which even intruded into the private lives of its members through a complex body of rules. The fact that at Ferdinand's court the right hand never knew what the left hand was doing becomes eminently apparent in one order issued in 1842: "*It is prohibited to employ even on a day-by-day basis individuals who have been dismissed because of a crime, violation or negligence.*"[15] In other words, anyone who was dismissed could be hired as a helper in another department without the knowledge of the main office which had fired him. The lack of oversight made dismissals and penalties ineffective.

Emperor Francis Joseph took over the reins of power from his uncle, Emperor Ferdinand 'the Good', who was quite popular among large parts of the population, known to be open-minded, yet because of his grave epileptic illness also severely limited, at a time when the ongoing threat of another revolution persisted and, as if this weren't enough, the empire was nearly backrupt. At one point, Francis Joseph and his family had to flee from the insurgents to Tirol and look on as the people dared to challenge the legitimacy of God-given Habsburg authority. He was proclaimed the new emperor in Olmütz, far distant from the imperial residence of Vienna. He could not abide his advisors, or any advisors for that matter, having seen what their counsel had done to his predecessor. At the tender age of eighteen, he prohibited the utterance of any unsolicited opinion in his presence.

During the first ten years of his reign, Francis Joseph trusted only two men: Prince Felix Schwarzenberg, his prime minister who decreed and enacted a rigidly centralistic government, but died in 1852; and Count Karl Grünne, his former First Valet, later appointed to be the all-powerful chief of his military office, the most hated and most feared man at the court of the young regent.

Count Grünne was the most contradictory personage ever to serve the emperor at close quarters. He was dyed-in-the-wool military in his views, ruthless in his personal ambitions, candid to the point of rudeness, intriguing and dishonest, yet at the same time relentlessly open-minded, did not shy away from conflict and the furthest thing imaginable from an eel-like courtier who changed with the shifting winds. He was utterly devoted to the young emperor. His friends praised his direct manner and unsparing openness, whereas the rest of the court thought him power-driven, uncultivated and crude. The court lady Therese Fürstenberg recalls: "*He was ignorant and ill-bred, like many officers of the day, but an incomparably sly dog, crafty as a fox. Cunning in his dealings with the court, rough-hewn and ruthless to anyone he did not need to handle with kid gloves. For that very reason, his friends nicknamed him a diamond in the rough.*"[16]

Count Grünne hastened to join the imperial family during their exile in Tirol, when he was 40 years old and already employed at court. At that time he was still undistinguished, except for one act of crass, ice cold venality. Before Grünne linked up with the young Francis Joseph, he was chancellor of the Palatine of Hungary, Archduke Stephan, who got caught between the opposing fronts when the revolution broke out. The Hungarians demanded independence from Vienna; the court in Vienna demanded uncompromising maintenance of the status quo. When Archduke Stephan relented, granting the insurgents a few of their demands, Count Grünne resigned theatrically from his duties and rushed to join the imperial family in their place of domestic exile, knowing quite well that they would occupy the center of power in future, as long as the revolutionaries were soundly defeated.

Not only the emperor's mother, also the conservative military officers were enthusiastic about Grünne's demonstrative rejection of any and all concessions to the revolutionaries. Due to his canny tactics, they became his most influential supporters at court. The implication that he had left his master in the lurch without a thought and exposed and embarrassed him to boot, was ignored. Count Grünne was appointed to the position of valet on the instant, began without delay to weave a spider's web of influence and power for his young master.

Emperor Ferdinand, despite reports to the contrary, was anything but a moron. He relinquished the power of the throne only unwillingly. The later adage attributed to him – "I rather liked doing it." – is pure myth. But he didn't stand a chance of withstanding the pressures which the closest family members and immediate advisors placed him under, he was simply too docile. He yielded without a fight, and placed the power of the Habsburg throne in the hands of his nephew.

As newly enthroned emperor, Francis Joseph was now master of the court of Vienna. But not only the monarchy as a ruling system, also the court itself was in crisis. The first shock for the emperor came from his Minister of Finance, Baron von Krauss. The state budget was in such bad shape that new sources of income were urgently necessary. The military budget swallowed the largest part of tax revenues, a veritable national bankruptcy loomed on the horizon. Even Count Grünne, who managed court affairs in the interim until Francis Joseph had appointed a Lord Chancellor, was in receipt of a letter from the finance minister. The essence was curt: if the court was not immediately reduced to a containable size, it was no longer possible to maintain operations. The ailing budget simply did not permit any further allowances or benefits.

Count Grünne acted immediately. The trenchant letter from the finance minister gave him precisely the opportunity he needed to appoint an investigative committee for the emperor. Grünne had long cast a suspicious eye on the courtiers at court. The degree to which longstanding court employees took privileges and benefits for granted; the endlessly cumbersome handling of court business; and the age-old rights and privileges of court officials were a thorn in the side of the spartanic and bold military man.

The emperor assigned Count Grünne to assiduously scrutinize the court from top to bottom in an audit. Not only the expenses were to be examined, even the working methods of the court administration had to be assessed. The emperor said he wished to be informed in meticulous detail of the findings.

Thereupon, Grünne and the officials he appointed to assist him delved deep into the affairs of court management. They zeroed in on the ways of processing reports and orders; read the entire correspondence of court officials and staff; examined the efficiency of administrative steps from the initial edict of one or the other director all the way to the implementation of a rule at the most menial levels. Grünne personally spied on the directors of the uppermost court departments, trying to gain an impression of the suitability of each one for the position which had been given him. During this investigation, not a word of his findings or conclusions was leaked to the outside. Not even the emperor himself received an interim report.

In April 1849, Count Grünne presented the emperor a sharply worded memorandum on the state of his court and its management which made the emperor cringe and which resulted in the most radical and far reaching reforms in the previous two centuries. The findings of the investigative committee made the depths of the failed system at court visible. They showed indisputably that not only austerity measures were necessary, the overall method of administrative processing needed to be disavowed.

The court administrative offices had no unified structure, the individual departments not only conflicted with each other in their approaches, they were so hostile to each other that decisions were often made for the sole reason that they would make life particularly difficult for other departments. The directors of many departments acted solely out of deep enmity towards their colleagues at court and did not shy away from extreme measures. Even under Emperor Ferdinand, these directors besieged each other with complaints and denunciations, something which the police of Vienna were incapable of coping with, having no authority to deal with anything at court (in the interests of avoiding scandals). Grünne accused the responsibile officials of frivolous and short-sighted leadership and having further bled an already meagre budget. He was able to prove systematic fraud in certain departments and criticised relentlessly the stupidity of specific officials. Their foolish directives were the cause of immense waste. Doubly and triply redundant actions, he claimed, impeded, indeed, precluded efficiency in carrying out the work at court.

Karl, Count Grünne was well known for his crude manners. He did not halt at administrative measures. He even leaned on the major officials at court, men from the highest nobility, with scathing criticism: "*They were often not well acquainted with the substance of their tasks; furthermore, were often preoccupied with completely different offices. This led them to only perform certain tasks and hope that the weight of their names would permit them to do things which were better left undone.*"[18]

The wastefulness of allocated funds was immeasurable. The most expensive departments were the most reckless. The office which assigned residential quarters at court to employees maintained accounts deep in the red, since for no conceivable reason apartments were exchanged every year, and each apartment had to be renovated for the new occupant at great expense. The Building Office often, and inexplicably, began building new wings onto the court buildings, hiring uncountable construction workers to perform the tasks simply to retain a large enough staff for any and all necessities. Precious furniture disappeared inexplicably whenever it was ordered to be transferred to another palace, since nothing was ever signed for on a receipt. This, in particular, incensed Grünne. The innumerable people who were given quarters in the court palaces of Laxenburg and Baden for short periods in summertime left behind devastated apartments when they departed which then had to be renovated at enormous expense by the Building Office each autumn. Moreover, there was not an official at court capable of pursuing this wanton destructiveness, they complacently continued to pay the invoices presented by the Building Office.

In the course of the thoroughgoing examination of the Office of Assignment of Quarters at court, Grünne and his team were in for a little surprise. In the more distant or isolated buildings belonging to the court, e.g. Schönbrunn, Laxenburg and Augarten, people who had nothing to do with the court and had never once been employed there or were related to anyone employed there, were found to be residing. How such "illegal" renters angled such apartments was easily explained: the countless widows of officials had often sub-rented their own large apartments in order to supplement their pensions and allow them the indulgence of a few additional expenditures; however, these sub-leases were rarely registered, and when they were, the quarters were always officially consigned to "nephews" or "nieces". In most cases, the responsible official never even checked the background of these renters. Over the course of decades, entire families came to occupy the quarters in these palaces, people who had literally nothing whatever to do with the imperial family or the court. Following the death of a renter, they continued to remain occupied. The Building Office never felt any necessity to check up on who was actually living there. And the court, which was ongoingly burdened by a lack of apartments for its employees and was even sometimes forced to rent external quarters for its employees somewhere near the palace, entertained phantom renters who lived free of charge.[19]

Grünne was also grimly dissatisfied with the organisation of the court's security personnel and with the guards on the court grounds. They were scattered throughout the grounds and the buildings and did not report to one superior, but to several. This made standards of discipline impossible, which was particularly dangerous, since the safety of the court had become the uppermost priority since the revolution. The security personnel also had another important duty, however: it was in charge of making sure that no court property, i.e. valuable objects, were "removed", since the losses due to theft were unspeakably high. Above all else, firewood and daily necessities were as a matter of course stolen from court and sold in the city. Even the guards in charge of security were reformed and accorded some efficiency after this audit. A new and much more effective alarm system was installed. The last thing the court needed was guards who once again could not protect the people and property of the court in an emergency.[20]

The biggest challenge at court, however, was its personnel. Both costs and employee morale were major weak links in the chain of command. Even at that time, the salaries and pensions of court employees took the largest bite out of the annual budget. In actual fact, it was not the salaries which were problematic, for these were quite low (apart from for the "additional services" which cushioned these standards). No, the real problem was the inordinately high number of people employeed. The court, simply put, had many too many employees, most of all, poorly qualified employees, a result of the nepotism of the previous decades. When new people were hired, persons were given preference who had been recommended by influential court patrons or were relatives of already employed officials and servants. Claimed qualifications were rarely checked on or verified. Thus, countless persons were taken into court service who had neither the required knowledge for their tasks nor the required standards of conduct. What Grünne found to be the very worst was the fact that automatic promotions of utterly incapable officials were habitual. Through that custom, the most important posts were run by people who were utterly unprepared and, for the most part, "not trustworthy".

Above all else, Grünne wished to break with the tradition of sending people into retirement as a disciplinary measure, particularly in the case of unwilling servants. It was customary at court for officials who had become untenable due to repeated warnings for lack of willingness to be "penalised" by early retirement. Since retirement for all court employees was connected to a drastic reduction in salary – just a third of their salary as a rule – this was a generally feared measure. In the middle of the 19th century, when the court did not have the social system which has prevailed for the last 40 years, retirement was not looked forward to, but delayed as long as possible. If the court continued to adhere to the principle of retiring lazy workers as a penalty, this would continue to burden the court finances far into the future. On the one hand, these people would receive a small pension, further burdening the court budget; and on the other, they would appeal to the court for special grants, since they were forced to makes ends meet on such a small amount of money. Requests for 'mercy payments' were hardly ever turned down, due to the generally prevailing dire straits among the population.

Grünne demanded a total reform of court employment and finances. One small staff should be the operative head of court organisation. The Lord Chancellor should be the central headquarters of all management business. Surplus personnel should be dismissed without delay. Employee morale had to be raised. To get on top of wasteful habits, all applications for payable services had to go through one central office. In future, no department outside the Chancellor's office could commission the slightest thing.

Grünne also demanded that centuries-old administrative structures be dissolved to permit drastic measures to be taken against all management failings. No court official had ever been forced to listen to such clear and harsh words about the incapabilities and failings of court management for their emperor, issued from the mouth and the pen of this trusted official. He was shockingly honest to Francis Joseph and refused to cushion the blows even when they were levelled against the emperor's closest friends in the nobility. Whenever he feared that he had demanded too much of the emperor, he closed his report with the words, "*The current conditions are so grave and urgent that respect for the age of a given practice is no longer sufficient to ensure its continuation. If it is proven to be damaging to the court, it must be ended.*"[21]

The young emperor reacted to the alarming report of his confidential advisor immediately. He launched without delay a complete re-structuring of the major court offices and departments. The current structure, more than 600 years old, divided into four sub-sections – Offices of the Chancellor, of the Chamberlain, of the Marshal and of the Stables – was retained, but all the expensive departments were placed under the supervisory budget control of the Chancellor, even if their expenses had nothing to do with his office. Thus, in one fell swoop, this became the most significant and powerful office at court. The entire management of personnel, previously distributed over four different departments, as well as the budget supervision of the other three departments was now placed under the sole control of the staff of the Chancellor, which amounted to the creation of a huge new authority. Effective immediately, the court was regulated in strictly centralised fashion. The independence of the four departments in terms of finances and personnel became a thing of the past. The Chancellor, as chief of this staff, was handed a measure of power through the coronation of Francis Joseph that he had never possessed before. Following the completion of this reform, the other departments were permitted to retain only their special, limited agendas: the Chamberlain's office retained authority for the art and court access; the Marshal's office, which had once managed most of the security personnel, was reduced to the legal department; the Master of the Stables remained in charge only of the imperial breeding farms and the Wagenburg vehicle fleet, although as a concession was still permitted to hire and manage his own stable personnel.

At the same time as a far reaching reform of court administration was announced, Count Grünne also decreed a whole series of prohibitions which help one to deduce what conditions had reigned at court until then. In a circular Grünne sent out to each department and to all court employees, he reminded the staff that, to name one example, they were not allowed to use imperial vehicles for personal trips. Entire families and circles of friends had been cruising around the city and surroundings in court vehicles. Official trips were suborned to go on journeys with the whole family. Some officials who had to make regular official trips took along sub-users with them, against all the rules re-channeling court coaches as taxis. In a cunning move to stem the tide of such misuse, Grünner simply ordered that for all official trips, only single-seat vehicles were to be used in future; ergo, when there was no room for passengers, there were no passengers.

One major problem persisted, particularly for appearances outside the Hofburg. Poorly paid personnel – coachmen, doormen and servants in particular – went begging for tips. Due to the base-bottom salaries they were paid, the custom arose for personnel to be given a gratuity for ordinary tasks which were part of their everyday agenda and the habit became anchored in everyday operations. More than anyone else, the imperial family regularly gave a penny to servants and coachmen who were amenable and helpful. The lowest level personnel who were gradually spoiled by the generosity of the emperor's family members began to see gratuities as a recognized employee benefit and thenceforth held out their hand ostentatiously for each appointed business visitor to the court management, especially to socially higher persons. The very first impression each visitor received was of servants begging. By the time a petitioner had wended his way through the labyrinths of court to the department he sought, at least eight different servants had held out their hands for a tip. From the coachman to the doorman, from the servant who escorted him to the correct department door to the low level official in the office itself, each of them claimed a gratuity for their service. A purse filled with loose change became an unavoidable necessity at court. Count Grünne made it absolutely clear that begging would no longer be tolerated. Anyone caught at it would be severely punished.

For another group of excesses and abuses, the imperial family bore a share of the blame. The highest members of the nobility usually had an open ear for the personal neediness of its staff. For example, court employees who needed the assurance of a job for their children, sick relatives who might need a loan, indispensable winter coats for families with many children – the requests with which archdukes and archduchesses were petitioned were endless. Since the nobility had personal contact with these employees and had a genuine desire to help, they always tried to fulfil the various requests. In the case of small amounts of money or material contributions, they acted at once; when it was a matter of a court appointment or transfer request, they had to ask permission of the Chancellor, who usually suffered pangs of conscience at such petitions. Even if an official bravely rejected a request for preference or patronage, he knew that his superior would be happy to fulfil the suit of a relative of the emperor. The patronage which Grünne was attempting to hunt down and prosecute had its weak link in the combination of well-meaning assistance and personal intervention in the hiring policies of the court. He reprimanded all court officials to desist with the practice of addressing petitions directly to the imperial family. He also informed the archdukes in a polite but decisive way that only the normal paths of officialdom were open to such applications. Even the mother of the emperor who often made special requests for the military was rebuffed. Of course, his unpopularity rose still another notch through these measures, but his action was backed and defended by the emperor himself. Only in exceptional cases, e.g. when Archduchess Sophie wished to engage a specific maid – in other words, in the most personal spheres of court affairs – did he permit special personnel requests to go through. For all administrataive positions, no suits which attempted to circumvent the normal channels would be considered. Moreover, no such petitions were permitted to arrive in the hands of the emperor anymore. Every coachman, every doorman who passed the emperor in the passages of court had until now pressed a written request into Francis Joseph's hand. The officials were now admonished and urged to submit such requests only to the Chancellor, under no circumstances was the emperor to be given such requests.[23]

Of course, highly placed personages from the nobility and bureaucracy continued to use the weight of their names to provide positions and take care of their protegés until the very end of the reign through their personal patronage. But at least appointments based solely on personal connections came to an end with the coronation of Francis Joseph.

Nevertheless, to one demand Count Grünne found the emperor to be utterly unreceptive. Francis Joseph refused to dismiss employees. It was almost too much for him to send old office workers who could no longer cope with the new rules into early retirement, naturally with full honours and the award of noble distinctions. He wished to spare these individuals malicious gossip. This social and moral commitment of Emperor Francis Joseph towards his court officials and household servants outweighed all efficiency considerations of Grünne's reforms. If thrift was imperative, it was better to effect it at once, but in Emperor Francis Joseph's code of honour, a Christian ruler never, ever threw out members of the court. The dictum of Emperor Joseph II about his servants – "I don't need them, but they need me." – was well anchored in young Francis Joseph's genes as well.

The finances of the imperial court were still in abominable shape even after the great reforms. The endowment for the imperial court was not enough to cover the first ten years of Emperor Francis Joseph's government. At regular intervals, the finance minister had to make special payments, often as soon as three months after the annual budget amount had been transferred. Former Emperor Ferdinand received the greatest bite of the money which had been allocated for apanages of the imperial family. As a crowned monarch, he was entitled to 500,000 guilders annually. And after his retirement in Prague, Ferdinand did not even entertain the notion of dispensing with his apanage for the benefit of his nephew.

Even weightier than his apanage was the fact that Emperor Ferdinand retained in his possession the largest part of the assets belonging to Emperor Francis I. As Ex-Emperor, he was forced to hand over the control of court assets and family funds, since only reigning rulers had the sole rights to dispose over these assets. Nevertheless, Ferdinand kept firmly in his hands the huge private wealth of Emperor Francis I (II), designated to be passed on to the next ruler only upon the death of his predecessor, which in the cases of Ferdinand and Francis Joseph had not yet occurred; in case of abdication, the former emperor was not compelled to relinquish his wealth.

Under these circumstances the wealthiest man in the family was not the emperor himself, but his uncle, the former emperor. It was assumed that there was ongoing contact between Francis Joseph and Ferdinand until it became known that whereas quick trips of the emperor to visit his uncle in Prague were frequently indicated, there are no sources to confirm that they ever took place in the early years of his reign. The trips which were assumed by Czech historians in particular[24] could have served no other purpose for the young emperor but to squeeze some financial support out of his rich uncle. Court protocol in Vienna documented every step taken by the emperor over the course of 68 years, but there is not one single mention of any trips to Prague. In the collection of handwritten records in the Vienna City Library, however, is a telltale letter of Count Grünne to the Master of Ordnance, Count Khevenhüller: "His Majesty will come tomorrow, on the seventh of the month, at about 12:00 noon to Prague and orders 4 postal coaches with four-horse teams to be waiting at the train station and prepared to continue the trip to Töplitz without any stopover. Please confirm upon receipt of this letter by special postal courier the immediate placement of the postal horses on the road to Töplitz and room reservations at the City of London Inn. The trip is being made strictly *incognito*, any and every form of reception is thus absolutely prohibited!"[25] These orders were not issued until late in the morning, Grünne having noted that they must be written *in code*. Thus, he had the letter encrypted so that no one who might see it would know its contents.

The emperor also secretly met his uncle and predecessor at regular intervals in the spa town of Teplitz, where Ferdinand often went, staying overnight at a rustic inn, to inquire whether his uncle Ferdinand might open his purse for him. This is pure speculation, but 17 years later on the occasion of the big savings programme of the emperor, Ferdinand played hard-to-get upon being asked to relinquish his apanage. Thus, it becomes clear that unselfish assistance for his nephew, who now sat on what was previously his throne, was not in the cards for Ferdinand.

In spring 1849, Emperor Francis Joseph appointed a Lord Chancellor for the first time. Until now, his adjutant, Count Karl Grünne, had held this interim position. After paving the way for his big reform package, Grünne wished to return to the office which had been created especially for him, Director of the Central Military Office, a position more suited to his overriding ambitions. Even if he had wished to remain in the position of Chancellor, it was prohibited for formalistic reasons, since princely background was a pre-requisite. The Chancellor had the uppermost rank at court, he was the only personage permitted to represent the emperor even on official occasions. Only someone whose lineage ranked him above the entire Austrian aristocracy could take on such a position. Someone from the lower ranks of nobility would have introduced an element of chaos into the complicated status system at court.

This great honour of being Chancellor, and thus the most powerful man at court, was granted to Prince Liechtenstein, who stemmed from an ancillary, non-reigning branch of the family dynasty. Liechtenstein, like Grünne, was a proud member of the military, where his network of contacts was based, yet could have not been of more contrasting character from the cold, ruthless, cynical Grünne. Liechtenstein was a tranquil and gentle spirit, father of two sons who were slightly younger than the emperor, and one of the most popular men in society circles of the day. Each Chancellor at the imperial court was not only an insuperable entity in aristocratic circles, but his public profile in Vienna was on a par with the mayor. Every Viennese knew the name of the Chancellor and knew a few stories about him.

In the course of his reign as Chancellor, Liechtenstein rose to become the most beloved personality in Viennese life, dubbed "the most courteous and urbane *Grand Seigneur* in Austria." In the words of the Russian emissary to the court of Vienna: "*Neither at court nor in society circles was there a more likable or a more remarkable human being than Prince Karl Liechtenstein ... Prince Liechtenstein enjoyed a rare breed of popularity in every sector, at every level of*

Viennese society. There was, I believe, not a salesgirl or salesman in the city who did not recognize him or tip their hat as he walked by."[26]

When he first assumed the office of Chancellor, Prince Liechtenstein was 59; based on his immense wealth he was financially independent and devoted his life, apart from his court responsibilities, to only two things: his children, whom he loved above everything else on earth; and horseback riding, based on the precepts and guidelines of his English ideal, a sport dedicatedly promoted by the monarch himself. Liechtenstein's four daughters and two sons were his one-and-all. Having lost his own parents at the age of 5, he compensated the loving care he sorely missed in his own childhood by drowning his own six children in his devotion. He furthered their education far beyond the contemporary usages which prevailed, having them tutored by the best instructors he could find – sons and daughters alike – in science and art. For his daughters, only the very highest of aristocrats were considered as worthy marriage applicants. Each of his daughters was married to the scion of a princely dynasty; for his sons, he cleared the way for the highest attainable positions in military or imperial service. The result of this combination of paternal protection, intelligent marriage designs, his own unsurpassable lineage and top position at court, was a family circle highly connected to the top of society which no one, even 40 years later, was able to circumvent when they wished to launch or pursue a high level career. And the same time, it provided an endless source of gossip.[27]

When Liechtenstein took office, the measures for the new reform were already decided upon, he merely had to implement them. But he did have to untangle one knot he inherited from Grünne: the bloated staff of court servants had to be reduced, but – a strict caveat from the emperor himself – without dismissals. In order to get on top of the gargantuan costs caused by the army of livery servants, Liechtenstein resorted to the only measure available to him: he talked the emperor into prohibiting his servants to marry for several years. This step, which initially appears irrational and bizarre, was in fact the one assured way to reduce personnel levels over the long term. Every married court official and servant had the right to have his family provided for if he was no longer be able to do so. That meant not only that a servant's widow and orphans received pensions in case he died; it also meant that if a servant earned very little, the emperor had to intervene with support payments for families with many children. And base level servants in particular tended to have many more than three children. Due to the low court salaries, this entailed support of virtually all the families employed there. In order to lower at least these additional costs, a general marriage ban was decreed. Liechtenstein planned to prolong its validity for as long as was necessary until the desirable number of servants was reached.[28]

Through natural staff reductions such as retirement or death, the number of servants would decrease over time, but not deplete aid and assistance funds due to ongoing families being started. The marriage ban was not repealed until 1867[29] and proved exceedingly hard on the staff members in particular. It led to a dilemma nine months later which no one had expected and which turned out to be quite embarrassing. Within a short time, the directors were confronted with a large number of illegitimate children – and that, at a strictly Catholic court! The office of the Chancellor made an about-face; due to "urgent necessities" court servants were permitted to wed, but had to sign a waiver of renouncement.[30]

Since one could not very well allow entire families to fall into penury, or for widows and orphans to live in poverty, court servants and their families continued to receive 'clemency pensions' which were paid, alternatingly, from a reserve court fund or the personal purse of the emperor. Furthermore, the court continued to award financial premiums to widows and orphans on all appropriate occasions. Thus, the problem was not really solved by this measure, and would not be solved until the next Chancellor, Konstantin Hohenlohe, fundamentally reformed the remuneration structures at court. In the 1850s, the court could not bring itself to take the necessary and expensive steps towards changing the methods of compensation, in itself partially due to its unsound financial footing, which chained it to unavoidably high costs for another 25 years. In the end, by virtue of postponing it for so long, these half-measures cost just as much as a full-fledged reform would have.

As a raw youth, Francis Joseph needed some time to grow into his new role as emperor. He could not yet count on the love of his people. Francis Joseph was still a long way from the nearly mythical devotion of his subjects which was accorded him in his later years. Many of his subjects currently refused devotion to him because of his harsh treatment of the insurgency and also because he depended so thoroughly on the military to shore up his power whenever necessary. The Hungarians, whose nation seethed under the harsh yoke of the military since 1849, hated the young, reactionary emperor (a Hungarian assassination attempt four years later was just barely prevented). Even a half-year after the uproar, Francis Joseph did not trust the calm which prevailed, perhaps even feared new popular outbreaks. This anxiety is demonstrated by a confidential memo from his Chancellor. Liechtenstein was asked to quietly find out what measures could be taken to secure the court from attack. He reported to his master that all the cellar and ground floor windows could be secured with iron window grilles; the public entries to the court grounds, however, would have to be blocked "*with iron poles cemented into the ground, iron-clad beams or even full-fledged walls.*" The emperor laid the problem *ad acta.* The notion of closing off the imperial residence at the heart of the city and blocking its main traffic arteries was unthinkable to him; there was also no money to finance such a mammoth project.[31] The emperor didn't merely introduce cost-cutting programmes for his employees, he also had to give up some of his own plans, even if the consequence of it was an abiding fear that the spark of revolution could theoretically ignite the imperial court at any time.

III
The Structures at Court

The administrative structure of the court remained fundamentally unchanged for the 600 years of its existence until the end of the monarchy. The simple reason for this was that it proved to be a viable way of handling and managing the vast operations at court, by and large. Single adjustments, such as combining small departments or shifting certain responsibilities to a different authority, had only minor influence on the overall work and administration of the imperial court.[32]

The age-old sub-division into four different, relatively independent departments was preserved by Emperor Francis Joseph: Department of the Exchequer (*Obersthofmeisterstab*), Department of the Chamberlain (*Oberstkämmererstab*), Department of the Marshal (*Obersthofmarschallstab*) and Department of Stables (*Oberststallmeisterstab*). At the head of these four departments stood the foremost officials or authorities of the court, aristocrats personally selected by the emperor. These men formed the sole link between the monarch and his administration, since the emperor did not issue edicts for the management of individual departments or intervene in their operations. The uppermost court authorities were the only ones who reported personally to the emperor and received personal orders from him. This buffer zone between monarch and administration secured the degree of aloofness which had always been the hallmark of the monarchy and was also the personal intention of Francis Joseph. If the emperor desired a change in administration, he informed his foremost charges. They were the ones responsible for making sure those requests were fulfilled.

Department of the Exchequer

The largest and most important department since the earliest days was that of the Exchequer, the *Obersthofmeisterstab*, the central heartbeat of court life, in charge of all administrative, financial and personnel agendas. At the summit of this huge department stood the Chancellor of the Exchequer, the most powerful and influential personage at court. The appointment to this position of honour was the greatest imaginable distinction for an aristocrat. It meant that the appointed person was not only entrusted with running the huge court complex but far more important, that the selected person enjoyed the highest possible personal confidence of the emperor. The appointment to Lord Chancellor meant nothing less than the emperor's placing into his personal hands absolute responsibility for court affairs, the court staff and the court treasury and, last but not least, the emperor's own personal assets. Each respective Chancellor was one of the most influential men in Vienna; he not only had the ear of the emperor, but was the only one to have access to the emperor his life long, since their period of service ended only with his death or that of the monarch.

The huge Department of the Exchequer comprised four main divisions, which in turn included countless lower sub-divisions: Office of the Exchequer, the Departments of the Exchequer, the Administrations, the Court Services. The actually responsibilities in these four divisions are not always clear to modern eyes and have to be elucidated through a description of their history, above all else. Evolving slowly over the course of centuries, most of the sub-divisions were left under the aegis of their original authority.

The first of the four divisions of the Department of the Exchequer was the Office of the Exchequer, the administrative heart of the overall department. Here all the threads of court life came together, from here they were defined, controlled and navigated. The Office of the Exchequer was the place of work of the Chancellor, here was his representative office, here was his chancellery direction, the spearhead of every movement at court designed to relay each instruction of the Chancellor to the appropriate department.

At the head of the chancellery was the current director, the highest civil servant at court and the highest position a bourgeois citizen was capable of attaining. The chancellery director was the only employee distinguished by the title of Court Counselor (*Hofrat*); he usually looked back on a long career at the Exchequer and was entrusted with the operations of court in the absence of the Chancellor. The chancellery director was free to assign and alter the assignments of the civil servants beneath him (even though basic approval of the Chancellor was required); and act independently at his own discretion to combat administrative problems which might arise. When, at the end of the 19th century, the chancellors deteriorated in professional quality and personal involvement, the power and influence of the chancellery directors increased in direct proportion. They became the only ones who knew every procedure, every department, every unusual situation and every danger lurking in court operations. And their awareness of that capacity made them correspondingly self-confident, bordering on arrogant. They knew well that their knowledge was crucial, their services indispensable.

Adjacent to the Chancellery Direction was a department which interfaced with it ongoingly: the Department of Ceremonials, which had its own ceremonial director. All ceremonial protocols were devised here and relayed to the appropriate places. For every court event, every reception, every grand entrance of the emperor, the ceremonial director went into action, publishing an individually designed set of rules for the given event. Each step of an event was precisely defined and devised beforehand: who would accompany the emperor, how the participants were to be arranged; who was permitted to precede whom. In designing the event, meticulous attention had to be paid to adhering to the hierarchical status and rank of the respective participants, so that no member of the higher classes would have reason to be socially offended by preference having been accorded to someone ranking below him or her. The work of the ceremonial director presupposed vast knowledge of centuries-old court guidelines as well as microscopically detailed acquaintance with the complex ranking system at court. Only after many years of practice as a ceremonial servant was one in a position to devise a protocol which did not lead to collisions and disputes. Together with the Court Commissioners, the Chancellery Direction and Department of Ceremonials comprised about 30 employees, all of whom had advanced education in jurisprudence, with their secretaries.

In the 'Human Aid' departments, all those sectors crucial for processing files and expediting postal shipments, *Registry, Expedition* and *Protocol,* were merged into one department with 40 employees. The *Registry* oversaw the entire body of written documents and correspondence at court, ordered and stamped each report and kept the diary which noted each and every written communication which left or was received at the Chancellor's office with a key word or a name. The number of written documents produced during the era of Francis Joseph defies imagination, developing exponentially in comparison with previous centuries. The ease with which a modern day historian can seek and find specific files or reports is only to be attributed to the perfectionistic organisational system which was introduced for filing purposes of such masses of documents.[33] *Expedition* was the department which sent off everything in need of external post. A fee was levied only for letters which contained cash.[34]

The second major sector was the *Departments*. The most important oversight organ of the Exchequer was the *Accounting* department, the controlling eye of all court business which was founded in 1867 after the Constitution was introduced. Under the supervision of the court *Accounting Director*, more than 60 accounting counselors were working in the financial management of the court in the final days of the monarchy. The accounting department oversaw the Payments Office, the cash window of court business with twelve paymasters and cashiers, which distributed salaries of all court employees, paid the invoices addressed to the court; this office remained completely in the hands of the accounting department as the foremost watchdog of the court budget. The accounting department hunted down any and all irregularities, making it the treasured policing authority of the Chancellor. This was the only office which ensured that the exigencies of the court budget would be fulfilled. If this department lost the overview of finances and payments, the way was paved for corruption and fraud in every niche of court business. The only astonishing thing is that such a system was not introduced until Francis Joseph, the penultimate ruler of the Habsburg monarchy.

The relatively small *Department of Travel* employed only one director and a secretary; it was responsible for all business connected with court travel, mainly the organisation of the emperor's trips or moving his household to Budapest or Ischgl. Apart from that, this department also bore the responsibility for organising the trips of all imperial family members and announcing the time of their safe arrival. All correspondence with the place of destination was also within its purview, as a way of ensuring that everything which the emperor might need on a trip was in the hands of one sole organising office. It was also the axis of a number of ancillary posts related to journeys, e.g. valets, chefs (who sometimes travelled along), doctors, Chancellor and many more besides, although it covered only private trips of the emperor or the imperial family's seasonal change of residence. Official state journeys, on the other hand, were organised by the cabinet chancellery. If the emperor visited the annual military manoeuvers, the military chancellery handled it.

The director of the *Department of Uniforms* had only a small staff. It handled completing, managing and ordering the uniforms of all court employees. Everyone employed at court had the right to one working uniform and one gala uniform for special occasions. Each official and servant was himself responsible for maintaining the uniform in good condition for at least two years of wear, after which certain parts could be renewed. Should a uniform become unusable after a short time, something which occurred not infrequently, leading the department to conclude it had been recklessly ruined, the price of replacement could be deducted from the uniform-wearer's salary. In the latter 19th century, the court changed its tactic: whoever had worn and preserved his uniform for a certain length of time received a bonus payment.[35]

The *Department of Buildings* employeed about ten construction engineers who were responsible for the safety of the court buildings. The Telegraph Office was under the supervision of the Office of the Exchequer, employing 20 postal officials in Vienna and Budapest. The *Department of the Chapel* employed about 40 priests, preachers and chaplains; and the ten *Court Physicians* had their own department. In addition to these were the *Salon Services*, which employed 50 doormen and announcers. The doormen were posted in the imperial residence round the clock and at every door of the official representative apartments.

Thus, the *Office of the Exchequer* employed approximately 250 staff members, not including the ever-changing number of employees, servants and lackeys, couriers and dispatch messengers, without whose services nothing would have moved, but whose ranks appeared too insignificant to be recorded in court employee files.

The third large department under the supervision of the Chancellor of the Exchequer was the so-called *Administration*, comprising a wide variety of different departments: the *Imperial Music Band* employed about 50 permanently engaged conductors, singers and instrumentalists, who were showered with all the benefits and privileges of employment at court. The *Imperial Pharmacy* had about 20 employees; it was not for the sole use of the court, anyone could order or purchase medicines here. The pharmacy had an excellent reputation and was extremely popular, especially among well-to-do Viennese. Due to its exclusive clientele, the pharmacy was the only department at court which was able to finance itself, and even show a profit. It was taken over in 1797 by the court when Emperor Franz I. purchased it from the widow of the court pharmacist, Elisabeth von Czerny, for 30,000 guilders. Until then the pharmacy had been privately owned and was merely permitted to call itself the Court Pharmacy. The pharmacy was part of the emperor's personal assets for 40 years. Not until 1837 did it pass into the hands of the Office of the Exchequer for the sum of its estimated value.

The *Imperial Prater Inspection* managed the beloved amusement grounds of the Viennese. Prater was part of the imperial asset portfolio but had been accessible to the general public since the reign of Emperor Joseph II. Its management, the Forestry Department, the Office of the Hunt and the granting of coffee house licenses were all in imperial hands. The *Menagerie at Schönbrunn*, today's Schönbrunn Zoo, was in the hands of the menagerie director, who not only bore the responsibility for the veterinarians and zookeepers, but also for the many exotic animals housed there and for stimulating public interest to visit the zoo. The department called *Imperial Building Management* comprised managing the main residences in Vienna and Budapest, the palaces of Schönbrunn, Belvedere, Hetzendorf, Laxenburg, Baden, Prague, Salzburg, Hellbrunn, Innsbruck, Ambras and Miramar; the Augarten Palace in Vienna, the so-called 'imperial buildings at the outer gates' and the management of the Imperial Theater (Burgtheater), the Opera House and the storage depots of the imperial theaters. The Imperial Building Management department employed a total of 80 people for the upper management echelon alone. At the various buildings themselves, a variety of people held their supervisory posts and were permitted to act independently in the interest of their respective properties. The *Imperial Gardens* supervised and maintained all the gardens and greenery which were under imperial control, coordinated the operations of countless gardeners and was in charge of sales (like the pharmacy, the imperial gardens also enjoyed revenues). Through the sale and despatch of cut

The imperial laundry

flowers and bulbs, this department provided for a part of its own income,[36] although it had far too many employees to maintain itself financially, as the pharmacy did. The administration of the *Imperial Hunting Office Gödöllö* and the *Tarczal Vineyards,* which provided most of the wines to the imperial wine cellar, was directed from Vienna, but only employed 20 people. The sale of imperial wines was a third source of revenue to the court administration.

The fourth major department was the Court Services, comprising not only all non-administrative departments but also the particularly cost-intensive departments, at the head of which was always a distinguished court official: an aristocrat enjoying the privilege of a coveted court directorship. To receive such an appointment required ancestry at least at the level of a Count, and the special favour of the emperor.

The most costly department by far was the *Household Utilities,* at whose head stood the *Master of the Kitchen.* This distinguished official was highest in rank, immediately following the four uppermost court offices. He had the ultimate control and supervision and bore personal responsibility for flawless imperial meals. He had to be present at every dinner, even assumed the place of the Chancellor when he was absent. He also bore the responsibility for the kitchen economy, supervising one of the court's highest budgets.

An imperial transport coach bringing laundry to the washhouse in Prater

The Master of the Kitchen reigned over 120 to 150 employees. Included in the Household Utilities were the *Imperial Kitchen, Imperial Pantry*, the *Imperial Wine Cellar*, the *Imperial Confectionery*, the *Firewood and Coal Depot*, the *Light Room*, where thousands of candles for court use were stored, and the *Imperial Laundry*. The laundry rooms handled 70,000 pieces of laundry ranging from tablecloths, napkins and kitchen towels to the emperor's underwear. The laundry was not washed at the Hofburg or at Schönbrunn, but in Prater, where the court owned its own washhouse. The laundry was driven to Prater in special transport wagons, was washed and pressed there, and returned to court, where it was checked off against inventory lists and closeted. The laundresses (women only) thus commuted regularly between palace and Prater. The *Imperial Silver and Tableware* managed the valuable table silver and the precious dishware and table linen.

The court was the biggest purchaser of food in Vienna, making it a coveted customer for all suppliers, since the court could always pay. For that reason alone, the vendors competed intensely to close deals with Vienna's biggest kitchen. In order to make sure that such food purchases were effected with all due thrift and as little waste as possible, an internal Controlling Office, headed by

An imperial laundress

the Court Controller who was independent of the Master of the Kitchen and responsible only to the Chancellor, watched over all the household purchases. Together with his invoice inspectors and household inspectors they ran the Office of Household Economy with eagle eyes, constantly on the lookout for any examples of waste or theft. All purchases had first to be cleared with the Controller, every invoice had to be countersigned by him; he watched over the stores in the pantry and was – apart from the head chef and the controllers of dining room and wine cellar – the only one to possess a key to every supply/storage room, to which no unauthorised person was permitted access.

For household purchases, the so-called "Price Negotiation Commission" met once monthly. Chaired by the Master of the Kitchen and the Controller, the suppliers' price quotations were submitted each month and examined carefully. If a supplier kept his prices at the same level as the month before, the commission made a note of this.[37] The commission did not invariably take the lowest price, but strove for a balance of price and quality. Those suppliers who had always provided outstanding quality were preferred, even if the court did not wish to become dependent on particular suppliers and often requested samples from new ones. If sev-

A glimpse of the court kitchen

eral suppliers provided merchandise of equal quality, the orders were alternated among them. Merchants whose wares were consistently of higher quality than those of their competitors were often chosen; the court was even capable of selecting the most expensive goods, as long as "the quality of the goods justified the price."[38]

The Master of the Kitchen had to maintain a close watch on the pendulum between finances and the pantry stores. Towards the end of the ninetheenth century, the Household Utilities was involved in a corruption scandal which resulted partly from the fact that the Master of the Kitchen did not have the major sectors of his area of responsibility in careful view.

The second-in-command of the household offices was the *Master of the Hunt*, director of the Imperial Hunting Office. Like the Master of the Kitchen, this official had to have aristocratic heritage, at least of a Count. He managed the imperial hunting reserves at Lainz, Laxenburg, Aspern, Hütteldorf and Auhof. This included the animal pens and fenced-in terrain in these reserves, the sale of hunting leases and the organisation of imperial hunts for purposes of entertaining visitors and foreign diplomats. The staff of the forest and hunting offices worked under the Master of the Hunt, who

Guards on duty in their service room

of course had to have well founded knowledge of hunting. Before Emperor Francis Joseph there was also a position known as Silver Valet, who was the head of the *Silver Chamber*, but this position was only sporadically appointed and in 1910, was suspended for good.[39]

The *General Direction of the Imperial Theaters*, i.e. Burgtheater and Opera, was also under imperial aegis. This office did not require aristocratic directors, yet remained under the constant supervision of the Chancellor. In this way, the chancellor also had direct influence on what works would be staged, since he was also the final censor. The General Director had about 250 people under him, from minor directors to stage workers and actors. He was always the problem child of the Chancellor. The disputes, the hard-to-handle artists, the cultural tasks seemed never-ending and stood in stark contrast to the cheerful entertainments demanded by the public. Moreover, the operations caused a deeper and deeper deficit, making its oversight anything but easy.

One office which occupied a peculiar rank in this universe was that overseeing the *Guards*.

The 150 to 200 guards were responsible for security. They had their own management and reported solely to the Chancellor, who was traditionally the commander of all the guards.

Department of the Chamberlain

At the pinnacle of the Department of the Chamberlain was the Lord Chamberlain, the second highest officer at court after the Chancellor. The Lord Chamberlain had two major areas of responsibility: managing the imperial art collections and supervising all those who came and went at court. The epicentre of the Department of the Chamberlain was the Chamberlain's Office, headed (as at the Exchequer) by a chancellery director and in whose hands all the threads of the entire sector came together. In the chancellery, consultants and secretaries, together with the notorious 'ancestral lineage examiners' worked, specialists in researching personal lines of descent, investigating every marriage certificate and family tree. The notice of 'permission to enter court' was only granted when all family members of the high aristocracy were truly proven to have been members of the upper aristocracy.

The art collections belonging to the Habsburg family also lay within the area of responsibility of the Chamberlain. The 'House of Habsburg-Lorraine Treasures', among which the jewellery and crowns numbered, were in the hands of a Master of the Treasury, accompanied by four or five jewellers. Their job was to guard, preserve and maintain the incredibly valuable old treasures of immeasurable value to the Habsburg monarchy. The diamond diadems and necklaces were removed from safekeeping only on the occasion of court balls or representational events, generally worn only by the empress, although archduchesses were occasionally permitted to wear them. Handing over the jewels was under the strict personal supervision of the Chamberlain. And even he was not allowed to deliver the items without a back-up. The Master of the Treasury also had a key to each respective glass safekeeping case, so that only the two of them together were able to open it. All this, as a matter of security.

A culturally significant position was the responsibility of the Chamberlain for the *Historical Art Treasures of the Imperial House* which since 1891 have formed the backbone of today's Kunsthistorisches Museum. This included the *Painting Gallery*, the *Antiques Collection*, the *Coin and Medals Cabinet*, the *Arsenal and Industrial Collection* and the *Imperial Library*. The library was not accessible to just anyone. Only court officials, imperial counselors, diplomatic representatives, university professors, private instructors and employees at public libraries, archives and museums were allowed to borrow books from its shelves.[40] The 30 custodians and consultants working at the art collections worked under the authority of the Director of the Administration Chancellery. The zoological, botanical and geological/paleontological departments, which also employeed 30 employees, were under the aegis of the *Imperial Natural History Museum*. The court sponsored scientific work on the collections, even of external institutes. In the art and natural history collections, scientific lectures were given, although they were always watched over by an employee of the Chamberlain's office.[41]

Department of the Marshal

At the head of the *Department of the Marshal* stood the Marshal, the legal representative of the imperial court. Until the 18th century, he also had jurisdiction over all the court employees; but by the time of Emperor Francis Joseph, the Department of the Marshal had been reduced to a purely judiciary department reserved for the exclusive personal use of the imperial family. Emperor Francis Joseph's large-scale civil law reform of 1895 was not implemented by the Marshal, who continued to work in accordance with the Josephine reform until the end of his tenure; this earlier reform was far more complex, but spared the imperial family one of the most delicate areas: the principle of openness. Public view of litigated cases was permitted for all court actions as of 1895 and it was necessary to protect them from the occasional embarrassments of legal actions being conducted against members of the Habsburg dynasty.[42]

The Marshal, like the Chamberlain, had to hail from aristocratic background at least at the level of Count and have completed a legal education. His department was the smallest one at court and cost next to nothing. The staff comprised just under 30 people, at the head of which stood the Director of the *Office of the Marshal*, employing mostly consultants, translators, experts for purposes of estimating goods, coins and antiques. The "*Judiciary Senate for Legal Disputes*" remained in the hands of the imperial family. Employees at court didn't come into contact with the Office of the Marshal unless disciplinary proceedings were being conducted against them. In such cases, the Marshal sat at the head of

View of the imperial stables

the disciplinary commission which, after three admonishments and threat of dismissal, was convened to handle the case.

Department of the Stables

The *Department of the Stables* was the second most expensive department at court, following the Exchequer. Preservation and maintenance of the imperial stables, the breeding farms and the Wagenburg, which housed the fleet of vehicles, were exorbitantly expensive. The care and maintenance of the horses themselves also swallowed immense resources (they sometimes numbered in the hundreds). The Department of the Stables ranked second in its number of staff members; most of the lower level personnel were employed here.

The Master of the Stables, fourth and last of the four uppermost ranking court officials, had to be an expert in all matters pertaining to horses, of course. This job required far too much expertise for it to be a position of pure honour. Emperor Francis Joseph only appointed men to this office who were distinguished by outstanding knowledge of keeping and breeding horses. They usually came from aristocratic families who enjoyed a reputation of great breeders and experts at the time of the monarchy, e.g. the Kinsky and Liechtenstein families or the Bohemian line of the Thurn and Taxis family.

At the head of this department was the *Office of the Stables* and its chancellery director, secretaries and other employees, a total of ten persons. The assignment of the *'noble boys'* – the sons of aristocratic families who served as pages at imperial events – also numbered among its responsibilities. The *'veterinary department'*, the *'riding schools'*, the *'railway stables'* including coachmen, animal feeding staff and coach maintenance staff, the *'Wagenburg'*, the *'forage warehouse'* and the imperial rifle loaders and lackeys including a total of about 200 persons all were under the authority of the *Imperial Marstal Stables*. This department also managed the *'Imperial Breeding Farm'* in Kladrub and Franzenshof in Bohemia and in Lipizza.

Hungarian Department of the Marshal

Not until 1895 was this department established. The Hungarian Marshal managed the Office of the Marshal in Hungary, the court and church in Budapest, the civil service of Budapest (which was also the palace administration of Gödöllö), the imperial gardens of Budapest and Gödöllö and the Hunting Office of Gödöllö. The Hungarian Marshal was subject to the authority of the Marshal in Vienna.

The *'Military Chancellery'*, the *'Cabinet Chancellery'* and the *'General Direction of the Family Fund'* were also part of the court, or more precisely, had their headquarters in the Hofburg but lay outside the Vienna court administration.

The *Military Chancellery* of the emperor was not a part of the state budget for the imperial court, but rather was financed by the military itself, although it was allocated to the emperor as commander-in-chief of the army. All correspondence between emperor and army was handled directly by the Military Chancellery, bypassing the government entirely. The Military Chancellery had its own chancellery director, its own registry, its own despatch service and a number of secretaries. The General Adjutant and the wing adjutants were on the staff of the Military Chancellery, their salaries paid by the War Ministry.

The *Cabinet Chancellery*, on the other hand, was the official link between the emperor and his state government. All communications from government ministers were received by this chancellery. It also had the responsibility to organise 'communication with the people'. All audiences were managed and supervised by the Cabinet Chancellery. As of the introduction of the Constitution in 1867, it was financed as a direct budget item in the overall state budget, strictly separate from the imperial budget. Even the cabinet direction had its own director and office, its own registry and its own consultants, senior assistants, secretaries, servants and messengers.

The *General Direction of the highest and most confidential private and family funds* managed the personal assets of the imperial house and was also quite separate from the court administration. The employees of the family funds were paid out of the emperor's private purse.

Even in the constitutional era, the imperial court maintained a special status in the state and for that reason insisted on a strict separation of its own and the state's administration. The court was not permitted to become an object of general public discussion nor be associated with political or military decisions of state; and for that reason was prohibited to correspond directly with state ministries. Any and all correspondence with the outside world, and also every public statement published by the court, had to go exclusively to the Foreign Minister, who acted simultaneously as 'Minister of the Imperial House'.[43]

The court lay outside the reach of sovereign territorial law. In accordance with Article 1 of the Municipal Laws of the Empire of 5 March 1862, all residences, palaces and other buildings, including parking areas, which counted as living quarters or temporary places of residence of the emperor and the highest members of his court were "excluded from the municipal laws of that town". Even the police had no jurisdiction in these sovereign court holdings over imperial family members or court employees. Only the imperial security forces designated for that purpose had the right to take drastic action or rigorous steps in these sovereign territories.

Department of the Exchequer
Chancellor of the Exchequer

Office of the Exchequer

- Chancellery Direction
- Department of Ceremonials
- Office of Assistance
  - Registrar
  - Expedition
  - Protocols

and as of 1895:
Hungarian Office of Imperial Marshal

under authority of Chancellor of the Exchequer

Departments

- Accounting
- Payments Office
- Department of Travel
- Buildings Department
  - Telegraph Office
  - Chapel
  - Doctors
  - Salon Services

Administration

- Music Band
- Pharmacy
- Prater Inspection
- Schönbrunn Zoo
- Building Office
  - Hofburg
  - Schönbrunn
  - Belvedere
  - Laxenburg
  - Prague, etc.
- Garden Administration
- Hunting Office Gödöllö
- Vineyard Administration Tarczal

Services

Master of the Kitchen

- Household Utilities
  - Oversight Office
  - Kitchen
  - Pantry
  - Wine Cellar
  - Confectionery
  - Firewood and coal depot
  - Lighting chamber
  - Laundry
  - Chamber of silver and tableware

Master of the Hunt

- Office of the Hunt
  - Hunting Office Administration
- General Direction of Theaters
  - Burgtheather
  - Imperial Opera

Guards

- Administration of Guards (separate adminis tration, but unde authority of Exchequer)
  - Imperial Life Guards
  - Hungarian Life Guards
  - Satellite Guards
  - Mounted Guards
  - Palace Guards

financed by War Ministry

Military Chancellery

Imperial Dynas

... the only link between co

Department of the Chamberlain
Lord Chamberlain

Office of Chamber-lain
- Chancellery Direction
- Ancestry Examiners

Imperial Collections
- Habsburg-Lothringen Treasures
- Historic Art Collections
  - Painting Gallery
  - Antiques Collection
  - Cabinet of Coins and Medals
  - Weapons and Indust. Art
  - Court Library
- Natural History Collections
  - Zoological Collections
  - Botanical Collections
  - Geological-Paleological Collection

Department of Marshal
Lord Marshal

Office of Marshal
- Chancellery Direction
- Examiner of Goods

Judicial Senate
- *reserved for imperial family*

Department of Stables
Master of Stables

Office of Stables
- Chancellery Direction
- Noble boys

Marstal Stables
- Riding Schools
- Draught horse stables
- Veterinary Department
- Wagenburg
- Forage Warehouse

Hofgestüte
- Kladrub
- Franzenshof
- Lipizza

Departments outside Court Departments

financed by national budget

Cabinet Chancellery

financed by private imperial assets

General Direction of Family Fund

inister (=Foreign Minister)

istry and outer world

IV
Life and Work at Court

"As far as concerns the Imperial Lighter of Lanterns, Franz Fuchs, who is known to be lazy, careless, drunken, unreliable, and has been repeatedly penalised, it is necessary to maintain an especially watchful eye on him, since the court is determined to act decisively against all disorderly and unreformable individuals with due severity!"[44]

What at first glance might appear as a harbinger of inevitable dismissal was in reality an everyday, customary proclamation, recited like a prayer mantra, of a pending dismissal which would not ever take place. The emperor and his court may well have been everything in the eyes of their employees and servants, but strict and severe they were not. All people working there were subject to periodic evaluations by their superiors, but there were simply never any consequences or penalties for poor performance.

For a long period of time, an 'especially watchful eye' was prescribed for the Imperial Lighter of Lanterns who, due to drunkenness was either not capable of lighting the lanterns to provide light at court after darkness fell or came dangerously close to burning down the whole establishment. That long period of time went on until it finally became clear that no improvement in his performance could be realistically expected. However, he was not fired, merely sent to work in the kitchen, to a place of work which also had something to do with fire, but was decidedly less perilous to other people if it should come to an anticipated mishap. He was appointed to be 'spitroaster', assigned to turn the skewer of meats over the open fire, always in view of the many chefs and kitchen assistants, to ensure that disaster was avoided. Anyone endeavoring to comprehend Francis Joseph's concept of rule has to take into consideration his behaviour towards his own employees at court. A job at court was generally performed slowly, without any particular effort, often sloppily, sometimes even negligently. Prohibitions and admonishments were repeated again and again, like a pious reciting of the Rosary, reprimands and cautions repeated *ad infinitum*. Yet penalties were rarely imposed, consequences rarely seen. By today's standards, and in fact even by the standards of the free economy of that epoch, performance at court was profoundly infirm. Yet no one clamped down, no drastic measures were taken, no dismissals announced. Whoever landed a job at court could count on remaining there until the end of his life. Poor performance was bemoaned, but not punished. The lowermost levels of service in particular were treated with astonishing degrees of forbearance and leniency. This was not always acknowledged by the subjects with gratitude.

What was it that bonded emperor and public servants together, if not a sense of common fulfillment of their respective tasks? The answer to that question is to be found in the ancient concept of rule in the mind of Francis Joseph. As much as he himself was forced to adapt his own conduct and policies to the exigencies of the modern era, insofar as the responsibilities for his court and his household were concerned, the emperor remained until the end of his days an old-fashioned monarch, a patriarch in the truest sense of the word. Francis Joseph's foremost task as ruler over the imperial court meant not only that he could count on the obedience of his employees; far more than that it meant that the people who lived and worked at court could count on his protection, namely, in financial, social and moral ways. Whoever became ill, frail or unfit for work was permitted to stay on at court and received assistance. In emergencies, the court employees turned to their emperor with requests for aid – which were granted without exception. All those who did their work particularly poorly were reprimanded, admonished or transferred. Dismissals were effected only in the very rarest of circumstances and even then, only when the violations were grave, such as theft or fraud. And even then, so that the person in question would not suffer additional burdens in his future life, no mention was made of the reasons for dismissal. Thus, even thieves and embezzlers were sent benevolently on their way.

A place of employment at the imperial court in the 19th century meant an extraordinary degree of social security. Whoever worked at court had not only a secure job, but enjoyed a wide-reaching social net which, compared to what other simple labourers could count on, seemed barely short of paradise. For, the living conditions in Vienna were catastrophic for the working class at the time Emperor Francis Joseph assumed the throne at the middle of the nineteenth century. Whoever did not have a higher education and was compelled to get a job as a simple labourer or house staff, insofar as he could find work at all, had to be happy if he was granted a primitive place to sleep at his place of work.

Those labourers who, on top of these obstacles, had to rent a room for themselves and their families, could simply no longer survive on their meagre wages. The rents in Vienna escalated by more than 50 % in the first 15 years of Emperor Francis Joseph's reign; by the end of his reign, they were seven times as high. In 1857, a one-room flat in the city cost about 230 guilders, already more than the annual salary of a servant. Making matters worse was the fact that the tiny, simple flats which a labourer might hardly be able to afford were especially expensive relative to the prices of larger apartments, due to the huge demand for small flats. This led to a deadly downward spiral: the lower your income, the higher your costs of living.[45] The upshot was that not only more and more people had to share one flat, but fewer and fewer were able to nourish their families from their salaries. Outside the city walls (today's Ringstrasse), impoverished districts began to spring up: "*... if you visit the lower end of Erdberg ... you can see the same picture of misery hundreds and hundreds of times. In one room, measuring barely 25 square meters, two to three families live, sometimes as many as ten, twelve, fifteen people, depending on the number of children, all pressed together in the same room ...*"[46]

Yet even those classes of society who earned what was considered to be a sufficient amount to live on were threatened by inflation and basic costs of living and endangered to fall into a downwardly spiraling eddy and into the abyss. The lowermost civil servants protested more and more often, more and more clearly, that their salaries had not been adjusted in the slightest for inflation and rising living costs for more than 50 years, were no longer sufficient to nourish their families. They formed special interest groups to fight for adequate remuneration. They would not receive it until 1873.[47] Whoever, on the other hand, had the good fortune to be employed at court and be permitted to live there, was wondrously shielded from this syndrome. One's earnings were low, but the social net balanced it more than amply.

At the imperial court, you could work as an *official*, an *officer*, or a *livery servant*. Officials were the highest ranking level of servants, sharply delineated from all those beneath them, and were skittishly allergic to being grouped with house officers or livery servants. The court officials worked in the chancelleries and writing rooms of the four departments, the military or cabinet chancelleries or at the general direction of the family fund offices. Their work was purely administrative; manual labour was considered unreasonable for a court official. For their work, a legal or, at very least, a business education was a necessary pre-requisite. Moreover, one had to begin at the lowest rung of the ladder. There were no opportunities to enter court service at a higher level, except when on one occasion Chancellor Hohenlohe assembled an effective and powerful cadre of top officials to force through his proposed reforms. Whoever wished to have a career as an official at court had to exercise great patience and even then a career was possible only as higher positions became available through the retirement or death of a superior. This was one marked disadvantage of the court policies which did not dismiss even those employees whose performance was miserable. Many hopeful and well qualified officials of the younger generation never got their chance to climb up the ladder of employment because the incompetent ones never left. Over the years, the court system passed over many valuable human resources due to this shortcoming.

A lifetime of employment always unfolded according to the selfsame pattern. One was 'tried out' as an apprentice, then hired after a period of a few months to maximum two years. Subsequently, for the next 40 years, one climbed slowly up the career ladder. Not every one of the officials succeeded in reaching the top rung open to them, but most retired from a significantly higher position than they had started out in.

Top positions at court were few. The highest which a bourgeois citizen could attain was the post of Chancellery Director at the Department of the Exchequer, comparable to a chief of section at a governmental ministry. Additional top positions were the heads of department at the Office of the Exchequer, i.e. Director of Ceremonies, Director of Household Utilities, Director of Payments, etc. However, it is fascinating that the careers of top officials, which like everything at court were fastidiously documented, show that even the highest ranking officials began without exception as insignificant apprentices and moved upward to the top only after thirty long years. Thus, it is clear that the court fetched its recruits from its own ranks, outsiders were never appointed to top positions. Although such positions must have been coveted, the emperor trusted only long years of experience as the stepping stone to higher ranks of service. Sinecures for influential members of society were taboo in the court administration. The emperor knew well that the key to a functioning court administration lay in the competence of employees who had long been entrusted with the daily responsibilities of court service.

The career of one of the first chancellery directors of the Exchequer, Franz Baron von Raymond, demonstrates in exemplary fashion the classic professional advance of a top court official in the monarchy's later years. Raymond commenced working at court in 1839 as an apprentice in the Office of Household Utilities, worked until he had a permanent court place of employment, laboured his way up every single step of the Household Utility Office until he was appointed as an official at the Office of the Exchequer after seven years. He then advanced to be an adjunct of the registry and five years later rose to become protocol director of the Department of Ceremonies. In 1864, after 25 years of service at court, he was given his first significant posting, appointed to be 'genuine court secretary', comparable with a departmental head, responsible for all ceremonial affairs. Five years after that, he was given the rank and title of a government counselor; and in 1871, after 32 years of service, was named Chancellery Director of the Office of the Exchequer.[48]

All officials at the court of Vienna, not only the top ranked ones, were highly regarded in city society; it was well known that they performed personal services for the emperor and were able to bask in the lustrous glow of his immediate circle. It was well known that they also enjoyed a number of social privileges which distinguished them from their confrères in civil service. But above all else, it was because of their magnificent imperial uniforms that they were the envy of one and all. There were three categories of uniform, depending on the rank of the official, although the actual differences were marginal. Everyone wore a ceremonial jacket of finely woven, dark blue cloth, boasting collar and lapels of black velvet with scarlet piping. The height of the collar was precisely predetermined; depending on the status of the official it was not permitted to be higher than six centimeters or lower than four centimeters, and was fastened with two rows of buttons on which the imperial double-eagle was embossed. The lap folds had to extend to just above the knees. The sleeves also had a double-eagle button. The highest ranking officials boasted gold borders on their collars and sleeves. The rank of a given official could be seen by the rosettes on the projecting collar. A cashmere or silk gilet in dark blue, a white neckband, a hat of black felt, modelled on military hats (which for high officials was adorned with black ostrich feathers), white leather gloves and a sword were part of the ensemble. As a cloak, dark blue cloth with a collar of black velvet served. For gala occasions, the monotone pants were exchanged for ones with gold piping down the sides.[49]

The Officers at court performed a higher level of service, with a fluid borderline distinguishing them from the livery servants beneath them. Those people were distinguished as house officers who performed a service at court which presupposed a special education or which was carried out in the immediate vicinity of the emperor or his family. A great variety of positions bore this title, for the grouping was nowhere near as unified as that of the officials, who all enjoyed the same kind of education. The kaleidoscope of employees in the second rank was quite colourful. At the summit were two officers in two completely different categories: the cook and the valet of the emperor. The cook reigned over a far larger area of responsibility (including the entire kitchen brigade and much of the purchasing staff), whereas the valet performed a more menial form of service but through his nearness to the person of the emperor enjoyed a higher level of prestige. Any activity close to the emperor himself outweighed the lack of actual responsibility tenfold.

Numbering among the officers were also the entire kitchen, confectioner's and room service personnel, the employees of the table service and silverware, the head preparer and wagonmaster of the Office of the Stables, the custodian of the bedrooms and setter of the table, all the craftsmen such as carpenters, upholsterers, polishers and machinists of the Building Office, the custodians of the imperial museums and the servants of all four departments. The Officers were the only ones who might have had a chance to find a job in the free economy, due to their special education;

A porter

nevertheless, next to no one chose to leave court service and to live on the economy, even though kitchen and bedroom staff were much sought. Any rich private household longed to decorate its house with a former court chef de cuisine or former valet; yet next to no one abandoned court service, even though not a few prosperous businessmen made tempting offers. A lifelong, secure job with guarantee of providing for oneself and one's family was something which could be had only at the imperial court.

The uniforms of the house officers, as well as those of the higher servants and lackeys, distinguished themselves from those of the officials. They wore uniforms of brown cloth with golden braids on the collar, knickerbockers with edge strips, an officer's cap or a so-called *chapeau claque*. Corresponding to a wide variety of professional tasks, they received in addition a cutaway suit, working shirt or kitchen toque, a jacket and knee-length dress, a uniform shirt and a black morning suit. The highest officers also were allotted a gala service uniform in rococo style of red cloth with knickerbockers, golden knee buckles and a sword.[50]

The third and largest group of court servants were the so-called livery servants, comprising all the working groups at court which had been educated to no specific activity or service. They

A garden assistant

were in the lowest working category, and performed all the menial tasks. Numbering among this group were the countless servants, the entire cleaning staff, the simple kitchen crew, e.g. maidservants and kitchen help, porters and wardens, roadworkers, woodcarriers, firemen, heaters, castle guardians, night watchmen, and numerous stableboys.

The uniform of the lowest level servants, doormen and porters included a daily work uniform, with hat, cotton kneesocks, calfskin shoes with buckles, gaiters and a coat, plus a gala livery uniform. For bad weather, those working outdoors also had leather boots, a fur coat (or special porter's coat); for in-house work they also had working dress, a linen smock and a cap.

The livery servants were the problem children of the emperor. They comprised not only the most numerous and, therefore, most expensive group of employees, they also had the least amount of working discipline, were slapped with the greatest number of admonishments and reprimands, including for alcohol abuse. The court administration conducted periodic controls through the ranks of these servants. Twice annually, so-called conduit-lists were devised for the Exchequer, on which individual employees were evaluated on their performance. On these lists, the following

A gatekeeper at Augarten Palace

points had to be recorded by their superiors: date of birth, place of birth, religion, class, profession, number of children, usefulness of service, conduct, languages, ability to read and write, tendency to make errors, and for which, and last but not least, has this person often been reprimanded and/or penalised?

An evaluation of these lists shows that livery servants consistently received the worst evaluations, both for their performance and their behaviour. Apart from that, it was evident that those who worked far distant from the central headquarters also received the worst marks. Not all the assessments turned out to be as bad as the following one of a fireman: "... *since it had already been ascertained that Johann Sühsenböck, imperial fireman at the Schönbrunn palace, was given to drunkenness; moreover, that he often left his post while he was on duty,*" his superior came to the conclusion that *"the persistent transgressor of rules, with inappropriate conduct and negligent dutifulness of the worst possible degree, would have to be punished by the complete and utter dismissal from the directorship of imperial services."*[51]

Another livery servant was, following three official reprimands due to extremely derelict performance of duties, even threatened with ultimate dismissal from court services.

Of course, not all livery servants were judged so harshly, nor did their evaluations all turn out so negatively, many performed their duties to perfection. Nevertheless, a large number failed to carry out their work satisfactorily.

Despite all the poor assessments, next to no one was dismissed. Emperor Francis Joseph's leniency towards the lowermost of his servants and the weakest persons living at his court might not have been solely a matter of his anachronistic attitudes, but also due to his awareness that livery servants in particular were expected to do all the backbreaking work. Firewood carriers bore very heavy loads on their shoulders day in and day out. Guards had to stand outdoors all day long, no matter how cold it was. Machinists worked under the most difficult conditions. The hay-binders in the stables, the heavy work of the cleaning crews, all of this exacted a price on physical health over the years. Francis Joseph was the first emperor to rescind the collection of the centuries-old court tax from the lowermost servants. It was a custom that each newly employed person, regardless whether official, officer or servant, had a court tax levied on him: one third of his first year's salary, deducted in twelve monthly installments. Chancellor Liechtenstein felt infinite pity for newly hired livery servants who worked hard to secure permanent employment in their recently won positions. He convinced the young Francis Joseph that this burden was unreasonable and should be repealed. "*There is no doubt that paying this tax from a very frugally measured salary is a great hardship for these people. For example, a lantern lighter or a floor washer in his first year, often after years of burdensome employment in overtime service in order to land this job, frequently has to pay 80 fl from a paltry annual salary of 240 fl, which means getting through the whole year on 13.20 fl monthly for himself, for wife and child if he has a family, for living expenses, clothing, firewood, light, school fees, etc. Since this is clearly impossible, these people have to go without the most basic things in life; and in case a minor illness or other emergency occurs which they cannot ward off, they have to count themselves lucky if they find someone who will lend them a certain sum to get through the year without charging them usurious interest, even if they then fall into a descending spiral when trying to pay back that loan on their tiny salary. It would not require an inordinately merciful attitude on the part of Your Majesty to liberate them from the worries*

A wood carrier

and abasements of such a situation, as well as from the temptations to which such a situation exposes them. I permit myself for that reason to humbly request that Your Majesty free the lowest servants at court from the payment of this service tax in its entirety."[52]

After centuries of this tradition, the court tax was duly abrogated for the lowermost levels of employees in 1852. This was the first step towards adjusting working conditions at court to the new epoch, but another 20 years would go by before the most fundamental changes were effected. Salary increases to acceptable modern levels and the introduction of a halfway-functional system for measuring and rewarding performance were still far distant measures.

The procedures for hiring officials, house officers and servants were identical. A written application was accompanied, ideally, by a number of personal references or recommendations. In spite of this, most applications were rejected. The court attempted to recruit most of its new employees from the ranks of children of current staff members. Since personal loyalty and allegiance to the imperial dynasty were just as important as a reference, the hiring officials felt more at ease hiring from the court's own established ranks. Not to be underestimated, the emperor himself felt called upon to look after the offspring of loyal court officials and servants by offering them an employment opportunity. The very large families of the lowermost servants in particular had little chance to find jobs for their many children. One difference from the children of higher officials jumps to view: the sons of top court officials did not as a rule work at court, but instead made their career in one of the government ministries. Whether this was because climbing the ladder of promotions at court was seen to be overly slow or insecure or because a ministerial career could be rationally planned, can no longer be ascertained. However it is certain that the sons of court officials tended to 'emigrate' to other forms of employment, while the children of simple servants tended to stay at court.

Many attempts were also made by outsiders to find employment at court. Letters of application, letters of reference and requests to hire a protegé of an illustrious personage flooded the Office of the Exchequer. It seemed that nearly everyone had someone for whom they wished to find a position at court. The court hiring services remained eminently unperturbed by this, fulfilling such special requests very rarely. Only the children of court employees or outstanding candidates were hired. One exception was the head chefs in the kitchen, who were usually wooed from service in private homes of the nobility or high cooking positions in France so that the niveau of meals served could measure up to the gourmet standards of the day at least on festive occasions. Were the court to always train its own chefs, educating them to the position, as it were, the cuisine would never have evolved.

Applicants for court service had to be younger than 35, had to have a flawless reputation and, ideally, glowing endorsements. Preferably, their parents already worked at court. After a longish trial period, the decision with regard to permanent employment was made, in most cases positively. For a definitive position to take effect, the employee had to take an oath in the Office of the Exchequer, the famous Oath of Service, which revealed most of what one needed to know about working at court. The most important thing was loyalty to the emperor and the dynasty; to adhere to the rules; and not to take advantage of one's nearness to the monarch by making special requests.

Oath

Solemnly vow to God the Almighty and swear on your honour and loyalty to be loyal and obedient to His Majesty the Highest Eminence, Lord and Master, Francis Joseph the First, by God's grace Emperor of Austria, King of Bohemia, etc. and Apostolic King of Hungary and Highest Eminence of those of the selfsame house and blood.

Once you have been appointed to the position of ... by His Eminence the Lord Chancellor, swear to ardently perform all the duties assigned to you by your superior to the best of your knowledge and ability; not only to keep the best outcome of service for His Imperial and Royal Apostolic Majesty and the Highest Eminence of the Court in view, but to also ward off all disadvantages and dangers, to adhere to the existing rules in the performance of your duties, to fulfil the special instructions which have been imparted to you, to willingly obey your superiors, to loyally and industriously fulfil the specific duties of ... and in general to conduct yourself in such a way that befits a man of honour and loyal servant of His Majesty the Emperor and King.

Should you have a request to make upon the Most Eminent mercifulness of your Master, it will take the form of a written request addressed either to His k. and k. ("imperial and royal") Majesty or to the Chancellor of the Exchequer, with full knowledge of your superior, if not directly via your superior himself, and in strict observance of rules pertaining to the submitting of a special petition.

It is strictly prohibited for any court employee to ask influential personages, regardless whether such personage is engaged at court or not, to put in a good word for you at the appropriate circle of court as may pertain to a request or a recommendation; or to disturb such persons with any form of request. It is imperative to always keep this prohibition in mind.

Swear also that you do not currently belong to a foreign group pursuing political goals nor will you ever do so in future.

So help me God!

> *... (name) swore this oath to me on ... and placed it into my hands.*
> *... (date)*[53]

Whoever had taken this Oath of Service was considered a member of the court staff. Apart from being the recognized recipient of a place of employment, he profited from a host of other benefits from his new position.

As regards remuneration, a position at court was not necessarily advantageous. The salaries were at the normal levels of the day, sometimes even below them. What made a position at court worth striving for was not the salary, but the many social benefits which enhanced employment there: the chance for lifelong job security, of being taken care of in all exigencies and emergencies, including old age, medical care for the whole family and a working day in a safe, secure environment.

One of the most important supplementary benefits at court was doubtless the right to living quarters in one of the many court buildings or a payment in lieu of such quarters, the so-called 'quarters payment' amounting to one third of one's annual salary. Most staff members chose an apartment at court, only higher officials – and even among those, only a small number – preferred to take a 'quarters payment'. All house officers and livery servants opted for living quarters in the Hofburg or one of the other court buildings. The reason was obvious: the rental crisis in Vienna would not have permitted menially employed people to rent more than a single room. Low level servants would have been able to manage no more than the rental of a bed, plummeting them into the notorious circles of 'bedrunners', people who literally rented a place to sleep by the hour.

The apartments at court were assigned to each person by the Office of the Exchequer. Higher officials, and even aristocrats who had a fixed position at court, such as court ladies, housekeeping directors or personal chancellors of the higher nobility, were assigned larger apartment complexes often comprising several rooms. Officials were given less splendid but usually several-room apartments. Servants received flats similar to those of officials, often equally large, since they had several children, a decisive factor in being assigned quarters. The furniture was also sup-

A salon doorman

plied by the court. Higher personages were permitted to select freely from the splendid inventory at the court furniture warehouse; simple staff were given the most necessary items, table and bed. Each apartment had a stove for heating purposes, toilets had to be shared until the end of the monarchy, with but one toilet per corridor.

All court employees who had a claim to quarters lived in a motley tumble together in the corridors of the Hofburg or Schönbrunn Palace, utterly detached from their social rank. No one had his own wing, neither noble staff nor stableboys. The assignment of quarters was made solely on the basis of availability, the only concession to the social rank of an occupant was the apartment size. As soon as quarters were vacated by someone, they were renovated and reoccupied immediately, since there was always more demand than supply. Repeatedly, the court had to rent quarters for its employees in nearby private houses, since the palace was fully occupied down to the very last room.[54]

Some effort was made to allow special consideration to higher ranking female employees. Thus, unmarried women who served

View of Chancellor's court apartment

as court ladies or executive secretaries at the exchequer who were often unmarried, despite their advanced age, were housed in the famous 'spinster corridor', one of the longest hallways in the old sector of court where only women were housed. These ladies, who were unaccustomed to social contact with men, were not forced to live cheek-by-jowl in close contact with simple, jolly men who might have little respect for their virginity. At the same time, one wished to spare them having to share a toilet with men. Yet even this 'spinster corridor' was colourfully mixed with all classes of women. Adjacent to mistresses of the chancellery and court ladies lived laundresses, clean-up servants and chambermaids.

The remainder of the apartments at court were simply handed out as they became available, without any master plan. Hired hands with their families lived one door down from officials; gas lantern lighters resided next door to kitchen chefs; a gardener was housed next to the custodian of the coin cabinets, etc. Only in those apartments which were on the ground floor and nearly had to be called cellar apartments did one try to place single men. These apartments were dark and loud, making them unsuitable for women and children.[55]

The interior of the residences could be altered according to individual tastes. The officials and court ladies in higher positions, in particular, elected to do just that, investing noticeable amounts in enhancing or decorating their apartments, i.e. built-in shelving, water conduits, expensive wallpaper. However, even before they took occupancy they had to sign a waiver that declared they were informed that such investments could only be reimbursed when they had been previously recognized as worthy of reimbursement.[56] Pets were never officially permitted at court, although one or the other court lady kept a canary in her apartment, without raising any objections from the Office of the Exchequer. For hygienic reasons, dogs were strictly forbidden inside the palace and were taken away immediately if one was discovered. The only exception to this rule was the empress.[57]

The apartments could be kept even after one retired from active service. This made it possible for many simple employees to lead a respectable human existence even in old age, since old-age poverty was highly prevalent in the everyday life of the nineteenth century. Elderly people who could not live from their meagre pensions and were forced to go begging were an abiding image of the cityscape. The huge advantage of a court apartment was that one could take in relatives who had fallen on hard times or were otherwise in need of assistance. The only requirements were prior approval and that no sub-lease payments were accepted for such hangers-on. For example, a servant inquired whether it would be possible to take in "*his mother, widow of an official, and his brother, into his apartment in the imperial stables building in front of the palace gate, since only by living together with these relatives would it be possible to improve the quality of his old mother's penurious existence.*"[58] The application was approved, like all such requests. However, only blood relatives were permitted in the rooms. The court checked up on these matters stringently after the investigations conducted by Count Grünne revealed that innumerable sub-renters were to be found in the court buildings who were in no way related to the employees.[59]

Each court employee not only had the right to living quarters, but also to a certain quantum of firewood. Each week, every resident received a contingent of firewood, brought to the apartment by the imperial wood carriers.[60] In many corridors of the Hofburg in Vienna, one can still see today the huge, dark, locked cabinets where the firewood was stored. Each court apartment had its own special shelves where firewood supplies were kept.[61]

Whoever worked at court and lived there was treated to wonderful meal programmes. All meals for court employees were cooked fresh and were of outstanding quality, nourishing and healthy. The subscriptions to the court kitchen for breakfast, lunch and dinner, which every employee could purchase, were for one week. Since the court was extremely generous in the meals it served its staff, entire families could live from one subscription. Employees who were ill often received special meals; for families with small children, supplementary rations of milk were added.

If a court employee or a relative became ill, there was the option of consulting one of the court doctors. In case of need, the patient also was given a prescription to be filled at the court pharmacy where he was given the appropriate medicines, either at cost or, in the case of low-level employees, free of charge. The medical care at court was first class. It was quite exceptional that simple servants or labourers were taken care of medically by their employer in that era. It helps to explain why simple people with very low salaries tended to remain at court. Every change to a different employer would have meant a lesser degree of coverage.

The low salaries were also enhanced by a number of material compensations of a different nature, for example obtaining merchandise at cost. Thus, firewood and food were nearly free, which protected court employees particularly during years when inflation ate away at the buying power of money to an alarming degree. The firewood prices in particular rose so quickly that many people earning low salaries were not able to adequately heat their apartments in some winters.

The salaries were paid punctually on the first of each month, in cash, handed to each person. The employees had to pick up the remuneration personally at the Payment Office and sign for the money received. At the start of the reign of Francis Joseph, it was still permitted for friends or relatives to pick up the salary for someone else. But after irregularities and disputes arose, it became necessary to require the personal appearance of each individual employee.[62] The salaries could not be impounded; this

Distributing pensions at Payments Office, usually on the 2nd day of the month

was an exceptional law applying to the court.[63] And so that hundreds of people did not have to stand in line at the Payment Office each month, and leave their work undone for that time, cashiers spread out throughout the hallways and gardens of court each month, distributing the largesse. For those employees who did not work in the Hofburg, but at external places such as Schönbrunn, Hetzendorf, Belvedere or Augarten, payment officials drove with accountants and a cash box to these palaces and temporarily turned an office into a payment depot. At the same time, other employees erected an official payment office out of folding tables at some central spot in the court gardens, set up the cash box and employee lists and paid the gardeners, labourers and porters their salaries outdoors in the fresh air.

Pensions were paid out on the second day of each month. Since many of the poorly paid livery servants could hardly survive on their meagre pensions (it was not until the 1870s that the pension system was reformed), many pensionists also received so-called mercy payments or reductions. Widows and orphans were also taken care of at court. If the head of the family died, the family could assert a claim for support payments. The income or individual savings of the wife did not need to be deducted.[64]

Apart from salaries, there was also a variety of extra benefits. The servants and house officers who had a tough time making ends meet, in spite of their salaries, could apply for a wide range of aid payments. The higher and highest officials at court profited from a series of exclusive luxury remunerations, e.g. top officials had access to an exclusive, lockable seat in a loge at the imperial theaters and the opera. The proprietor of these seats could, if he wished, use the reserved seat at the imperial theater or opera daily. The proprietor of a locked seat merely had to leave word at the theater by 11:00 am whether he would be attending the theater performance that evening, otherwise the seat would be sold at the evening ticket window. Mid-level and higher officials did not receive a locked seat, but had regular free-of-charge access to theaters.[65]

Whoever wished to live, work and enjoy such privileges at court had to adhere to the severe moral strictures of court life. All officials and servants had to attend church every Sunday and holiday in accordance with church rules. Disport and merrymaking in public places and participating in street festivities at Carneval were not permitted. And court residents had to present to the outside world a portrait of dignity and uprightness which reflected the Apostolic Court at its best.[66]

The court exercised enormous influence on its residents' private life as well. If an official or servant wished to marry, permission first had to be obtained. Name, profession and class of the potential wedding partner had to be revealed. For the court, this was not so much a question of marriages adhering to class barriers, since the court did not really care if an official married a poor farm girl, but rather, whether the particular employee in question could 'afford' family life. The marriage of a lower-level livery servant was no private matter, on the contrary, it was an occasion which the court would receive the brunt of, financially speaking. Each court employee had the right to have his family taken care of financially if and when he was no longer in a position to do so himself. If a poorly paid young employee working as a simple livery servant or porter married and had children, it was just a matter of time before he applied to the emperor for aid payments to supplement his paltry salary, since the official amount was in no way enough to raise a family. The court always helped out, whether through aid funds or out of the emperor's private purse, but tried to prevent such marriages when it was clear that the money would not support family needs. That meant for the servant in question that marriage permission could not be granted until that employee had been promoted to a higher salary category (which occurred automatically with each passing year). Permission to marry was generally refused at the lowest salary level.[67]

To maintain discipline inside the Hofburg, the court guards bore the responsibility. Since so many people lived so close to each other, friction and disputes were inevitable. The biggest ongoing problem at court was drunkenness, particularly among the lowermost ranks. Generally, the authorities tended to make the response to such things quick and painful: if an employee caused a stir, got involved in a dispute or was seen to be drunk and became dangerous, the guards fined him. This measure was only used to defuse the heated situation on the spot, and almost never led to further consequences. Once the delinquent had sobered up and quieted down, he was sent on his way. Unseemly behaviour or poor conduct was quickly forgiven, the court was known for its great leniency.[68]

Only for grievous violations such as fraud or embezzlement, or very poor performance at work or refusal to work for a longer period of time, did the court officials become active. Whoever had been reprimanded three times, had received one threat of dismissal and/or committed a crime, had a disciplinary action opened against him. This process followed a certain, well laid out scheme. First, the staff where the person in question worked investigated the accusations. The results were then presented to the disciplinary commission, consisting of one lawyer from the Office of the Exchequer and four high officials from various departments in order to have a balanced group of viewpoints to decide upon the person's fate. The members of the disciplinary commission then had one week to examine the case, interrogate witnesses and hear the version of the defendant himself. Thereafter, they related their ruling to the Office of the Exchequer in writing. The judgments were similar, for the most part. Most said *"as a penalty, transfer to a different department and reduction of salary."*[69] What is interesting is that the protocols demonstrate that disciplinary processes occurred in all departmental staffs and at all social levels. Not only household servants and coachmen, art restaurators and secretaries fell out in dispute and were in need of reproval, also commissioners and even a captain of the palace in Prague were subjected to disciplinary proceedings. The simplest labourers were reported because of repeated drunkenness, the higher officials were reported due to irregularities in money matters. Next to no one was dismissed. Between 1903 and 1928, for example, there were 86 disciplinary trials, of which only one ended in a dismissal. Even those who were still in their apprenticeship period of trial employment and had to be disciplined were permitted to remain at court, and suffered no impediment to their barely blossoming court career.

V

Court Society
Glamour and Representation

During Francis Joseph's reign, the society throughout the Danube monarchy evolved into a multi-layered, fluid structure. The political predominance of the nobility had been broken by the Land Restoration Act of 1848, the middle class had gained a foothold in the society of the day, economic barons navigated the financial fortunes of the empire; as of 1861, about a third of adult males were granted the right to vote and elect their representatives in the federal states, national parliament and imperial council.

Yet inside the court, the structures still reflected the ancient class order. As much as the emperor was forced to bend to the demands of the age, he persisted in his ultra-conservative stance with regard to the hierarchical societal composition at court. The aristocratic families remained as the emperor's own personal circle; they were the only ones who had unlimited access to court and persisted in positions at the very top of the pyramid. They numbered no more than three to four hundred families; until the very end, they were like gods on Mt. Olympus, cavorted exclusively among themselves as if the world around them had not changed a whit.

This small group of old nobility made up "court society". They were the elite who passed all the tests of "ancestral lineage examination" with flying colours, who were permitted unlimited entry to court based on the pristine purity of their ancestral background. This exclusive group did not need to shine through achievement, it already possessed the requisite glamour from their heritage as princes, counts or barons. Whoever could prove eight maternal and paternal ancestors stemming from a noble line of flawless credentials and whose own ancestors had not broken this longstanding chain through marriages with partners beneath their standing could legitimately lay claim to the seal of approval generally dubbed 'admissable at court' (*hoffähig*). The ancestral lineage examination was supervised by the Lord Chamberlain, who was also responsible for the imperial art collections as well as all comings and goings at court itself. The specialists of historical investigation and verification of heritage ardently took apart and hunted down every family tree, examining it with a magnifying glass to make sure no one gained entry to court who did not belong there. Whereas in England, France and Prussia wider classes of society, particularly wealthy industrialists and entrepreneurs, had gained court access by the mid-nineteenth century, those same great industrialists and their ilk were held at arm's length from court in Vienna. Due to these strict standards, the Habsburg court was widely known as the most illustrious and elite court in Europe, and was subjected to harsh criticism for its refusal to relent. Even the Rothschild family, despite their immense influence, did not gain permission to enter court until the late 1880s.

Not only *vis-a-vis* the outside world, but even among themselves strict rules for the upper nobility were rigourously adhered to. The complicated ranking at the court of Vienna, which at the time was a science unto itself, guaranteed each and every aristocrat precisely that status at court festivities which his heritage accorded him, no more and no less.

The hierarchy of Austria's aristocracy is closely enmeshed with the history of the Holy Roman Empire of the German Federation, whose emperor, more often than not, was a Habsburg. After Emperor Franz I. became the first to accept the title of Austrian Emperor over the lands of Habsburg heritage and ownership (to date the title of Habsburg Emperor referred only to the Holy Roman Empire of the German Nation, whereas the traditional lands of the Danube monarchy were simply the private property of the House of Habsburg) and then two years later brought the selfsame monarchy to a final end by laying down the imperial crown of the German Nation, thereby ringing in the demise of the Holy Roman Empire, the hierarchical structure of the nobility at court had to be reformed. This was because in the young empire of Austria, apart from the empire nobility, i.e. the nobles who had an 'immediate connection to empire' inside the Holy Roman Empire, there were also the Austrian nobles of longstanding heritage. The Biedermeier court had a hard time reforming these structures; not until 1837 did Francis Joseph's predecessor Emperor Ferdinand reform the hierarchical structures of rank at court, which then endured until the end of the monarchy.[70]

In first and foremost place in the hierarchy ranged the families of princes and counts who were 'intimately connected' to the kingdom before the end of the Holy Roman Empire in 1806, in other words held sway even within the German kingdoms and – this was the key factor – were not subjects of any of the numerous German sovereigns, but only to the emperor himself; and moreover, possessed both a seat and a vote in the former council of princes. Within this highest echelon of nobility, the internal sequence was arranged according to the date of elevation to the rank of prince. The highest ranking families were Arenberg, Lobkowitz, the branches of the Salm family, plus the families of Dietrichstein, Auersperg, Fürstenberg, Schwarzenberg and Thurn and Taxis. The famous Liechtenstein family ranged ahead of the aristocracy, since it was the only family of still reigning princes.

In second place came those families who were also 'intimately connected' to the empire, but until the end of the Holy Roman Empire possessed no seat or vote on the council of princes. This rank included the families of Croy, Esterhazy, the various branches of the houses of Hohenlohe, Schönburg and Waldburg, the families Trauttmansdorff and Windisch-Graetz, to name but a few. Thereafter followed the dukes of heritage lands, i.e. those of Austria whose reign did not lie inside the Holy Roman Empire, such as the families Lubomirski, Lamberg, Kinsky, Palffy and Collato. Immediately after that came the families of counts and barons.

As complicated and precisely defined as the ranks of the aristocratic families were, they were treated with the corresponding degree of respect both by the court and by the panoply of families themselves. The ceremonial, the way of dealing with this structure of ranks on official occasions, had to reflect the position of each and every member of this class. The court ceremonies until the very end of the monarchy were far more than an organisational scheme, they were a visible display of every living aristocrat's position at court and in present day society.

Those who were permitted to appear at court were of course not allowed to simply show up arbitrarily at the festivities, but had to adhere to ironclad rules. In the run-up to court festivities, the Office of the Chancellor held its own ceremonial rehearsal to ascertain and affix the place of each individual in the approaching festivities. Guests were not allowed to enter in terms of where they had the best view of the gala affair; they had to stand in the spot foreseen by their rank, namely, following the next highest ranking person and preceding the next lower ranking person. And even for the aristocracy, it was not sufficient to be able to prove an eminent lineage. In order to be integrated into court ceremonials, it was necessary to actually make the effort to obtain official court recognition. Only persons who had been granted such recognition could be a part of the retinue of the emperor on official occasions. They were then, and only then, permitted to follow the emperor, the Habsburg family and the uppermost dignitaries of court in the magnificently staged performance of state visits, court ceremonials or the famous festive procession for the Feast of Corpus Christi, and thus, become a part of the production.

For aristocratic males, this was best embodied by an appointment to be an imperial chamberlain; for women, it was an application to join the equally illustrious Star of the Cross order. Male aristocrats over age 24 could apply for the distinction of chamberlain. For the appointment to this rank, the applicant had to pass the ancestral lineage examination, be an Austrian-Hungarian citizen, have a flawless political and social reputation and command a degree of wealth commensurate with one's class.[71] For the aristocracy it was a point of great importance to be integrated in the festive events at court, it was part and parcel of its glamour.

As a chamberlain, one received a chamberlain's uniform with its own badge of honour[72], the obligatory golden valet key. This meant one was now allowed to appear in official court robes. The distinction of chamberlain was a supremely high honour, yet at the same time a burdensome duty to fulfil for the emperor. For, as chamberlain one had to be present at all representational affairs of court, barring a timely announcement of illness as an excuse, and take one's place in the famous 'courtège', the *entourage* of the emperor. A chamberlain received no remuneration for his services; the honour of being part of the highest level of court ceremonies alone was sufficient. Since there were hundreds of chamberlains, the groups were assigned to service in revolving fashion; each took his turn, each fulfilled his duty in sequence. Chamberlains were summoned to appear for the proclamation of newly-named ambassadors of foreign states, for the highest receptions and ceremonials of court. If one had been summoned to appear for revolving duty, one had to stay in Vienna in order to be at the ready for this task.

Emperor Francis Joseph was far more strict with the nobility than his predecessors had been. Under Emperors Franz and Ferdinand, attendance of the aristocracy at the often quite strenuous ceremonials at court had slackened off noticeably, not least because of the personal lifestyle of the two Victorian Age emperors, who led the reclusive lives of a homebody. From the very start of the reign of Emperor Francis Joseph, the court paid particular heed to the involvement – and that meant the regular attendance at court – of the nobility. Whoever had not appeared for a longish period of time had to answer to inquiries about why they were not performing their obeissances to the emperor.

In 1869, Francis Joseph altered the pre-requisites leading to the chamberlain distinction. In the most formalised procedural way possible, he let it be known that this was not a sign of distinction or honour but a 'genuine court service'[73] The newly regulated, stricter chamberlain edict was the emperor's chosen method to discipline the aristocracy. As lenient as Francis Joseph was towards low-level officials and servants, he was severe and rigid with the uppermost ranks of society. Whoever enjoyed great benefits in society through the blessings of his/her birth had to bear the burdens of additional duties which were attendant upon that extraordinary status. In the mind of the emperor, that meant for the aristocracy: an impeccable lifestyle and the fulfillment of duties both to their respective family and to the state. If an aristocrat did not fulfil the high ideals of his given position, i.e. if he incurred debts or got involved in a scandal which became public, Francis Joseph matter-of-factly revoked the chamberlain distinction from the person in question, which was a terrible disgrace for the entire family. For most aristocrats, it was a matter of course – and, beyond that, a great honour – to be selected for such honourable service. After all, the court was the last exclusively held bastion of the aristocracy; it alone signalled what level of society a person had hailed from since ages past and how close he stood to the reigning monarch.

Apart from the aristocracy, people who either fulfilled a special function or had been awarded a special distinction were also permitted to appear at court, even if not a member of elite court society. The right of appearance at court in its furthermost extension was also granted to high military, political and church dignitaries.

The emperor also had the option of influencing the rigid ranking system himself by distinguishing persons who had performed services of extraordinary value to the state or the imperial house but were without aristocratic background, by awarding them a position of particular distinction in the court ranks. The appointment to privy councillor (*Geheimer Rat*) was the highest distinction the emperor could confer. With this award, one obtained entrance to court ceremonials, the title of *His Excellence* and a special rank in court. Since this was a matter of personal selection by the monarch himself, the privy councillor were even permitted to file into court ahead of the chamberlains. The Prime Minister and cabinet ministers who were often of non-aristocratic background, almost invariably received this honour, in isolated cases also men who in the emperor's eyes were deserving of special distinction because of their efforts in one field or another.[74]

For the newly created nobility, as well as the so-called letter aristocracy, those bourgeois families who had been elevated to the aristocracy over the centuries, usually at the end of a long military career as officer or as a high official of state, or else of powerful economic barons whom one wished to distinguish particularly, there was one sole way to appear at court: by being appointed a 'seneschal'. These filed in behind the privy councillor and chamberlains and were permitted to appear at court for major ceremonials and take their places at the imperial dining table.[75]

Not every newly ennobled person was permitted to appear at court, however, since that honour was a personal distinction and not automatic. But more than that, the court simply didn't have room to accommodate all the newly ennobled ranks. During the Francis Joseph era there were more than 5,700 elevations into the lowermost ranks of nobility, an enormous numerical increase over previous epochs. This bourgeois aspiration to enter the ranks of nobility is an additional demonstration of the strong mental bond the people felt towards the monarchy.[76]

In principle, the emperor rejected frivolous ennoblements, particularly when it was a matter of catapulting someone into the upper ranks of nobility, i.e. creating a baron, in accordance with the nobility law of 1877. With the letter aristocracy he had fewer qualms. The title "Knight" or "Noble" was an untroubling matter to him, compared to creating a Baron (*Freiherr*). Francis Joseph's remark on the petition of a German who hailed from a venerable dynasty for an Austrian baronial title: "*If he desires an Austrian baronial title, he can have it; I myself find the age-old nobility he already has to be preferable.*"[77] To the emperor, an age-old standing in the upper classes of empire, even if the title itself was ostensibly lower, was worth more than any elevation in the modern age.

Of course the emperor couldn't stem the tide of the movements and values of his age, and for that reason, countless men were raised to the nobility. But it was always a matter of importance to him that not only those people who donated large sums of money to public causes were ennobled, but in particular, those who had served the state and the emperor with distinction and loyalty. Nevertheless, towards the end of his life, the emperor approved more ennoblements than ever before, "*often for people whose one and only service was shoring up the court funds,*" as one skeptic noted.[78]

The emperor showed himself to be stubbornly unwilling whenever his ministers or governors handed him ennoblement petitions from people with lots of money but few services to distinguish them. Francis Joseph's son-in-law, Archduke Franz Salvator, made great efforts to secure the elevation of a filthy rich property developer whose daughter wished to marry one of his regimental comrades from an elevated noble family, who were a bit ashamed to permit a bride utterly without noble credentials into their family. He asked Governor Kielmansegg for assistance in making this ennoblement a bit more palatable to the emperor. As a rule, the emperor wished to have nothing to do with such elevations, which had purely financial motivation. Governor Kielmansegg, not without a certain cynicism about the convoluted path which was necessary to convince the emperor while at the same time doing the state a favour: "*The developer earned a fortune from the railroads, but had done little for them. A newly planned railroad, however, happened to be a local line promising little in the way of revenues, but whose construction had great political significance. The Director of the Ministry of Commerce, Ritter von Wittek, needed a subscription of common shares for this railroad to the tune of about a half million crowns in order to begin construction. It was his intention to tap it from this fellow who hungered for a noble title.*

He reported this to the emperor, whose response was: 'Let Wittek pump him for all he's worth.' The squeeze job worked, and nobility certification was the reward. A better title for the fellow would have been 'von Bahn Pump'" [79]

Those permitted to appear at court had to accommodate themselves to the official annual court calendar. The year's first important function was to pay one's respects to the emperor on the 1st of January each year at the famous New Year's Day Reception at court. All the aristocrats and the entire diplomatic corps and other dignitaries of state made their pilgrimage to the Hofburg to transmit their heartfelt New Year's wishes to the emperor. Thus, the year commenced with a demonstration of respect to the throne. The monarch personally received these good wishes only from the highest diplomats, his highest court dignitaries and the sovereign princes of the realm. All the others delivered their wishes to the Chancellor, the official representative of the emperor. The ladies declared their good wishes to the empress's chancellor; the empress also received the wishes personally only from the diplomats.

Shortly after the New Year's Day ritual, the two court balls took place, the first was the official Court Ball, the second merely a 'ball at court', at which the aristocracy were compelled to appear. The ball at court was the smaller of the two, to which only the aristocrats and the diplomats were invited. It was markedly more intimate and personal, and much more exclusive than the Court Ball.

At the Court Ball, which was considered the offical State Ball and was the largest secular event at court, anyone could participate who enjoyed entrance privileges at court: the whole court society, the diplomatic corps, the dignitaries and bearers of awards and distinctions, as well as active officers of the Vienna garrisons, who were the only ones permitted at court who had no official 'court admission recognition'. Since the emperor was the commander-in-chief and made a point of emphasizing the importance of the military whenever he could, the officers were granted the privilege of attending this ball. It was an honour designed to outweigh slightly the fact that military service under Francis Joseph was anything but glorious. The officers were paid miserably, were often not permitted to marry for lack of adequate funds to support a family, yet at least enjoyed a high social status.

The Court Ball took place at the end of January, the exact day always being set by the empress. The emperor – who was immeasurably overjoyed if Elisabeth simply appeared – adapted to every extent possible to the personal plans of the empress. He himself always informed his Chancellor with a brief written note about the days which were preferred by the empress: *"The empress wishes for the Court Ball to take place on Wednesday, the 27th of the month and the ball at court on Wednesday, the 3rd of February. Please prepare everything for these dates."*[80] Sometimes, however, the empress kept the Chancellor waiting with her decision, making the officials responsible for the preparations increasingly nervous. No one was permitted to simply check in with the emperor with an inquiry; generally the emperor himself intervened, trying to spare his officials any undue stress, and moved the matter along himself, regardless of the empress's indecisiveness: *"The empress wishes to set the date for the ball at court 12 days before the event. Nonetheless, the invitation list could be prepared."*[81]

Only the highest guests were actually sent invitations to the Court Ball, for the others a 'court announcement' had to suffice. In other words, the date of the ball was posted, there was no r.s.v.p. required and whoever enjoyed general admittance at court was permitted to attend the ball. As of the 1880s, ball attendance had to be limited generally to the military. Only about 700 tickets were distributed among the military because the numbers of other visitors avid to attend the ball had risen so swiftly in the years previous that their security could no longer be guaranteed. The ball announcement also made clear the standards of appearance: dignitaries must wear their court uniforms, military personnel their military uniforms, for all others a cutaway evening suit was compulsory. Ribbons and orders were permitted. The ladies were to appear in 'round-necked' dresses, which was the going euphemism giving the all-clear to strapless, decolleté gowns.

For ladies, ball attendance caused an enormous outlay of expenses. Evening vestments cost in the region of 300 – 500 guilders[82] (as a point of reference, a court servant earned 300 guilders annually). And most of the ladies wished to make a certain splash, socially speaking, i.e. make a grand impression on the other ladies through an especially splendid evening gown, but they also wished to read about who was 'best-dressed at the ball' in the next morning's newspaper.

The ball season was a significant stimulus to the economy. The mercers and clothiers, designers, top sales establishments and ateliers for custom-made dresses could count on big cash flow at the beginning of the year. For the wealthy aristocratic women, the Court Ball was also one of the few opportunities they had to show off their old family jewels, their precious diadems and necklaces, which had to remain locked away for most of the year.

The day of the Court Ball got underway quite early in the morning, at least for the ladies. Whoever could afford it had an appointment at Vienna's best coiffeur, Monsieur Ardelliano. This Italian hairdresser hardly knew how to cope with all the ladies who wished to have his own personal touch on that day, so opened his portals at 7:00 am. Those who had greater cachet angled an appointment with him just before the ball began that evening. The less fortunate ones who could only land an early-morning appointment then had to go through the whole day with a pompous, delicate hairdo, often with the family jewels entwined in their artistically staged plaits – entailing twelve long hours of careful maintenance.[83]

All this time, the Hofburg itself resembled an anthill of activity. The two court balls were the largest events which the court had to organise, comparable with state visits. The court kitchens were running at high speed from dawn. An exquisite buffet was organised and prepared for nearly 2,000 guests. Whatever could be prepared ahead of time was already in the cooling rooms, ready to be served. There were canapés, soups, small hot dishes, superb finger food, huge artistic pyramids of delicatessen specialties. Every kitchen employee was on duty helping to prepare these enormous hillocks of food. The supplies were delivered days ahead of time, the confectioners worked round the clock fashioning hundreds of creamy tortes, cakes, meringues, candies, chocolate cremes and frozen desserts. From all other areas of court employment, assistants were requisitioned for kitchen work. For the immense buffet, chamber servants were specially schooled as waiters in an effort to accommodate the waves of ardent ball visitors.

The gardeners had begun to decorate the ballroom and festive salons the day before, of course. Huge palm trees and shrubs were brought from the imperial nurseries by the dozen and distributed throughout the ballroom and the staircases. The gardeners bred the most magnificent varieties of cut flowers in greenhouses and then arranged them to form spectacular bouquets for the walls and niches. The festive rooms and official entrance staircases unveiled a vast sea of flowers in the middle of winter. The most precious wall hangings were fetched from the imperial storehouses to adorn the stairwells, adding their own inimitable charms and sense of luxury. The storehouse for dishware and table silver brought out its best offerings of cutlery, glasses and china; the laundry room wheeled in backbreaking piles of damask tablecloths.

The livery servants placed new candles into all the chandeliers. For court balls, there were even several rows of candles lining the mantlepieces and door jambs to ensure that the festive rooms would be bathed in the splendour of unlimited light. The cleaning crews then went through one last time to make sure everything was perfectly placed, every glass spotless. Temporary cloak rooms were established at the foot of the staircases and servants were schooled in the handling of expensive fur coats and capes. For court servants, cooks, doormen, waiters and waitresses and cleaning crew, the Court Ball was an exercise in concentrated, unalloyed and unlimited stress, linked to lots of overtime hours of labour. As a bonus, they received an extra week's salary.

The Court Ball traditionally commenced at eight o'clock p.m.; thus, as of 7:30, the coaches began to drive up and unload their occupants. In the memories of those who attended these balls, they were like a fairy-tale sprung to life, a dream come true. Merely driving up to the Hofburg was a memorable experience.[84] A long, long column of coaches inched its way forward from the Ringstrasse to one of the many designated entrances. At the gates and in the courtyard, mounted Hussars formed an honour guard with glittering sabres. If it happened to be snowing, everything looked as if it had been sprinkled with confectioner's sugar and the brightly illuminated palace became downright magical in the snow-covered accents of its brightly uniformed guards.

Court society entered the Hofburg via the Diplomats Staircase, the entranceway for the diplomatic corps being on the Bellaria, whereas the military generals and officers accessed the palace through the Augustiner Bastion. Lackeys in gala uniforms opened the coach doors, assisted the ladies to step down. As soon as the guests entered the palace, they were relieved of their fur coats and capes and the hurly-burly crowd burgeoned forward in full splendour, diamonds glittering everywhere, precious robes brushing against one another, words of greeting, the acoustic level rising to nearly intolerable. At precisely eight o'clock the guests had to be assembled and ready for entrance. The magnificent tangle moved amorphously towards the Ceremonial Salon, passing by a number of other salons against the walls of which the emperor's bodyguards stood in impressive formation. Once in the Ceremonial Room, the guests continued their chatter until the moment of imperial entry was announced. The salon was aglitter with light, jewels, flowers and silk, particularly the ladies were recalled in later years as having broken all the boundaries of splendour. Prince Gottfried Hohenlohe, son of the Lord Chancellor, represented his father at the ball festivities at the Czar's St. Petersburg palace in 1891 and later reported to him about what a poor showing the Russian ladies made compared to the *belles dames* of Vienna: *"But the society! Agh, nothing but foul, poorly dressed and raggedy women without the slightest charm, very little in the way of jewels, in other words, a hodge-podge of invidious females who look like they got dressed in the coach on the drive here, complete with crookedly pinned flower coursages on their heads!"*[85]

All the while, the imperial family and the sovereign princes and princesses who were poised to take part in the ball festivities were gathered in the Alexander Salon. Precisely at half-past eight, the Chancellor reported to the emperor that everything was ready for the entry of the *crème-de-la-crème* of Viennese society. The imperial family formed a cortège in pairs, at the head of which was the emperor with the empress, each followed by an archduke with an archduchess. In the Room of Mirrors, the diplomatic corps awaited the imperial formation in their most elegant garb, chests dotted with orders and ribbons, the ladies in their priceless gowns. Each diplomat who had not yet made an official appearance at court was then introduced to the emperor and empress, who chatted with him briefly.

At precisely half-past nine, the imperial cortège set into motion. They marched into the Ceremonial Salon, the diplomatic corps entered through a second entrance. The flocks of ball visitors waited, laughed and gossiped in small groups, refreshing old

Emperor greets the Diplomatic Corps before Court Ball gets underway

acquaintanceships, tensely awaiting the emperor and empress until they heard the classic three-time thud of the heavy staff at the only door which was still closed. Silence prevailed on the instant. The Ceremonial Director opened the door and the sea of visitors parted in a matter of seconds, in utter stillness. The Lord Chancellor knocked his golden staff thrice on the parquet floor, and the grand entry got underway. The Ceremonial Director moved forward to the far wall, the Lord Chancellor immediately behind him, then followed by the emperor with the empress, the emperor wearing the traditional field marshall's gala uniform, with white jacket and red trousers, the empress in a gorgeous ball gown, adorned with diadem and necklace from the Imperial Treasury; they were followed by the archdukes and archduchesses. The ladies in the room curtseyed low as they passed, the gentlemen performed a deep bow. At the same time, the diplomatic corps entered the room through its own separate entrance.

The grand entrance of the imperial couple wound to an end at the dais with two golden chairs for emperor and empress, surrounded at a certain distance by other chairs for members of the imperial family. The emperor usually stepped without delay onto the dance floor to perform the 'cercle' – the mandatory chat with

Entry of the imperial family at the Court Ball

selected visitors. The empress performed her 'cercle' while remaining seated. To the right of the dais, along the wall, sat the row of princesses. Only the wives of the highest nobility were permitted to sit in this coveted spot. They sat in strict observance of their status, the highest ranking princesses closest to the imperial couple. Two at a time, a princess and the wife of a diplomat were called forward to greet the empress, to converse briefly. Each took a seat in one of the two armchairs on either side of the empress for the short interval of their talk. When their moment was over, they had to withdraw walking backwards, something challenging in itself in their long gowns, including a few stairs which had to be mastered, curtseying the while. The ladies whose gowns had a long train needed to be eminently careful that they didn't take a spill, to the malicious delight of the others, something which happened not infrequently.

When the Dancing Master gave the signal for the orchestra to begin, dancing commenced, usually opened by an archduke and archduchess. The dance programme had been written up with great precision long before. On the small, white, gold-bordered card could be read: *"First waltz from 9:30 until 9:37 pm, five minutes intermission, first polka from 9:42 until ..."*[86]

During the dancing, the elaborate rules devised long-previous for military officers tended to cause problems for the ladies. At court festivities, all officers had to be dressed in strict adherence to military guidelines; not seldom the emperor made a disparaging remark about too high a collar or some such blemish, and the person in question was discreetly told to leave the palace at once. The all-seeing eye of their commander-in-chief was well known to the military and they were usually tense about fulfilling the rules to the letter. That meant, among other things, that to avoid imperial disapproval their leather footwear – in the case of the cavalry, high leather boots – had to be polished to a deep shine. But for the ladies, such highly polished footwear was lethal poison, since the whole ballroom not only reeked of shoe polish but the extremely expensive gowns of the countesses were bordered in black before long, sometimes blackened for the whole lower third of the material, and thereby ruined, since shoe paste could not be removed from such delicate materials. Over the years some ladies developed the habit – since they had often been able to wear a new gown only once for that reason – of putting on 'just an old rag'. Only after many years of complaints did an official finally take his heart in hand and apply at the highest office, where the emperor always had an open ear for the concerns of the ladies, whereupon patent leather boots became a part of the rules.[87]

The Court Ball was also the official occasion for introducing the new ladies at court to the empress, thereby making their right to appear in court society publicly demonstrable. The young aristocratic ladies, who were generally referred to as 'countesses' until they wed, were also introduced officially to court society by being presented to the empress at the Court Ball. This presentation took place at a precisely designated time in the highly regimented agenda of the evening at the ball. Following the first quadrille, the empress withdrew to the Privy Councillors' Room, where the Lady Chan-

Emperor honours ball visitors with his conversation

cellor escorted and presented the young princesses, countesses or court ladies.

Following the second quadrille, the empress usually withdrew to the adjacent rooms with the archduchesses and a handful of selected ladies to sip tea at tables pre-set for that purpose. Tiny cards in diverse colours had previously been distributed to the highest ranking ladies of court society, indicating precisely where they were to seat themselves for this occasion. The best table was, of course, reserved for the empress. It was set up in the Room of Mirrors, had white-coloured cards and was designated for the duchesses and female ambassadors. At the three other tables, with pink or blue cards and table linen to match, the ladies were ranged, with a high ranking duchess at the head of each table.[88]

While the empress sipped her tea, the huge buffet was opened in the large Redouten Hall, which soon turned into a veritable battleground for the coveted dishes and delicacies, particularly by the military.[89] More than any other regiment, the Royal-Imperial Ulans, a particularly self-assured unit of the cavalry, unwittingly gained a notorious reputation through their behaviour at the ball buffet. They were known to be not averse to removing their helmets and piling them high with sweets from the long tables, for

Emperor in conversation with a visitor to the ball

the simple reason that they could transport more in their helmets than in their two hands.[90]

There was not, in fact, much dancing done at the ball. This was largely due to lack of space to move in. The cotillion was the high point of that activity, at which the gentlemen were given corsages to present to the ladies. The flowers had the same form as in Maria Theresia's era, were bound with wire and ensconced in curled sleeves. The couples dancing the cotillion were observed by the aristocracy with eagle eyes. Whoever danced a cotillion twice in sequence with the same partner was considered engaged to marry.

The last waltz closed with the precision of a watch at exactly a quarter past midnight. The official exodus of the court took place in precisely-mirrored reverse of the entry. The imperial family formed in a double line, the guests opened a wide swathe for them to pass, the Director of Ceremonies led the cortège with his golden staff, followed by the Chancellor and the imperial family. When this upper crust of the court had exited, the doors were closed behind them and the ball was over. The guests then moved towards the exits designated for their use, picking up their wraps at the cloakrooms, each receiving a box of sweets from Demel, the court con-

Traditional 'battle of the buffet' at the Court Ball

fectioners, as they parted. Servants assisted with the coats and helped the ladies into the coaches.

As soon as the last guest had left the hallowed halls and the last coach had rolled through the gates of the court grounds, the servants and cleaning crews began with the rough stage of the clean-up. More than 10,000 candles had to be safely extinguished, the most valuable dishware had to be washed right away in the middle of the night, so that it could be returned forthwith to the silver and dishware vaults. The employees of this division were long aware that despite their care and diligence, a not insignificant number of small dishes and pieces of cutlery regularly went missing after court festivities. The remains of the buffet were packed together, to be sold the next day. The profits went to the servants, chefs and confectioners who had worked overtime to make a glittering evening come about. On such occasions, the work continued unabated all night long. Early next morning, the gardeners appeared to haul the huge palm trees back to the greenhouses, and the next cleaning crew arrived to slowly bring the rooms back to their proper state.

Slightly less than two weeks later, the whole thing would start all over again. That was the moment when the emperor sent out invitations to the 'ball at court', which always came after the Court Ball. The ball at court was much smaller, and far more exclusive, since only the most important dignitaries and personages from court society, aristocracy and military received invitations. A personal invitation was sent to each guest, this being not a state occasion, but rather, the emperor's personal soirée. The driving up of the coaches and entry of the court unfolded in the selfsame manner as at the Court Ball, merely somewhat earlier in the evening, since the official introductions and presentations which took so much time had all been completed at the Court Ball.

For the aristocracy, the ball at court was, of course, much more attractive. Instead of 2,000 guests, only 700 were present, making it possible to dance. More important, the aristocrats were among themselves and it was far easier to speak to the emperor and empress personally. But above all else, the honour of dining with the emperor and empress was treasured by these guests. At this ball, there was no buffet, everyone was served at table in the Room of Mirrors, the Radetzky Salon and the Stephan Apartments. As at the Court Ball, the tables had different coloured table linen, matched by different coloured cards marking the place where each guest was to sit. Here, too, the placement cards were ordered strictly according to status: uppermost aristocracy was nearest the emperor. Nevertheless, all guests could eat sitting down at table.

The table decorations were magnificent: huge floral arrangements as centrepieces, the most valuable china the court possessed, and glass from the treasury of tableware stores. At each place, the gold-bordered menu card was placed. The dishes never varied at the ball at court. There was crème d'orge en tasse, fish with mayonnaise, patè, a roast and ice cream for dessert. Wine, beer and champagne were served with the meal, by countless servants in gala uniforms who buzzed back and forth between kitchen and dining tables in quiet routine. Following dinner, the guests returned to the ballroom. At twelve midnight, the ball was over. Thereby, the two traditional social duties of the court were absolved; the small additional balls which were given by the mother of the emperor, now deceased, had terminated by the 1860s at latest. The initiative for small-scale events of this kind during carneval season had always been the purview of the first lady at court, but the young empress expressed little interest in such optional extras, much to the disappointment of court society.

Having got through the two court balls and the New Year's Day duties, the aristocracy was nearly finished with its compul-

Only at the 'Ball at Court' was it possible to dance, due to fewer visitors

sory duties. At the presentations of ambassadors, receptions of foreign sovereigns or official court business, only those chamberlains whose turn in revolving service it was had to appear. The next mandatory appearances for the aristocrats were the holy day festivities; and then, the court society also had to appear in full plumage at the Easter Week ceremonies. In their spectacular old coaches, they drove up to the palace and took part in the church ceremonies. The most important date of the year, which was even more important to the emperor than the court balls, was the Corpus Christi procession.

The traditional procession of the court at Corpus Christi – fondly dubbed 'God's Court Ball' by the Viennese – was the most significant festive day on the calendar to the imperial family, since this holiday celebrated and demonstrated the longstanding close ties of the dynasty to the Catholic Church. Everyone had to appear at the procession, including those who were not assigned to march in the parade itself, since the emperor viewed this as his foremost representational duty. Unlike at the court balls, the general population was able to follow every detail of this event. The parade always marched from the Imperial Chapel across the palace courtyard and through parts of the inner city, the Lord Chancellor distributed tickets for onlookers in the courtyards, since they would otherwise have burst at the seams from the crowding. Tickets in various colours indicated which zone the visitor was allowed to stand in. It was important to the emperor that this ticket distribution be effected fairly, utterly uncoupled to a visitor's social status. Repeatedly he told his Chancellor to tell the guards: *"Please be so kind as to instruct the guards to apply the selfsame courtesy and liberality in admitting the public to the palace grounds and dealing with them as they showed last year."*[91]

Higher ranking citizens and dignitaries were given apartment tickets, enabling them to stand at a window of the palace itself to view the proceedings. Two hours before the ceremony began, the entrances to the palace grounds were closed and locked, only those with valid tickets were permitted to pass. When the bells began to peal, everyone knew that the church ceremony had commenced. Then the parade got underway from the imperial chapel and was soon visible to all as it stretched across the palace grounds. The impression it made on spectators was staggering: *"Whoever sees this imposing, richly coloured panoply even once will not easily forget it. The glittering gold, the sparkling ribbon orders on the uniforms of the illustrious dignitaries, the magnificent dresses of the ladies, whose gold-embroidered trains were carried by pages or lackeys, the glory of the ecclesiastical vestments, the ramrod-straight guards in their picturesque yet quaint uniforms, the crowds of court servants from stableboys upwards, all in gold-rimmed, medieval-looking livery and costumes. And in spite of this immense variety of individual appearances, the overall impression was utterly harmonious."*[92]

The whole procession wended its way amidst the ringing bells and the choral song of the court choir. Trumpets, kettledrums and percussion accompanied the song. Three priests headed the procession, followed by 100 court employees, then came 20 priests, then a huge number of seneschals and chamberlains, followed by the high state dignitaries, the privy councillors and the Prime Minister, behind whom followed the imperial ministers. Then came the Archdukes, behind whom came the golden baldachin whose four tassels were held by four chamberlains. Beneath the baldachin, the court priest carried the Holy of Holies, behind which strode the Lord Chancellor and behind him, the emperor. As a sign of humility, he wore no hat, appearing in his field marshall's gala uniform with the linked chain of the Order of the Golden Fleece draped over his shoulders. Adjacent to and behind the emperor strode his captains of the guard and adjutant generals. Behind them came the empress, the archduchesses and the ladies of the palace in their most splendid garb, richly adorned with jewels. The onlookers gaped at the glamour and the glory of the court.

The Corpus Christi celebrations are the only court festivities for which there exist photographs. It was permitted to take photos in the courtyard of the palace, and some houseowners had photographers perform their task from the upper story windows as the parade passed by. Thus, there are documents bearing witness today to the splendour of the court of that time. Neither from the court balls nor from state banquets nor from the glamourous diplomatic presentations do we possess any such pictures.

With the completion of the Corpus Christi procession, court life had absolved most of its ceremonial responsibilities. The period from January to June was the busiest of the year; after that, the court withdrew on their sojourns to Ischl, Budapest and Schönbrunn and did not return to Vienna until September. In the latter part of the year there were no large ceremonial duties for the aristocracy. Members of the highest nobility were regularly invited to dine at court or to accompany the emperor on an imperial hunt, but the compulsory attendances were over. Most left the city after the Corpus Christi procession, retiring to their country estates. The cycle of court attendance did not begin again until the New Year.

VI
The Fateful Years: 1866/1867

The year 1866 was a traumatic one for Austria. In the war against Prussia, it suffered a systematic defeat, which in turn cost Austria its preeminent position in the German Federation. This, in turn, led to a profound transformation of the politics of the monarchy, but also – as a domino effect of this – substantial changes in the court itself. As of the lost battle of Königgrätz, a domestic avalanche was unleashed, by the end of which a completely new positioning of the imperial court within the state had been generated.

The defeat of Austria was a sign to Hungary that the time had come to finally loosen its bondage to the hated Austrian reign. A rekindled Hungarian attempt at liberation could not – as was the case earlier, in 1849 – be militarily fended off, since after the catastrophe of Königgrätz the military resources were no longer available. Moreover, Austria was isolated after Königgrätz; Russia had supported Austria in 1849 against the Hungarians, but was still piqued because of Austria's neutrality in the Crimean War.

Thus, a solution had to be found for the burgeoning Hungarian revolt. If Hungary left the protective fold of empire, it would set a disastrous example to other, still quiet, but dissatisfied provinces. The only possibility to keep Hungary inside the union of Habsburg lands was to permit it autonomy, which gave the Hungarians a certain, partial independence but yet did not reduce the boundaries of Francis Joseph's overall empire, since Hungary would agree to remain a part of it. The upshot of the long and difficult negotiations between the emperor and Hungarian politicians was that Austria was redesignated as a double monarchy, dubbed "Austria-Hungary", which led to Francis Joseph being crowned King of Hungary. Only the Foreign, Finance and War Ministries were henceforth to be shared with Austria. The Ministry of the Interior could now be run by Hungary on its own. The political supremacy in the overall empire was now to be shared by the German and the Hungarian populations, to the disadvantage of the Slavic segments of the population. This would prove to be the most devastating implication of this agreement.

With heavy heart, Francis Joseph agreed to the settlement. The liberals finally got their long desired Constitution; in 1867, Austria became a constitutional monarchy. Once and for all, the emperor had to share his power with popular representatives. He could appoint governments, he could dismiss governments, but the laws were now to be written and passed by parliament; the emperor retained only the right to veto them. Foreign politics and the military remained the prerogative of the crown.

But above all else, the emperor had to relinquish his seigniorage over the state finances. This was doubtless the most far reaching consequence of the political changes for the court, since the very thing which had previously been unthinkable for the monarchy now occurred: henceforth, Emperor Francis Joseph had to have his court budgets approved by the parliamentarians! The emperor was fully aware of the ramifications of such a step, even as the negotiations with the Hungarians were still in their early stages. For the first time in history, the amount of the court budget would become known to the general public; anyone could attempt to create a political issue out of this or that aspect of the situation. Public discussions about putative waste of state money, or arguments about the permissible line-amounts of the court budget, were simply incompatible with the dignity of the imperial monarchy.

For that reason, the emperor began to make preliminary provisions for this coming change as early as the year 1866. He ordered a rigourous thrift programme for the court. The year 1866 was destined to be important for another reason: it was the year when the emperor appointed a man who would set his stamp on the court as no other had ever done before, in the office and person of the Lord Chancellor: Prince Konstantin Hohenlohe-Schillingsfürst.

The appointment of Konstantin Hohenlohe was the most important personnel decision Francis Joseph ever made. Hohenlohe would become the most colossally important Lord Chancellor in the entire 600-year epic of the Habsburg court. He assumed his office at a turning point in history, just before the constitution was introduced. The old court structures were giving way, a transparent and thrifty court economy needed to be introduced. Not one thing could remain the way it was. At the same time as Austria was coerced into the modern age, the court was able to transform itself into a modernistic structure under Hohenlohe's aegis. The

Young German Prince Konstantin Hohenlohe-Schillingsfürst

old imperial court transmogrified into a large enterprise, although it naturally maintained old fashioned and longstanding attitudes on the part of the emperor towards his employees.

Hohenlohe rewrote the terms of employment at court, placing them on a modern footing. He introduced social programmes. Talented bourgeois citizens were hired in the chancelleries and trained; Hohenlohe raised the educational level of court officials and did not shy away from taking highly unpopular measures. When Konstantin Hohenlohe died, after more than thirty years in his office as Lord Chancellor, he left behind a well trimmed and perfectly functioning administrative apparatus, peopled by outstanding and industrious officials on which the monarch could depend without reservations until the very end of the monarchy. The modernisation of Francis Joseph's court, the successful high-wire act between the demands of empire and those of a cost-cutting administration which had become necessary in the constitutional era, the at long last achieved transparency in the finances of court management, were all inextricably linked to the name of

Hohenlohe. Without him, none of it would have taken place; with him, it was achieved to perfection.

Prince Konstantin Hohenlohe-Schillingsfürst was the youngest son of one of the most venerable German princely houses. He became the founder of a younger, Austrian line of the overall dynasty of Hohenlohe. He was considered to be extremely ambitious, utterly focused on his goals and willing to work hard to achieve them. He was small of build, an utterly prim and prudish man who was taciturn to all but his most intimate friends. Hohenlohe was, however, highly respected and there was nary a critical word to be heard about the way he conducted his office. Due to his enormous capacity for work, his untiring efforts for the court and the unsurpassed power of example he was able to set personally, he was appreciated by one and all at court, from the lowest servant to the highest aristocrat. Most of all, the employees treasured the fact that Hohenlohe was utterly incorruptible and had not the slightest patience with patronage uncoupled to performance. For Hohenlohe, achievement alone counted. Whoever proved to be valuable and was industrious could count on his support. Requests for favours, no matter how high the perch from which they stemmed, were coldly ignored. Since Lord Chancellor Hohenlohe, just like the emperor, insisted on looking at all the files and invariably endeavored through tenacious conversations with his staff to fill every last gap of information, and moreover always formed an unprejudiced opinion, he managed – in stark opposition to his predecessors – to become and remain fully informed about all procedures and affairs at court. For that reason, corruption, intrigues and nepotism didn't have a chance with him.

In Viennese society, the rumour was spread that even while he was still a junior cadet he had mapped out his future in meticulous detail. Purportedly, he once told his amazed schoolmates: *"I am going to Austria, where a young emperor reigns. I shall make great efforts to please him, to advance to be appointed his adjutant, to marry a rich woman and thereby reach the highest imaginable position at court."*[93] Even if the truth of this anecdote is unproven, the very telling of it in Viennese society bears witness to the single-minded fixity of purpose attributed to Hohenlohe.

Konstantin Hohenlohe entered military service in the Austrian army in 1848. He took part in the campaign in upper Italy, was placed in the Adjutant Corps in 1856 and advanced a year later to become Wing Adjutant of Emperor Francis Joseph. In the same year, he married a rich woman, as he had planned: Princess Marie zu Sayn-Wittgenstein-Berleburg[94], who brought a dowry of vast landholdings in what is today the Ukraine, thus putting the finances of the newly founded family on a firm footing, since Konstantin Hohenlohe, as youngest son, had no claims to the family fortune, which traditionally went to the eldest son of the family.

Exactly how Emperor Francis Joseph first became aware of the later so obvious and indisputable abilities of Hohenlohe cannot be ascertained from court literary sources or the private correspondence. It was highly surprising for the emperor to appoint the barely 36-year old Hohenlohe to be interimistic Court Director after the death of Chancellor Liechtenstein in 1865.[95] It can probably be assumed that the emperor was hesitant to entrust the administration to the sole responsibility of such an unexperienced man, since such a trial period for the position of Lord Chancellor was not customary.

It is possible that Emperor Francis Joseph knew well of the far more challenging and difficult situations which Hohenlohe had grown up in and coped with, in contrast to Liechtenstein; in any case, he wished to first test the suitability of his adjutant. After all, a number of large-scale projects needed to be realized which could no longer be put off, pressing reforms were piling up. It was quite possible that Francis Joseph was not quite sure how these urgent projects were to be solved. Regardless how felicitous the Hohenlohe appointment proved to be, in the year 1865 he was without the slightest experience in tackling such enormous economically and socially complex obstacles.

Yet it is also possible that Emperor Francis Joseph was convinced of Hohenlohe's abilities from the start, but wished to protect him and his highly unpopular reforms from the critical crossfire, since the success of those reforms was anything but certain. Were Hohenlohe to have failed in implementing those projects, this phase would protect his name from being viewed as having been the cause of the failure. The interimistic director of a staff, in lieu of a Chancellor of the Exchequer, simply did not carry the same burden of responsibility as an appointment to Lord Chancellor. Completely apart from such considerations, a Chancellor always served his emperor until death, either his own or that of his master. Resigning from an office at court was virtually impossible. The embarrassment of the appointment of the court's very highest official, personally undertaken by the emperor himself, being seen as an error would have been great. It is highly understandable that the emperor wished to be quite sure of the aptness of his choice before appointing this man to the vacant position of Lord Chancellor. The future would prove him to have been not only correct, but prescient: Hohenlohe was the ideal man. He was capable, he was willing to fulfil the high expectations set in him and was – and this would prove to be his greatest strength – not in the least shy of conflicts.

Three days after Königgrätz, Hohenlohe was appointed as Deputy Chancellor,[96] the number one man at the court of the imperial emperor, a German prince whose brother Chlodwig (in his position as Prime Minister of Bavaria) was at that very moment demanding the exclusion of Austria from the German Federation. This demonstrative appointment of Hohenlohe was a powerful symbolic act. Francis Joseph, who had to observe Austria being excluded from the German *Bund*, gave the highest appointment it was his to confer to a German prince, a loud and clear signal to Prussia.

Konstantin Hohenlohe's origins and family heritage produced a bizarre picture. He himself was a German prince, but worked in the highest position at the court of Austria. His eldest brother, Chlodwig, was to begin as the Bavarian Prime Minister and ardent advocate of German unification under Prussian leadership and later become Reichskanzler. His second brother, Victor, was member of the leading Prussian parliamentary chamber; and his youngest brother, Gustav, was a Cardinal of the Catholic Church. One comment of a statesman was rather cynical: "*The Hohenlohe gentlemen have generally done quite well: one of them toils for family success at the Austrian court, the other at the Prussian court, the third in the challenging position of Ambassador to France, the fourth is a Cardinal and priest in order to grant indulgences to his brothers for the sins they are required to commit.*"[97]

Hohenlohe's first, formidable task as Chancellor was not designed to increase his popularity among the high officials at court or with the imperial family. Upon request of the emperor himself, he had to concoct a package of measures to reduce court costs.[98] With an eye on the approaching Constitution and the parliamentary examination of all court expenses which would be an integral part of it, the emperor wished to present the court as a lean and thrifty enterprise. He therefore decided on a drastic savings policy. In place of the already long approved budget for the year 1867 of 7.4 million guilders,[99] on which the various departments at court had counted, they suddenly had to save 2.5 million within 6 months, amounting to a third of the entire annual budget. Since the customary methods at court, namely, lowering costs through restructuring and long term hiring reductions (dismissals continued to be taboo) were not feasible in a six-month period, Hohenlohe resolved on a more radical course. He asked court officials, to start with, to go through their costs with a fine tooth comb and exercise an 'all-round economizing' at every possible step; at the same time, however, he cancelled 36 percent of the allotted budget of every single department. Hohenlohe permitted no objections to be considered, he insisted on cost-cutting and every department had to make its contribution. The purchases for art collections and the court library were cancelled in entirety. Yet even such drastic measures were insufficient to save the necessary 2.5 million guilders. Hohenlohe then decided to sell court assets and began to carry it out without delay. These sales proved hardest for the Office of the Stables. The Chancellor of the Exchequer resolved to sell half the horses the court owned. That entailed the immediate sale of 70 lipizzaner and 30 horses from the breeding farm in Kladrub. The *Wiener Zeitung* published a huge headline announcing the auction of these horses.[100] The general public could hardly believe their eyes. The court was parting with its beloved lipizzaner, and through the method of a public auction at that! Count Grünne, current Master of the Stables, genuinely believed it was a joke being played on the Viennese by Hohenlohe. When he discovered it was bitter truth, he went on a rampage and sent bitingly caustic complaints to the emperor. "*In the middle of the year* (he was) *forced to sell, dump, destroy everything which had been built up through such arduous labour and meticulous care over the course of twenty years.*"[101] Grünne wrote scathing letters to the Lord Chancellor, accusing Hohenlohe of thinking only of his own staff, complained to the emperor about the unjust distribution of cost-cutting in his opinion. But there was no helping it. The stables were reduced. Hohenlohe got his way.

Only in one single department of court did Hohenlohe dispense with such cost-cutting, and for personal reasons: namely, at the Zoological Gardens of Schönbrunn. Hohenlohe said to the emperor: "*This collection is so beloved by the general public and is visited every Sunday and holiday by thousands of people. 'Panem et circenses' is the old, but also politically apt and popular adage which, along with theater productions, is also fulfilled by the animals in a menagerie. ... Such public amusements and merrymaking simply must not be cut! The reasonable costs they incur are well spent.*"[102]

Even the members of the imperial family were forced to perform measures of thrift. The archdukes and archduchesses would have to forfeit a third of their retinue, proclaimed Hohenlohe in articulation of the emperor's desire. Francis Joseph reported to Empress Elisabeth: "*Hohenlohe is journeying to Ischgl today, then to Salzburg, then Innsbruck, to announce to the ladies and gentlemen there that they must now forfeit a part of their retinues.*"[103] Konstantin Hohenlohe fulfilled the emperor's wish. He managed to cut court costs for 1867 from 7.4 down to 5 million. That masterpiece assured his permanence at court.

At the same time as the major money-saving policies were being implemented in 1866, a new department was created which was intended to assure the ongoing thrift and efficiency of court expenses in future. Through establishing the "*Department of Accounting*"[104] the Office of the Exchequer created for the very first time a bookkeeping and cost-oversight department as such function is understood today. Until then, there existed only the Court Payments Office, which handled the management of court funds, but only as receiver and payer of money, i.e. as the cash flow office. The Court Payments Office received at the beginning of each year the annual court budget from the Finance Ministry and dispensed the money. Each month, the budget went out to the four major departments and the salaries were paid to their employees. The Court Payments Office collected like a well behaved pupil the signed receipts, but failed to do one important thing: namely, check that the money was actually spent on the things for which it had been designated. In order to do that, the Office of the Exchequer created the Department of Accounting; it was henceforth to control all spending at court. The larger the court became and the more differentiated its spending and administration, the larger the staff at the accounting department grew to be. Hohenlohe sought out the best bookkeepers he could find in 1866, established and recognized experts in their field with experience in managing the budgets of the noble classes. The best employees from the Court Payments Office were given additional training by no one less than the president of the Accounting Department. This department became the apple of the Exchequer's eye, for only with its help was Hohenlohe able to uncover weakness and waste in court spending. It was an utterly independent staff which reported only to the Lord Chancellor.

In November 1867, Konstantin Hohenlohe officially became Chancellor of the Exchequer.[105] As of then, he not only received the offical salary of just under 13,000 guilders, he also was assigned the Augarten Palace in the second district of Vienna as his residence. The Augarten Palace was a court property, but was bestowed on Hohenlohe as an added bonus. All staff members at the palace were supplied by the emperor, horses and coaches came from the imperial stables.[106] The fact that Hohenlohe was granted such luxurious perquisites from the emperor was not due to Francis Joseph's gratitude that the Lord Chancellor had shored up the court finances so quickly, but rather to the representative role which the Hohenlohe family bore and was accorded.

Konstantin and Marie Hohenlohe were poised to play the leading role in the cultural life of the residential imperial city. As soon as Hohenlohe took up his quarters there, the Augarten Palace instantly became the heartbeat of Vienna's cultural scene. The balls, soirées and dinners given here became the stuff of legend. Leading personages from the worlds of diplomacy, the army, artistic circles met here. The center of the family was Hohenlohe's wife Marie, one of the most extraordinary women of her class. She drew artists, writers and musicians to her like bees to honey and she herself loved having them around her. Princess Marie Hohenlohe was a woman who had well founded and highly educated knowledge of all the arts of the time. She herself had led a life worthy of literature. Her childhood and youth appear to have been penned by a novelist and germinated the seeds of her later knowledge of art. Marie's mother was Princess Caroline Iwanowska and was mar-

Marie and Konstantin Hohenlohe-Schillingsfürst

ried at a young age to Prince von Sayn-Wittenstein. Caroline was a good match, since she brought immense landholdings into the marriage, but was anything but a quiet and docile housewife. She was an intellectual, carried out her own philosophical studies, even wrote a commentary on Goethe's Faust, a work which was considered immoral in that era and which hardly was considered to be appropriate reading for a lady of high society. In short, Princess Caroline was highly unusual for the feminine aristocracy of the day. And yet, her life was destined to become far more unusual still. When Marie was ten years old, her mother met Franz Liszt in Kiev, a meeting which would have a huge impact on Marie's future. Caroline Wittgenstein and Liszt fell in love and Marie's mother, whose marriage was unhappy, decided to take an unconventional and dramatic step, one which would have done honour to Anna Karenina. She abandoned her husband in order to live together with Liszt. To take that step, she had to give up everything she had. She forfeited her good reputation, her position in society and even had to leave behind her own personal fortune that she had brought into her marriage. (Her children would later receive this huge fortune back.) Caroline lost her homeland, since both the church and the Czar rejected the divorce proceedings which she filed at court. Caroline and Liszt had to flee to Weimar. Caroline Sayn-Wittgenstein lived utterly for her new love, Franz Liszt. She re-tailored her life to the requirements of his career, opened their house to all artists and scholars. Richard Wagner, Alexander von Humboldt, the painter Friedrich Kaulbach, the writer Friedrich Hebbel, the poet and later director of the court opera in Vienna, Franz von Dingelstedt, and even Gottfried Semper, the later designer of Vienna's Ringstrasse, came and went regularly.[107]

Young Marie grew up in this tingling, stimulating, champagne-prickly atmosphere not unlike *La Bohème*. She became a cultivated and well-read woman, bursting with adoration for all forms of art. The court lady Marie Festetics recalls a "*lovable women, highly cultivated, full of interest for art and poetry it is certain that she had only the very best influence on her husband.*"[108]

Marie Hohenlohe corresponded with the leading artists of the time. They, in turn, treasured her acquaintaince. She recognized with unfailing instinct where real talent lay, was unprejudiced in her judgment and brought promising young talents to the Augarten Palace. She was the connecting link between the cultural scene and the Court of Vienna. Marie Hohenlohe made new acquaintances with ease, and gathered them with astonishing speed; she asked the artists present in her salon to report to her of any new and promising talents. She sought only quality, was modern and courageous, and drew only the very best to the attention of her husband. Nearly all the architects, painters and theater people whom Konstantin Hohenlohe engaged or patronized at court in his capacity as Lord Chancellor found their way to him via his wife. Those architects and artists who were to make dazzling careers in the latter part of the 19th century were direct or indirect results of Marie Hohenlohe's patronage. She brought men she already knew to Vienna, such as Gottfried Semper; she patronized promising young artists. The writer Ferdinand Saar, Friedrich Hebbel and the Austrian composer and conductor Felix Mottl are but a few of her selected luminaries. The parties at Augarten Palace were splendid happenings, with a mixture of aristocrats, architects, writers, musicians and painters that could be found nowhere else in Vienna. The emperor himself assisted these soirées by visiting them regularly. What's more, he had blind trust in Marie and Konstatin Hohenlohe's taste and their selection of artists.

The emperor may well have seen Marie Hohenlohe as a special cultural emissary of court and supported her in that role. For, Empress Elisabeth refused to develop any such cultural functions or activities. She appeared for her official court duties – the two court balls, the Corpus Christi procession and a few charity appearances – but even those only sporadically. She had no ambitions whatever to play the traditional role of empress, namely, by promoting culture and the arts through her own personal involvement. By extending personal invitations, giving dinners and sponsoring events, Elisabeth might have brought many new artists and culturally active invidivuals to the court at Vienna, which in turn would have exerted a certain political influence of no small significance. Through her refusal, the court was prevented from a position as a leading art patron to lend an artistic identity to the era and the court itself. This, in view of the decreasing powers of the emperor in political spheres, was an aspect of power and propaganda which could not be ignored.

Francis Joseph was quite open to the artists and their themes. Moreover, he knew how important art and artists could be in the service of the dynasty, even if he himself did not have the time to devote himself to these concerns. Thus, he provided backing to Marie and Konstantin Hohenlohe in their hands-on involvement in finding the most important artistic movements of the time and bringing them into court circles, regardless whether in the realm of painting, music or literature. The Augarten Palace became, in effect, the external office for this part of the empire.

Hohenlohe's initiation in office was during the first part of the building of the Ringstrasse in Vienna. Nearly all architects and artists of the Ringstrasse Era were selections from Hohenlohe's circle of acquaintances, stemming from the talent pool at the Augarten Palace. But the Hohenlohes also moved with the times. They began to invite scientific personages, discoverers, world travellers and actors to their home. Hohenlohe himself even tried to have recognized and accomplished scientists invited to official dinners at court, by intervening on their behalf with the emperor.[109]

Konstantin Hohenlohe (right) with his sons, Gottfried (left), later Austrian Ambassador in Berlin and husband of Archduchess Henriette; and Konrad (center), later Prime Minister of Austria, whose daughter married Emperor Karl's brother

Through Marie and Konstantin Hohenlohe, a new family ascended like a shooting star in the immediate vicinity of the emperor. Apart from the Liechtenstein family, which had lived in close connection with the imperial family for a long time, the Hohenlohes became the most influential family in the monarchy. The sons of Konstantin Hohenlohe continued this intimate connection to the Habsburgs. They became Minister of the Interior and Prime Minister, as well as Austria's ambassador to Berlin under Emperor Francis Joseph. The last emperor, Karl, appointed another son of Konstantin to be his Lord Chancellor and even married the children and grandchildren of Konstantin Hohenlohe into the imperial family.

VII
The Golden Years

With the appointment of Konstantin Hohenlohe to Chancellor of the Exchequer, a golden age began for Emperor Francis Joseph. Once Hohenlohe had solved the most urgent financial problems, he initiated a wide ranging reform programme, in the course of which he changed nearly everything which existed at court. No emperor before Francis Joseph had ever reformed the court as comprehensively and as uncompromisingly; no emperor had ever employed such a decisive and unswayable Chancellor who, moreover, did not shy away from conflict in the slightest.

That Hohenlohe succeeded in modernizing and reforming the court in such a decisive manner was in part due to his complete and utter independence. His family network was in Germany; his wife, Princess Marie, had her relatives only in Russia and Italy. Hohenlohe was utterly detached from the webwork of families in the Viennese aristocratic society. He did not need to take anyone into consideration, was beholding to no one, had no one for whom he needed to perform favours. He was appointed directly and personally by the emperor without having had anyone smooth the way for him. He cultivated few personal friendships in the Austrian aristocracy and those whom he counted as his friends were just as unusual as he was. His closest friends were the famous adventurer and art patron Count Hans Wilczek and the former Austrian ambassador in Paris, Prince Richard Metternich, son of the famous chancellor. Both of them were just as critical of outdated systems as Hohenlohe himself; both were highly eccentric examples of the aristocracy of the time. Wilczek was a sponsor and participant of the Austrian-Hungarian expedition to the North Pole and one of the discoverers of a group of islands unknown until that time, which was then named Franz Joseph Land. Richard Metternich, on the other hand, made a name for himself as a composer. The new Lord Chancellor distanced himself from the exclusive society at court. Konstantin Hohenlohe was able to set about the work of reforming the court from top to bottom without the burden of those who pursued their own egoistic purposes, who made personal claims or to whom he owed a debt of gratitude.

Before Hohenlohe got started in modernizing the court, he assembled his team inside the chancellery of the Exchequer. The old chancellery director was sent into retirement; and dynamic, young people hired – not from court circles, but from external sources. Hohenlohe wanted to begin utterly anew. He hired talented and highly engaged lawyers who had no contact with the court and had not been infected by its slothfulness. He sought young professionals without familial commitments who under his tutelage with all due detachment would undertake to change the court from inside out. He started by recruiting the best staff he could find among those of his class. He 'borrowed' well trained personnel from the staffs at the family estates of Schwarzenberg, Liechtenstein and Wilczek: young men whose parents were often farmers on these noble estates whose studies had been paid for by the landowning nobles, based on their conspicuous talents and academic suitability. After their studies, they had to demonstrate in the chancelleries of their sponsors that they deserved the privilege of being permitted to study. For that reason, they turned into high performing, highly valuable employees in those chancelleries. They yearned to show, through their high degree of involvement in estate affairs, that even simple peasant sons merited the honour for which they had been selected.[110]

From the Office of the Exchequer itself Hohenlohe took only the very best, tried-and-tested young employees. With this new staff of well educated and performance-oriented men at his side, the Lord Chancellor launched his great project.

Following the great cost-cutting project of 1866 and the final clarification of court finances when the Constitution was introduced, Hohenlohe initiated his daring plan to place employment policies at court on modern, efficient foundations. What that came down to was simple: the court had to find a way of turning an old-fashioned system of providing for its employees in the manner of a patriarchy, in which each individual was guaranteed security but not urged towards any achievement, into a modern, achievement-oriented system of employment which compensated work and accomplishment in appropriate ways. The processes to date, completely divorced from individual performance, provided equal benefits to all staff members and thus, were utterly devoid of incentives to do anything or develop any new attitude towards work. The tricky part, of course, was that Hohenlohe, just like his predecessor, was told that dismissals were taboo.

Lord Chancellor Konstantin Hohenlohe perceived the basic problem in an instant: the low wages, which were cushioned by a variety of entitlements. The court employees earned very little, but didn't have to make much effort to secure for themselves a life full of entitlements and without risks. And even those who might make great efforts gained no benefit from it, apart from a clearer conscience, since higher degrees of effort or performance were not rewarded in any way. The employees had what they needed to survive, and could not afford the slightest extras or put anything away into savings. There simply was no reason to make any effort, it gained them nothing. Hohenlohe was certain that better work and higher performance could only be attained through the incentive of higher, and above all else, individually adjusted compensation.

Hohenlohe knew that the system of remuneration had to be reformed from top to bottom. All salaries had to be recalibrated on a contemporary basis. Moreover, the multi-layered pyramid of employees had to be re-ordered into a new hierarchy of rank and status. The Lord Chancellor did not wish to assume what was essentially a task of the state, since he was aware that civil servants had been wrestling with the government for years over the establishment of a standardised system of orderly remuneration; moreover, a national reform was withing striking distance. Since as of the moment the Constitution was introduced even court employees were considered civil servants (although the term was never adequately defined and legal experts had grave misgivings as to whether such a simplified definition did not endanger the loyalty distinctions of such employees; they preferred keeping civil servants quite separate from imperial servants) the court desired to carry out its own reform at the same time as the corresponding reform of the state.

At very least, the lowermost salary classes had to be revamped without delay. The menial servants at court and lowest rank of officials had extremely low base salaries. The court was never capable of raising salaries in a standardised and contemporary way, instead approved new supplements and entitlements in ongoing fashion, since the problem of low base salaries was well known. On the one hand, a low salary provided little impetus to work hard. Through the countless additions to that salary, the officials and servants were able to heighten their financial compensation noticeably. To make matters worse, the jungle of supplementary payments and entitlements mushroomed over the years so that the departments completely lost any overview of what they were paying out, compared to other departments (often identical payments under different names). To name but a few examples, there were supplementary allowances for firewood, candles, meals, children, orphans, boots, uniforms, coats, shoes, furniture, etc.

The paradoxical situation came about that persons who had exactly the same base salary received wildly divergent sums of money, depending on how many bonuses they were able to secure for themselves. The path to more money did not lie in delivering higher performance, but in the departments in a position to grant extra pay. Motivation and discipline were the stumbling blocks; in fact, no one was in any way driven to make a special effort, since court servants knew that not the industrious were rewarded, but the ones who knew where to apply for it. Many servants received regular allowances from the Imperial Care Fund, and a host of others (who applied for 'mercy payments') created a heavy burden on the emperor's private purse.

Hohenlohe raised the lowest quarter of court salaries measurably in 1869.[111] Through this step, those who were financially weakest were assisted. At the same time, a Care Fund for widows and orphans of court employees was established.[112] For a paltry fee, court employees could take out a supplementary insurance policy for their widows and orphans. In actual fact, this fund was by and large financed by money from the imperial family and chancellery fees, which were levied for every court appointment.

The long overdue salary raises were no more than superficial cosmetic measures, yet an essential first step towards contemporary remuneration reform. The court still had to provide small pay supplements for four more years, which was how long it took to provide service contracts for court employees; yet Hohenlohe fastidiously kept up-to-date on the negotiations between the government and the civil servants, demanded to see every interim report of their progress to assemble materials which would serve as a basis for court reforms. In 1872, when the major points had been settled, he began with his team to rewrite the remuneration and status system for court servants and officials, despite the fact that in the interim the payments had to be dispensed yet another time, due to inflation.

At the beginning of 1873, he was ready. At the same time, civil servants of the state and officials at court were escorted, legally speaking, into a new era. The hard-fought reform of employee status and compensation was just as significant for the court as it was for the nation. All court officials and servants were calibrated into a new, unified, obligatory system of ranks and remuneration. Every person could see exactly what rank he had, how high his salary was. Moreover, and this was perhaps most important of all, servants finally received a salary corresponding to the era.[113]

Hohenlohe defended the costs of this reform to the emperor by arguing that maintaining the old system would cost the same as creating a new one, although it would not take the form of a single sum, but rather countless items in complicated distribution. It was much preferable, he argued, to spend one large amount to regulate future financing of the staff once and for all.

The huge reform of categories of remuneration was a monumental break in the history of the court. For the first time, officials and servants had a precisely defined position. For the first time, all officials and servants occupied a slot in one all-encompassing system of status and ranks. The rise of each and every official was mapped out. Injustices were removed. Through the introduction of this reform, the bonus payment system was eliminated. A servant or an official received his salary, a regular advance, quarterly allowances and free meals at court. Allowances were now possible only for emergencies or as extraordinary assistance in case of illness or unforeseen catastrophes.

Even the salaries of the aristocrats who were employed at court, the uppermost rank of court officials, the possessors of court offices such as Master Chef or Master of the Hunt and the court ladies had their salaries raised, although not until 1875, well after the salaries of lower level court employees had been lifted.[114] Since the nobles, even including court ladies, were forced to earn money, they did not like the idea of getting a fixed salary, which seemed to place them on an equal footing with court employees; for that reason, the salaries for the aristocrats were re-named 'representational compensation'.

The second major change was in the sector of pensions, where the big winners were once again to be found on the lowest rung of earners. Until now, the court had to dig deep into its pockets again and again to provide pensions for the lowermost employees – and that included into the private purse of the emperor. Pensions amounted to about one third of salaries; this resulted in amounts on which the lowermost employees could not survive, which in turn made regular supplementary allowances unavoidable.

The monthly pension payments set down by the court budget were now deposited into a savings fund, which then had other revenues from court added to it: taxes, chancellery fees and supplementary payments supplied by the emperor, i.e. Christmas money and Jubilee bonuses. The objective was for the court to pay into this fund until an overall balance was achieved which, together with adequate interest accrual, ultimately had enough assets for the pension fund to subsequently finance itself. The goal was to liberate the court over the long term from this immense budget item, while at the same time secure the pensions of its employees. *"To achieve this goal, several decades at least will be necessary, assuming positive background conditions."*[115] The implementation of this in itself commendable idea which would have removed a great burden from court finances – since then as now, salaries and pensions took the biggest bite out of the annual budget – was not achieved by the time the monarchy ended in 1918. Nevertheless, the new pension fund was an advance whichever way one looked at it. The lowest pensions, the widows and orphans fund, were raised; and the account repeatedly handed out bonuses to those in need.[116]

After court finances had been refurbished, the most urgent cost-cutting measures realized and the salaries and pensions of court employees placed on a modern basis, Chancellor Hohenlohe could launch his next step: to create a programme of social benefits for those who were not permanently employed at court, yet performed regular services there. These were the labourers or seasonal workers. A year after the pension reform took effect, they, too, were given life insurance for the benefit of their widows and orphans. The coverage now extended to all those who worked at court, either permanently or at least regularly.[117] No widow would any longer be put in a position of penury if her deceased husband had worked at court. For his children, additional care money was paid, apart from the orphan fund.

The 1870s and 1880s were marked by the introduction of many social benefits. The court learned to economize and the Lord Chancellor was finally able to implement many of the social plans which he had envisioned. To relieve the burdens of the most menial livery servants and stable personnel, he built a kindergarten in the stable building, Court Child Care, where teaching nuns supervised children whose parents were occupied with their work at court. The wives of court servants were forced to hold down a job in order to earn enough additional money to support families which often had many children. They usually found employment in performing the lowermost tasks at court, as kitchen maids or in the clean-up crew. To keep their children safe and occupied, and prevent them from meandering around the court, which endangered them in the constant coach traffic, they were now watched over. The kindergarten was free of charge for the lower employees; it had its own budget, into which the women of the imperial family made contributions on their respective birthdays and at Christmas. With this money, coats, shoes and eyeglasses were purchased for needy children. At Christmas, a Christmas tree was set up in the kindergarten, and each child received a gift from the imperial family, together with assorted sweets. For as long as the emperor's youngest daughter, Archduchess Marie Valerie, lived at court, she remained patroness of the imperial kindergarten.[118]

Medical care at court was also reorganised. Among other things, a permanent medical service was established.[119] During the day, several doctors practiced at court and enjoyed a high frequency of patient visits. Anyone who was ill and anyone who was the victim of an accident could count on medical help. At night, the situation was quite different, since next to no doctors lived at court. The one court resident, Dr. Ritter von Bielka, who resided in the stable buildings, was the sole physician who could be fetched in times of urgency during the night. He was soon called out nearly every night, until he had suffered enough. He forbade "strictly, during his residence in Vienna, during the time from 9:30 pm until 9:30 am to be disturbed." Even if his protest was formulated a bit too rigourously, Chancellor Hohenlohe showed a modicum of understanding. He took the opportunity to establish a permanent medical service, which above and beyond the irritations of Dr. von Bielka, was a general necessity. All court doctors were assigned to a revolving cycle of daily duty, which extended from 9:30 am until 9:30 pm, and included stints of night duty. A special room was set aside for the doctor on duty, to which he could retire.

At the same time, strict quarantine regulations were also outlined and made mandatory. Each physician had to report every illness which occurred at court. The patient was assigned to a separate ward at court, his family had to move into quarters attached to it and remain there for the period of incubation. Only after it was established that no contagion or danger of infection existed were they permitted to return to their apartment.[120] The patient himself was not permitted to return to his apartment until he had completely recovered. This extreme caution at court was the result of the high rates of transmissibility of illnesses at court. People lived at such close quarters and came into contact with so many others that contagious diseases spread with the speed of wildfire. Due to the many cholera epidemics in the 19th century, the court had learned to be prudent.

For the same reason, compulsory innoculations were introduced at a very early date at court. Smallpox vaccinations, for example, were required for all court employees. The Office of the Exchequer kept innoculation records for all employees, including those who were newly hired and had never had such vaccinations before. If someone failed to appear twice for an innoculation appointment, he was cited to the Office of the Exchequer and warned. The court made great efforts through these strict measures to avoid the outbreak of contagious diseases.[121]

With that much medical supervision and privilege, there was inevitably a large amount of abuse. The doctors and pharmacists were regularly admonished for giving prescriptions of free medicines to those without any entitlement to receive them. Only the most menial court employees received medicines free of charge. The better earners had to pay a certain share of the cost. Even in the earliest years of Francis Joseph's reign, the doctors and pharmacists had to be reminded that very few members of the court staff were entitled to received medicines without payment. The Lord Chancellor knew well that many prescriptions were written for staff members, but were ultimately intended for someone outside of court. "*So-called prescriptions as a personal favour for people not entitled to receive them are absolutely prohibited!*"[122] Since the number of such cases mushroomed, the doctors and pharmacists were threatened with disciplinary measures if they did not improve their watchfulness.[123]

The court was also quite strict in supervising the prescription of medicines which served cosmetic, rather than genuine medicinal purposes. Random checks repeatedly uncovered that the highest ladies of court nobility down to the lowest servants had bath salts, mouthwash and even cognac and wine prescribed by doctors. Official documents repeatedly drew attention to the fact that "*hair oil, shampoo, losenges, aids for corns and herbal oils*"[124] (to enhance hair growth) were not covered by the court medical plan. The warnings and admonishments were unending: "*Since it is the will of the uppermost office at court that while nothing important should be lacking, the costs for unimportant medicines should not be higher than necessary, His Royal and Imperial Highness issues the edict that it is a duty of particular significance to request only absolutely necessary medicines for healing purposes and dispense with all those which serve good taste but contain no ingredients with any medical efficacy towards healing, e.g. schnaps, fruit syrups, etc.*"[125]

The admonishments didn't help much, but the court stuck with its promise of social supports and services nonetheless. Towards the end of the century, the emperor even extended the medical assistance policies to cover day-workers and weekly employees as well, i.e. all those who performed only short term services for the court. As of that decision, even a day-long worker had a claim to medical services at court, i.e. court doctors and the court pharmacy. When such short-term workers fell ill, they received 70 percent of their daily pay for a period of five months maximum. If they had to go into hospital, they were consigned to the Merciful Brothers Hospital in Vienna, and the court paid the hospital bills. Only if such temporary help were discovered to themselves be the cause of their illness or accident or had acted contrary to the instructions of the doctor did they forfeit their claim to assistance. And even then, they were not left utterly in the lurch, but nearly always were provided some kind of solution. Not only staff families received payments if the provider died, even the families of day workers had the funeral and burial costs paid.

Apart from the large and regular payments made by the court, there were also many small assistance payments which bolstered the salaries of the low earners. For example, nothing was ever thrown away at court. What had served its purpose was not sold, but auctioned off. The revenues were then distributed among needy court employees. This included court bed linen, which was often simply given to the laundry employees for a certain basic sum, and was then handed on to needy staff members.[126] Until the end of the nineteenth century, the leftovers from the imperial dining table could be taken home by the staff of the dining and silver chambers, and sold. This tradition was introduced in order to give employees something without having to raise their salaries, but over the course of time it came to be seen as a perfectly legitimate bonus to which they were entitled. As of 1896, the court conducted the sales itself and fed the proceeds into the assistance fund for its staff. Those employees who were then prevented from selling those things themselves received a compensation. The dining table leftovers were sold at the famous restaurant 'Schmausbabel'[127]. Even the emperor's clothes which had worn out were auctioned off, and his servants have recorded that demand for such items was high. The revenues were funneled into aid funds for the staff.

The Office of the Exchequer also had its own fund, into which all taxes which had been levied were paid. For every court appointment, a so-called appointment or chancellery tax was charged by the Office of the Exchequer. At year's end, the Lord Chancellor added an additional 30% of the balance to the account. After office expenses and tips were deducted, the annual profits were paid out to the lowest ranking officials and servants in the Office of the Exchequer, the simple messengers, servants and couriers. Over the years, the officials themselves successfully endeavored to gain access to this money, thus improving their amply endowed salaries. Again and again, those who had no need had to be driven away from this honeywagon, warned by the court that those who enjoyed fixed incomes had no entitlement to additional bonuses. Even the very last Lord Chancellor had to issue a strongly worded admonishment in 1914 to make clear that the fund was not there to provide bonuses to officials, but to aid employees who had been struck by unforeseeable events such as illness, emergency or had particularly large families to obtain a reasonable bit of supplementary assistance.[128]

If one poses the question of whether the work levels at court decisively improved following the adjustments of all salaries, the introduction of a just remuneration system, the initiation of comprehensive social benefits and emergency supports, the objective answer would have to be a decisive no. Until the demise of the court, the selfsame warnings and admonishments continued to be issued, the same prohibitions, the same corrections perpetually made. *"In order to discourage simulated illnesses on the part of court employees, the court doctors are forced to exercise the strictest precision and conscientious examination before granting an employee sick leave."*[129] The lackadaisical attitude towards work, disciplinary shortcomings, alcohol abuse and waste in grand style remained significant problems until the end.

As late as the 20th century, a newly hired adjutant showed some annoyance over the poor working performance at court and was astonished and touched by the leniency of his employer: *"His Majesty was surprised at the neglected state of the floors, and stood shaking his head for quite a while over them as we walked to lunch. The wood is worn down, true, but it might be waxed once a year, especially when eminent guests are expected!"*[130]

The court employees were the ones who profited most from Hohenlohe's reforms, not the emperor or his court; they, after all, had finally been accorded proper wages. Yet they went on living in their old attitudes and ancient habits, even if both had now become outdated. But as long as Emperor Francis Joseph persisted in his own patriarchal approach even in the constitutional era, running his own court on the basis of care and leniency rather than performance, the antiquated customs which defined life and work at court through every possible standard other than achievement were doomed to persist.

Chancellor Hohenlohe also wanted to open the court towards the outside. He wished to make it visible that it was more than just the residence of the emperor and glamourous stage for exclusive festivities. The court was a symbol, an emblem of a centuries-old ruling tradition which stood for continuity through the ages. The court was supposed to remain something apart, but the residence of the emperor might be visited and examined by all the citizens. That meant only the ceremonial and dining rooms, of course, not the private chambers of the emperor himself. In this spirit, the Lord Chancellor distributed for a paltry fee a number of admission tickets to visit the splendid apartments at court; upon prior arrangement, small guided tours were given.[131] The visitors were watched over by the doormen who kept an eye on the grand apartments at all times and whose only responsibility was to open the splendid doors.

Until the middle of the 1880s, these guided tours caused no problems. But in the course of the years to follow, more and more thefts were registered. In Francis Joseph's day, the rooms were more replete with *objets d'art*, vases overflowing with flowers, containers and trays of tobacco and sweets, silver photo frames, books, and many signs of real life in the apartments, than today, since they were actually lived in. As the numbers of missing preciosities began to rise, the Office of the Exchequer investigated how such a great amount of theft was possible. There seemed to be sufficient numbers of doormen present, making it puzzling how so much could be taken right in front of their eyes. The result of the investigation accorded perfectly with the historic patterns with which the reader is now familiar. The visitors were able to pilfer so much for the simple reason that the doormen were always asleep on duty. In the special training sessions which were subsequently introduced, it was drummed into them that they had to be not merely bodily but also mentally present while they were on duty. Above all, their eyes should not ever be closed, and napping on their feet was prohibited. Thus, even after Hohenlohe's great reform, conscientious and orderly work performance remained an unattainable ideal.

VIII
The Court Finances

Before Francis Joseph ascended the throne, the imperial court was financed by the 'Court Chamber'. The lands of the monarchy had to pay the so-called 'chamber quota' – the remaining sum, after their administrative expenses were deducted – to the Court Chamber in Vienna, which paid the expenses for the centralized administration and the court expenses from this money. Traditionally, the Court Chamber managed the assets of the empire and was under the authority of the ruler himself, who was permitted free access to the chamber assets. Shortly before Francis Joseph's coronation, the Court Chamber was dissolved, replaced in 1848 by the Finance Ministry. Even after this transformation, the emperor retained the sole right of access to the finances. However, he was not able to take much, since every court expense reduced the remaining pot of assets. For that reason, Emperor Francis Joseph, from the first moment of his assuming control of the state, spent a great deal of effort in keeping court expenses as low as possible. The economic situation in the 1850s was catastrophic: the military sucked away unimaginable sums, shoddy economic policy and lack of confidence in the political security of Austria on the part of foreign investors led to enormous fluctuations in the value of the currency.

The emperor set the endowment amount to pay for the court, which as of 1868 was known in the files as the *civil list*.[132] At the same time, he urged his officials to calculate their expenses at the thriftiest level possible, since every large expense was a great burden to the state. The not yet separate financing of court and nation did not mean that the emperor could take from the general pool of assets as he wished, but rather, that he was responsible for both. For that reason, he desired to be as thrifty as possible at court. First, the state finances had to be secured; then, those of the court.

Determining the costs of running the court is an enormous challenge for historical researchers. For, the famous 'court payment books' and files from the accounting department in which all revenues and expenses were precisely listed, are the only historic documents in the court archives which were lost in the change-over of ruling system in 1918. On orders from the commissioner of the national government, for reasons of saving space, as well as the fact that they were 'no longer current', they were destroyed (despite protests of the state archivars). The company hired to destroy the files, which amounted to more than 8,000 kilos of valuable materials, soon reported with pride that it had succeeded in manufacturing 550 kilos of usable paper from the destroyed documents. This is a statement which brings tears to the eyes of any historian.[133] The files and records which were in the personal possession of Emperor Francis Joseph were among those which were destroyed.

On the other hand, relatively reliable data could be obtained from the monthly accounting lists of the Office of the Exchequer about the costs of running the court and the retinues of the imperial family. The disadvantage was that this source became weaker and weaker towards the end of the monarchy.

Maintaining the imperial court at the beginning of Francis Joseph's rule cost approximately 350,000 guilders monthly. It rose steadily until the Constitution was introduced in 1867, which brought with it a change in the methods of accounting, to the amount of 500,000 guilders monthly.[134] This rise in costs by nearly a third for unchanging goods and services can be attributed to the poor economy and the fluctuations of the currency.

Converting these amounts into modern currencies and sums must be undertaken with great caution, due to the currency fluctuations which prevailed in the first third of the emperor's reign in particular. Conservative estimates calculate that 350,000 guilders in the 1850s amount today to about 5.3 million euros. The annual costs of maintaining the court of Vienna thus amounted to about 63 million euros in the mid-19th century.[135]

In practice, adding new line items and making payments for the court budget were carried out according to a strict scheme. The Lord Chancellor informed the emperor at the end of each calendar year of the sum which would be required for the coming year. The emperor checked the estimates and generally showed great unwillingness to raise the costs for any given sector. If the Lord Chancellor needed more money for something in the approaching year, he had to defend it assiduously and support it with comprehensive data. During the years of Neo-Absolutism, the budget barely rose at all, since Francis Joseph reigned with great thrift during his first ten years. The next step was that he commissioned his Finance Minister to transfer the required sum of money to the court payments office. The payment office subsequently transferred the money to the Lord Chancellor in monthly installments. The Office of the Exchequer then funneled the money to the four departments. At the beginning of his reign, the budget was so closely calculated that the emperor repeatedly had to inject additional payments, which always were made to the assistance fund because of employees who had fallen upon hard times.

A listing of the monthly court costs shows that most of the money was spent not on the imperial family or the costs of representation, but for salaries and meals of the employees. The expenses for salaries, pensions, emergency payments came to 80,000 guilders, with an additional 40,000 guilders as an additional supplement each quarter. This amounted to one third of the entire court endowment. In second place were, alternatingly, the costs of upkeep (food plus firewood and candles) and the costs for the stables, which included the high expenses of the breeding farms. The costs for the household economy and the stables fluctuated between 30,000 and 50,000 guilders monthly. Thereafter followed the costs for the maintenance of the court buildings and the guards and guardians (whose salaries were listed separately) which came to 15,000 guilders monthly.[136] In fifth place ranged the expenses for the imperial family, containing the retinues of all the family members, amounting to 12,000 guilders monthly.

The sub-divisions of court expenses

The annual costs of the imperial budget in descending order (in %)

Salaries and pensions	26.4 %
Court stables and breeding farms	19.8 %
Household utilities (food, wood, etc.)	16.3 %
Palace maintenance	11.6 %
Gardens	5.7 %
Costs for imperial family	3.6 %

Imperial theaters and opera	3.5 %
Hunt	3.3 %
Art collections	2.8 %
Imperial gardens and zoo	2.3 %
Social assistance and foundations	1.3 %
Support funds	1.2 %
Chancellery orders	1.2 %
Supplements for cabinet chancellery	0.7 %
Imperial Music Bands	0.1 %
Liveries	0.1 %
Other costs	0.1 %

Interestingly, just how much Francis Joseph received was never recorded, unlike the retinues of his family. It is unknown whether he was paid anything at all or perhaps relinquished any claim to payment from the budget allotted to the retinues. Given his distaste for financial luxury, this would not be surprising. Just how much his precedessor and uncle, Ex-Emperor Ferdinand, received is recorded: 50,000 guilders monthly. This sum was not an item in the court budget, but was listed and paid separately as the sum which a reigning monarch received and which the former emperor refused to disclaim, since he was not compelled to, legally speaking.[137] Thus, Ferdinand not only had his immense personal wealth, but also the largest retinue budget and did not even consider permitting his nephew to get any part of it. Until Ferdinand's death in 1875, Francis Joseph was forced to beg his uncle for funds again and again.

The introduction of the Constitution in 1867 brought about major changes at court. Through the transformation of Austria to a constitutional monarchy, the emperor had to relinquish his sole authority over state finances; in fact, he even had to have his court budget approved by parliament. Certain parliamentarians probably looked forward to juicy debates about the precise expenses of court and the amount of the overall court budget, since before then the exact expenses and, far more important, the way in which court finances were managed, were a closed book to the public eye. But the Finance Minister and the imperial family prevented this kind of examination. The Habsburg family members, the upper chamber of parliament, in which only loyal aristocrats personally appointed by the emperor had seats, made it immediately known that they had no intention whatever to vote on an approval of the court budget, since that was considered to be beneath their dignity, to subject the emperor and his family to such public measures. The Finance Minister communicated to the elected representatives that they indeed had the right to disapprove the court budget, but it would not be permitted to discuss individual line items of it. It was incompatible with the national respect for the imperial dynasty to discuss and vote on individual items, ranging from food purchases to firewood, all the way to the retinues of the imperial family. The court budget proposed by the Lord Chancellor could only be approved or disapproved as a whole. The Finance Minister also made quite clear that the parliament did not have any right of control over the court and that all court affairs lay beyond the authority of the responsible ministry. The intervention of parliament was limited to setting the court budget, whereas how, when and why such items were included was purely a matter of court discretion.[138]

The members of parliament had to swallow it, for better or for worse. The court budget was deducted as 'Chapter 1 of the State Budget' as the very first thing from the overall state expenses and voted on; only then was the rest of the budget discussed and voted on. Through the transformation of Austria to a double monarchy, the court budget was also split between Austria and Hungary, each state responsible for half (unlike the state budget, for which Hungary paid only 30 percent). Since Hungary and Austria were associated in a 'person-oriented union' (the emperor was the only connective link, as King of Hungary) Hungary had to shoulder half of the court expenses.

Until 1869, the court budget was determined annually; as of 1870 it was changed to a ten-year plan, the endowment set for the coming decade and paid out each year. In 1912, it was changed back to an annual arrrangement, probably because of disputes between the Hungarian and Austrian parliaments, due to rising allocations. In 1870, the court budget came to a total of 7,300,000 guilders annually, meaning 3,650,000 guilders for each half of the empire.

The court itself was a pure expenditure, with closely calculated expenses. Its administration had minor revenues, but not enough to make a decisive contribution to the running costs. Ongoing profits were enjoyed only by the popular court pharmacy and the court nurseries (which sold not only cut flowers, but also exported bulbs and seed to other countries).[139] Revenues from leases and licensed hunting regions by the Court Hunting Office yielded a surplus, despite the high costs of the Hunting Office. The administration of the vineyards of Tarczal and Tolcsva brought minor profits. The court theaters, as the best in Vienna, might have brought in big profits, but always ran a deficit and, in fact, required continuing, large financial payments from the court.

The court generated little in the way of revenues, but had its own assets, which were considerable. The palaces, gardens and distinguished art collections belonged not to the emperor as a private person, but to the imperial property office (*Hofärar*). This office was, by definition, a closed asset enterprise whose purpose it was to enable the monarch and head of state to maintain a princely household establishment. The court had sole right of utilisation of its assets, but was not permitted to sell anything from the imperial property office. It was state property, made available for the exclusive use of the current ruler. The emperor was therefore not permitted to bequeathe the castles, gardens and art to his children, since their use automatically was passed on to the next ruler upon his death. In the property registers, these assets were entered as belonging to the property office.[140]

Strictly separated from the administration of court assets was the personal wealth of the imperial family under the title of "General Direction of the Highest Private and Family Fund". This clear distinction in personal wealth of the dynasty had existed since the time of Maria Theresia, whose husband, Franz von Lothringen, not only brought immense assets into the marriage, but was also a proven financial expert and through clever investments and nimble speculations on the stock market managed to build up a significant fortune. When Franz Stephan died, his heirs – Maria Theresia and Crown Prince Joseph – used the greater part of his legacy to pay off state debts. They also designated a large part of his great fortune to establish a family care fund, designated to provide for the members of the imperial house in ways fitting to their station without having to ask the state for such funds.

The management of this family fund was traditionally in the hands of the head of the household and ruling emperor, however it did not belong to him personally, but rather to the whole family. Each individual member of the Habsburg family had a claim to a fixed percentage of the fund, but direct access to the fund was the sole right of the emperor.

Emperor Francis Joseph had next to no personal wealth before 1875. The private wealth of Emperor Franz was bequeathed to his precedessor, Ex-Emperor Ferdinand, who also inherited the legacy of the Duke of Reichstadt, comprising huge landholdings in Bohemia and a large horde of cash. Apart from that, Emperor Ferdinand, who was usually called simple minded, made a fortune on his own. He invested at the right moment in highly profitable enterprises, possessed large packets of shares in three railroad lines. The childless Ferdinand named his nephews as his heirs, which made Emperor Francis Joseph himself a rich man upon his passing. Parts of this fortune were written over to the family provision fund, some parts he kept for himself and later bequeathed to his daughters and grandchildren.

The imperial private fortune comprised properties in Lower Austria and Upper Austria, Eckartsau Castle, rented buildings in Vienna, huge estates in Bohemia and Moravia and large shareholdings. In 1938, the value of Habsburg assets in Austria alone was estimated at about 93 million euros. And the significant assets and investments which today are located in the Czech Republic were not even counted.[141]

The private and family funds were a part of the inner court administration, but their staff, consisting of about 200 people in Vienna and Prague as well as people at the properties themselves, were financed by the emperor alone, from his private purse. The employees of the family fund were not court officials, but private employees of the emperor; all salaries and pensions were paid by the family fund, not out of the court budget. Family members received regular dividends from this fund, but most of the profits were reinvested in order to ensure the maintenance of the family in the future.

If at year's end the imperial family fund was in the red, it was not because of poor money management, since the emperor had outstanding asset managers working for him, but because he had once again used the customary method of preventing the worst of scandals from getting out of hand. He paid without objection huge sums in order to keep still worse things from happening. A deficit of more than 200,000 crowns, for example, in the year 1907, was solely for imperial 'direct payments'. Just under 400,000 crowns were paid by the emperor to his former niece, Marie Larisch, to prevent her from writing memoirs about her deceased aunt, Empress Elisabeth, and also to keep her far away from Vienna. A lady by the name of Caecilie Obermayer received 100,000 crowns for ending her relationship to Archduke Heinrich Ferdinand, who stemmed from the Tuscan branch of the family.[142]

After the end of the monarchy, the assets in the imperial property office devolved to the state, the private imperial fortune was passed on to the war veterans fund. And Habsburg family members are still engaged today in legal actions in order to reclaim parts of their former fortune.[143]

IX
Art and Culture at the Court

By and large, Emperor Francis Joseph is not associated with any particular acumen or involvement in the arts. The prevalent viewpoint is that the emperor had little interest in music, equally little in the fine arts, literature and architecture. Only theater sparked his interest, but even then, he was attracted only to lightweight pieces.

However, if one examines the actual facts, namely, the major appointments to the opera house and the Burgtheater as well as the Ringstrasse architects, an entirely new picture of Emperor Francis Joseph and his appreciation of the arts emerges. A dearth of information on his personal preferences has one simple explanation: the emperor could not permit himself personal preferences in matters of cultural policy. This restraint was due not to lack of interest, but to his awareness that any personal engagement on his part would conflict with the official cultural policies of the empire, which elected to promote and support each sector and movement in equal measure. That meant that even artistic leanings and music developments which the emperor himself could not enjoy or grasp were supported by the court. Francis Joseph saw himself not as a private patron of the arts, but as a statesman, which as it happened, also included decisions in the fields of art and culture.

Nonetheless, the most momentous policy changes in the worlds of theater, opera and fine arts during the era of Francis Joseph can be attributed to the emperor personally, together with his Lord Chamberlain and Lord Chancellor. The most important cultural institutions were under the sole management of the court of Vienna: the court theater (Burgtheater), the court opera (Staatsoper), the court art collections (today's Kunsthistorisches Museum), the natural historical collections (today's Natural History Museum), the painting gallery in the Lower Belvedere, the Treasury Chamber and the collection at Ambras Castle in Tirol.

In the early years of Francis Joseph's reign, art and culture issues were in the sole hands of the Lord Chamberlain; in 1867 the authority changed hands to the Lord Chancellor, who then assumed control of all stage theaters. The Lord Chamberlain functioned as unofficial cultural minister, thus deciding on all purchases for the imperial collections, subsidies for certain art academies and directors of the Burgtheater and Opera House in collaboration with the emperor. The selection of the ideal Lord Chamberlain was the first decision of import which the young emperor had to make. All seven Lord Chamberlains appointed by Emperor Francis Joseph possessed well founded knowledge of the arts, a widespread acquaintance with artists and were open to all the artistic movements of the day.

For a long time, historic art research has claimed that Emperor Francis Joseph had no personal involvement in matters of art, relying utterly on the competence of his Lord Chamberlain; moreover, that he was utterly ignorant of the current movements in various art fields. Purportedly, he let others select who was to be sponsored, what was to be purchased, and showed no interest whatever in any particular promotion.

More recent historical researches have provided an assessment which is diametrically opposed to this view.[144] Francis Joseph, contrary to all evaluations to date, was profoundly interested in the fine arts and attempted assiduously to support a new wave of artistic endeavor.

In the past, the Royal and Imperial Academy of the Fine Arts had submitted proposals for commissioned works of art and artists worthy of support to the Office of the Lord Chamberlain. Under the emperor's two predecessors, Kaiser Franz and Kaiser Ferdinand, these proposals were never questioned, merely carried out. What resulted was seldom of outstanding quality for the court. All too often, artists of little talent were promoted, who furthermore charged exorbitant prices for their works and rarely delivered them on time (delays of up to two years were common). New movements went unheeded; historical painting was in a state of coma.

The members of the Art Academy believed they would be able to manipulate the 18-year old emperor to the same degree as they had his predecessors. But Francis Joseph made very clear at the outset that it was his express will to promote works oriented towards the history of the fatherland and to new, burgeoning artistic movements. When the academy presented him with works of genre painting and conventional portraits, he reacted with visible irritation and ordered that not a single one of the recommended works be purchased.

Francis Joseph then neutralised the art academy and appointed a new art commission. He had little confidence in the distinguished gentlemen at the academy who had advised his precedessors and his uncle so poorly, and so appointed very few academy members to his new commmission. In their stead, he gathered an assembly of private collectors, patrons and a variety of artists and ordered them to implement commissions and promotions in future which adhered to clearly articulated guidelines of the emperor himself. Even if the historical paintings the emperor loved so much proved to be less successful than he hoped, the personal involvement of Francis Joseph was pronounced. He had a modern, hands-on approach to art and defended himself vehemently against any and all attempts to manipulate his taste or his purchases.

Even in the world of theater, Francis Joseph pursued his own, novel path: for the important appointment of Heinrich Laube as Director of the Burgtheater of the Court of Vienna (the first Director under Emperor Francis Joseph) in 1849, the first Lord Chamberlain was responsible: Count Karl Lanckoronski, a member of an ancient Polish dynasty much treasured by the Habsburg family. Lanckoronski was serene, very restrained in manner, an amicable fellow who hated conflicts.[145] That Count Lanckoronski of all people would have made such a courageous appointment to the court theater shows both his far ranging knowledge of the requirements of theater life as well as how ingenious Francis Joseph's appointment of First Chamberlain was.

Through the appointment of Heinrich Laube as artistic director of the Burgtheater, the most decisive step towards the meteroric rise of this theater to the apex in the German speaking regions of Europe was taken. Nonetheless, the appointment was disputed, since Laube was anything but unknown at the time. Notorious for having been been an active member of a fraternity believed to cultivate revolutionary tendencies since his student days, he was an ardent admirer of the July Revolution in France. He was banished by the government of Saxony as a political agitator and convicted by the German Federation to seven years in prison for sedition. Thanks to influential friends, his sentence was reduced to 18 months.

After serving his prison sentence, Heinrich Laube went to Paris, studied French literature, began to write stage plays in Leipzig and launched an association with the theaters in Vienna around 1845, while still remaining politically active. Following the March Revolution in 1848, he was given a mandate in the democratically elected parliament of German Bohemia. The fact that Francis Joseph could countenance the appointment of a man who was active in a revolution, because of which the emperor had to flee to Tirol but a year earlier, is a startling demonstration of the clear-headed and emotionally neutral objectivity of which Francis Joseph was capable. If Laube was able to raise the Burgtheater to the rank which Francis Joseph envisioned for it, his revolutionary background was not deemed to be an obstacle.

Thus, Heinrich Laube's appointment by Lord Chamberlain Lanckoronski was highly unusual, but the ways in which the theater profited from it were indisputable. For, only under Laube's direction did the Burgtheater rise to become the topmost dramatic institution in the vast firmament of theaters in the German speaking world. His wide ranging repertoire included exemplary classic pieces as well as conversational novelties, but he also promoted contemporary plays and was a particular supporter of Franz Grillparzer.

Laube's period of directorship was the most formative, tradition-building era of the Burgtheater. Under his aegis, which began at nearly the same time as the reign of Francis Joseph, Austrian cultural life gave birth to a unique patriotism towards the Burgtheater, and its nearly mythical rise began. The theater became the center of ambitious reporting in the media, the schedule of plays and the attractions of the actors and actresses became the subject of daily boulevard gossip. Theatrical discussions resonated in the coffee houses and salons of the city. The directors provided both an artistic and a social backdrop in which Vienna's cultural needs and desires could evolve to perfection. The Burgtheater became something akin to an invisible link between the court and the citizens, since there was no other sphere of life where the elite court of Vienna touched the bourgeois world of the people more directly than in its guardianship of Vienna's court theater.

In 1867, the year of the settlement with Hungary and the introduction of the Constitution, the emperor appointed his former adjutant, Count Franz Crenneville to the position of Lord Chamberlain. This was a man whose unsuitability for matters of art and culture seemed unbeatable. Crenneville came from the military, was thought (unjustifiably) to belong to the war faction at court, was considered to be extremely conservative and was, to top it off, highly unpopular. That he had any inkling of art was simply unimaginable to his enemies. And yet, Crenneville was the one who guided the imperial art collections into the modern age. No one but his closest friends (and the emperor) knew that Crenneville had profound affinities to the world of art and possessed vast knowledge of the fine arts. Thus, the surprise was enormous when it turned out that the new Lord Chamberlain not only had a very refined concept of what the future art collection policies should be, but also, in disputes between court offices, on one side of a dispute, and artists and scientists on the other, invariably took the side of the artists.

Crenneville was one of the most important Lord Chamberlains under Emperor Francis Joseph. He not only promoted a series of individual artists and stars of the scene who had a big impact on the general public, he also invested in entire branches. And more than anything else, he patronized the neglected stepchildren of the art scene: the copper engravers, restorers, scientists and art historians. Crenneville stood up for the coming artistic generation, and distributed imperial stipends to many who lived abroad. Lord Chamberlain Crenneville viewed such measures to be investments in Austria's future and made great efforts to get sufficient funds appropriated by the Lord Chancellor.

The court also was attentive to the younger generation of artists in its official purchases. The cultural editors of the *Wiener Zeitung* proclaimed: "*... not only the creations at the top rung, but also artists who show talent and promise of great things to come are given consideration. This gives encouragement to young artists and inspires them to push forward their own education and personal development. It hardly needs to be said that the worthwhile principle of imperial patronage of supporting not only art which is recognized, but art which is in the process of germinating merits the applause of every art lover.*"[146]

In selecting works to purchase for the imperial art collections, Crennevelle had limited funds at his disposal. That meant that high-prestige objects could only be bought from estate inheritance auctions, since regular sales were prohibitively expensive for the imperial art budget. As a rule, the endowment of the Office of the Chamberlain was not enough to pursue a concrete purchasing policy; that meant the emperor repeatedly had to dig into his personal purse to provide necessary funds and keep his acquisition wishes alive. But Crenneville shied away from no effort to find and acquire new works for the collections, which in the end contained works from every epoch.

The art collections and the natural history collections grew to such an extent that there was no room to house them anymore (today's Kunsthistorische Museum did not yet exist). The two large museums as we know them today were parts of the huge Ringstrasse architecture project. While these new exhibition buildings were in the planning stage, internal revisions also took place. The collections had to be newly positioned and adapted to future exigencies. Lord Chamberlain Crenneville was assigned to work out a general concept for the future progress of the art programmes. In May 1876, Crenneville submitted his proposed agenda to the emperor in which the scientific objectives and the future internal structure of the collections were mapped out for the coming generations. In this very modern, well thought out concept, it was recorded that the art collections would never have a great deal of money at their disposal. "*Therefore, it is determined to be preferable to aim towards collecting narrowly defined works of outstanding quality rather than pursuing a vast, but nebulous goal in all directions, which in the end would still be full of gaps.*"[147] As far as personnel policies were concerned, the Lord Chamberlain demanded of the directors and custodians to hire "*without exception the best and most scientifically qualified*", since only in such ways could one be sure "*to appoint unconventional men to the right place of employment.*"[148]

The general programme can be seen as Emperor Francis Joseph's avowed commitment to culture, since the proposals of the Lord Chamberlain were implemented precisely as they were presented to him. Only scientfically qualified personnel were placed in leading positions at the museums; the collections focused on extending the existing art movements; public taste was not catered to, since he recognized that what was popular and modern one day

Emperor Francis Joseph visits an exhibition

might be spurned the next. The court thought in epoch-spanning dimensions, rather than in satisfying the cravings of the moment. The crowning point of decades of enlarging and transforming the imperial collections was the opening of the two museums on the Ring Road in 1891.

Also in the world of opera, the court revealed a highly modern approach. Lord Chancellor Montenuovo, who was responsible for the opera, reflected in his policies the latest musical trends at the turn of the century. The artistic renewal of the Court Opera House can mainly be attributed to his decision to engage the highly disputed Gustav Mahler as director of the opera. The era of Gustav Mahler turned out to be immensely important for the opera of Vienna. It was made possible only through the personal support of the Lord Chancellor for an ingenious yet uncomfortable and uncompromising artist. Mahler's first years as director were one prolonged battle between the director, the court authorities and the press, whose reports rippled with anti-semitic attitudes. Neither the civil servants at the court agencies nor the press had any comprehension of Mahler's emancipating endeavors, for his contract with the court permitted him only very little artistic self determination. They saw Mahler's stubbornness with regard to artistic autonomy as a permanent intractibility against the authorities of court and an unruly rejection of the taste of the times. Montenuovo supported Mahler in his efforts for greater artistic freedom and often tried to protect him from the onslaughts of the bureaucracy. The blossoming of high officialdom at court often led to caustic criticism of opera director Mahler and his staff. When these officials were about to open yet another critical dossier on Mahler, Montenuovo censured them sharply, enraged about the "*unjustified and stubbornly bureaucratic methods of making a mountain out of every molehill, creating paper trails for every tiny decision, so that a great deal of brouhaha is created, yet no thinking!*"[149]

Montenuovo's support for Mahler paid off, most of all financially. In the first five years of Mahler's direction, the incommodious director not only opened the court opera to modern works, he also raised revenues to unseen heights. However, Mahler's efforts to not only handle the administration of the opera, but also pursue his personal work as a composer, led to ongoing disputes with the court. When after the initial glorious years the numbers of opera visitors declined, Mahler let it be known that he saw his true calling more in composing than in running the opera house. At this juncture, Montenuovo decided to let the director go. Mahler departed full of decorations and awards, Montenuovo himself saw to it that Mahler, due to "*his restless striving to bring new life to this institution*"[150] receive the highest possible pension as well as a high dismissal settlement, which the emperor approved personally. Mahler is said to have claimed years later that Montenuovo "*was the ideal theater boss, full of understanding for the necessities of artistic operations.*"[151] The officials responsible for cultural affairs at court showed an astonishingly modern face in their unflagging support of Mahler, whose opera direction was lampooned continually in the daily papers to the point of resembling a veritable witch hunt.

But as much as the court tried to answer and reflect the needs of modern art, in one area neither the emperor nor his preeminent counselors recognized the need for fundamental renewal. In spite of all its problems, the court could simply not manage to get rid of its bureaucratic censure, which reviewed all new pieces. Even the pre-selection of pieces to be considered for production at the Burgtheater was far too complicated. The Court Censor Office, which operated completely apart from the State Censor Office, worked against the backdrop of post-revolutionary confusions in the police department of the Prime Minister's office during the early years, and later on was carried out by appointed functionaries. When the constitutional monarchy was launched in 1867, the General Director of each theater was also the censor, who in turn coordinated his decisions with the Lord Chancellor. After the death of the highly self-assured and decisive Hohenlohe, a new spirit took hold of the Censor Office around the turn of the century, partly due to the delicacy of censuring modern theater in a new age.

Neither the General Theater Director nor the new Lord Chancellor Liechtenstein wished to bear the final responsibility for such a tricky task. They handed on the Court Censor responsibilities to the office of the Foreign Ministry, which was also the Ministry for the Imperial Court, and all along had had a voice in the choices made by the Court Censor. But Foreign Minister Goluchowski had misgivings about the ramifications of his new responsibility and refused to assume it before the principles of censure were precisely defined.[152] Liechtenstein, on the other hand, had no desire to do that, in fact was incapable of laying down the principles of censure and told the Foreign Minister that *"it was only a matter of adhering to moral and aesthetic principles, as well as consideration of the imperial dynasty and political conditions."*[153] This back-and-forth of who should bear final responsibility led ultimately to a division of authority, which made future examination of any pieces extremely difficult. Both court and foreign ministry agreed on one Chief of Section at the Foreign Ministry whose official function would henceforth be censure. But since this person was equipped only with the right to prohibit, but not to approve, the General Director of the Theater still had to provide the pre-censure selection. The upshot of this fragmented authority was an unnecessarily complicated, time consuming and utterly opaque bureaucratic path which led to immense criticism of the court, and went so far as to question the value of court criticism to begin with.

The struggle revolving around court censure is a portrait of the kinds of problems the court was confronted with in the final years of its existence. The theme of censure was, in the mature legal state of the late Francis Joseph era, such an indefinable and treacherous subject that no one wanted to be responsible for it without solid back-up. The appointed authorities at court refused to bear the responsibility themselves. The state agency also refused to make the decisions without extensive guidelines and directives. The result was a kind of Kafkaesque catch-22 which managed to make court decisions utterly intransparent to the general public and remained full of clique-oriented intrigue and backroom decision making, precisely the reputation which the court tried so hard to avoid.

The moral strictures and ethical guidelines new plays had to fulfil were, fascinatingly enough, quite well defined. The inviolability of the statecraft of the imperial family, a resistance to all tendencies hostile to the dynasty and the omission of any and all tendentious judgments or symbolic references to the various nationalities of the Habsburg empire or offense of any regional populations; moreover, no insulting of church or priests. These were the most important criteria of the censure.

The court felt no antipathy to modern plays. After all, the major authors of the Young Vienna Group had already had their debut at the Burgtheater, often to the great displeasure of the conservative theater audience. Nor was the court reluctant to stage unconventional plays. Hermann Bahr, who was known more than anything else for his acrid attacks on court offices and the Burgtheater director, was put on at the Burgtheater.[154] Politically explosive authors were repeatedly engaged by the court. Even in political works, the emperor showed himself to be not at all skittish, his person was untouchable at the top of the empire and he was the ultimate guarantor of that empire. Yet emperor and court agencies simply could not manage to dissolve the Censor Office, even though it was no longer necessary – all one had to do was declare that emperor, state and regional groups could not be offended, period. If one tries to figure out why this step was not able to be taken, one can only conclude it was perhaps a certain fear of the unknown and of the unimaginable. Even if the Censor Office caused far more problems than it solved, an abiding fear of scandals stayed the court's hand and left it in place.

If releasing plays for production was complicated and delicate due to the Court Censor, it really got difficult for authors when individual members of the imperial family tried to have works cancelled after they had already been approved for production. Any official intervention of court appeared downright grotesque when a play got cancelled, i.e. removed from the programme, without it ever having been censured or having violated any perceptible lines of correctness to begin with. Arthur Schnitzler's play "The Green Cockatoo" suffered precisely this fate. Due to the personal interference of the emperor's daughter, Archduchess Marie Valerie, who voiced moral objections, the play was cancelled. For an artist, such interference by a conservative member of the imperial family was a disaster. On the one hand, it meant the play was taboo from that moment on, the author also forfeited his royalties, and other stages couldn't put on the play either, since he was tied legally to a contract with the Burgtheater. In the case of the "Green Cockatoo", Schnitzler was forced to beg the theater to actually prohibit his play publicly, since that was the only way the contract he had signed with the Burgtheater could be annulled, which would then at least permit him to sign a contract with another theater. But the Burgtheater couldn't admit that a play which had been officially approved by the Court Censor subsequently had to be cancelled because of objections by an archduchess.

It was through such inofficial prohibitions that the court authorities aimed to carry out the wishes of the imperial family, but they merely poured salt into the wound of what the public perceived as an utterly unreasonable and anachronistic court authority. Both the public and the theater audiences sensed the true reasons for plays being cancelled which had already been staged more than once and, based on those feelings, let loose bristling criticism of the court. The press took advantage of these incidents to agitate against the theater directors, thus indirectly against court authorities. The outdated and overly complicated Court Censor which due to poor organization needed months to approve a play for staging; plus the arbitrary cancellation of certain plays due to objections of imperial family members were the main reasons for the skyrocketing criticism of everything relating to the court in Vienna.

X
The 'Private Life' of the Imperial Family

In Emperor Francis Joseph's day, the number of archdukes and archduchesses was higher than ever before. The various branches of the House of Habsburg blossomed to such an extent throughout the 19th century that the earlier concern about a lack of male heirs under Charles VI evaporated completely. The challenges which Emperor Francis Joseph had to face lay less in securing the succession to the throne than maintaining discipline in the vast family.

The hierarchy was just as strictly defined within the imperial family as it was for the aristocrats at court. At the top stood Emperor Francis Joseph. His word, quite literally, was law. The family statutes of 1839, i.e. the Habsburg family's own constitution, gave the reigning emperor full and complete power over all the branches of the family, and to a far more profound degree than in the previous centuries. Francis Joseph alone decided upon the place of residence of all his relatives, made all the decisions relating to their own courts and determined the course of education, training and career for all male members of the family (military careers, in general). He was the final instance in dispensing permission to marry, determining the amount of money for an apanage and could even exclude archdukes from the imperial dynasty, should their conduct merit it.

Francis Joseph was very strict, bordering on severe, with his own family. He measured his relatives by the selfsame standards which he applied to himself. His family felt deep respect for Francis Joseph, even as a young emperor, occasionally even fear. The emperor was incorruptible and had not the slightest patience with individual urges for unusual lifestyles, which he viewed as a breakdown of duty, driven as he was by his own inordinate sense of responsibility and willingness to sacrifice everything for the fulfillment of his tasks. A Habsburger had preordained responsibilities which were placed upon one's shoulders at birth: a dignified representation of the family through irreproachable conduct, support of the ruler in his efforts and responsibilities and, above all else, a life spent serving the dynasty.

Since Emperor Leopold II, Francis Joseph's great-grandfather, there had been five families in the Habsburg-Lothringen line. The main family branch of the emperor; the Tuscan line (stemming from the former Grand Dukes of Tuscany until 1859); the Rainer line (former Viceroys of Lombardy); the Hungarian Joseph line; the line of the Hungarian Palatinate who lived in Hungary; and the military line of Charles, offspring of the victor of Aspern, Archduke Charles. The position of each family member was determined by the family branch and the nearness to the throne. First came the emperor, his son, his brothers, then the Tuscan family, the Charles family, then the lines of Joseph and Rainer.

Even if all the Habsburgs had adhered to this ranking, the system in practice was doomed to lead to blossoming tensions inside the family, particularly since the Habsburg-Tuscan line came in such numbers to Vienna after the end of their reign in Italy in 1859. They occupied only the second rank in the family tree, after the emperor's closest family, but since the newborn Italy had confiscated a large part of their assets, they had very little personal fortune remaining at their disposal and needed financial support from the emperor. On the other hand, the lower ranked part of the family, the Charles line, was highly thought of and wealthy. Together with Archduke Charles and Archduke Albrecht, they not only produced the only successful field marshalls of the Habsburg family in the 19th century; but because of their wealth were completely independent of the emperor, financially speaking. Archduke Albrecht was the doyen of the family, following Emperor Francis Joseph, although he formally ranked behind the youngest of the far less wealthy and not very well based family members of the Tuscan branch. Archduke Leopold, who quit the ranks of the family, recalled: *"The unusual constraints of the family ranking system led to people being treated according to family branch, not only within the dynasty but within a given family itself. This status was a predominant part of daily life from earliest childhood and often became an issue of import. One grew up with it and accepted it without question."*[155]

To all appearances, the rank was strictly observed and respected, only at family functions or get-togethers were these ranks dispensed with, where seniority alone held sway. No young archduke from a high ranking branch of the family would ever have used his rank to supercede an aged Archduke Albrecht or Rainer.

The personal lives of the Habsburgs were also subjected to severe strictures on behaviour. The educational agendas of the children had to be reviewed and approved by the emperor. Young archdukes were compelled to enter military service and launch a career there. Females born as archduchesses had the sole responsibility of marrying into the highest of ruling families and submitting to the demands of their husbands' families. Those marrying into the Habsburg family were expected to be perfect mothers and wives, adopting occasional supplementary responsibilities in patronizing orphanages or kitchens to feed the poor. Their public responsibilities were limited to social tasks. The protectorates which were given to archduchesses were, in the main, cultural. Individual lifestyles were unthinkable for a Habsburg. Insisting on pursuing such, or entering marriages not countenanced by the emperor, led to the most profound family discord imaginable, which could even lead to family exclusion. At the turn of the century, the number of young Habsburgers who were rankled by these strictures and no longer willing to submit to them rose dramatically, thereby intensifying the family crisis.

Only those family members who had their own private wealth, either through inheritance or marriage, were in a position to live outside the walls of the Vienna palace, and thereby escape the observation and censure of the emperor. Archduke Albrecht and his family lived in the Albertina in Vienna and in the Weilburg near Baden; the emperor's brother, Karl Ludwig, built his own palace in Vienna in the 1870s; Archduke Rainer lived with his family in a palace in Vienna's fourth district. Whereas whoever was financially dependent had to articulate financial needs regularly and thus was observed regularly, the emperor often turning down financial requests based on reports which reached his ears. Members of the imperial family who had no great personal wealth had a right to an apartment in the Hofburg or one of the other palaces; had the right to a small court and a coach from the Stallburg. The Tuscan branch of the family received the right to the Imperial Residence in Salzburg after they were exiled from Tuscany; when in Vienna they had apartments in the Hofburg.

Families who were financially independent of the emperor had no claim to palace apartments, coaches or servants, nor to a state apanage which was the privilege of every Habsburg family member. However, they had far greater freedom to lead the lives they wished and dispense with the severe etiquette of the family. The daughters of Archduke Friedrich, heir of the very wealthy Charles line, for example, lived an extremely modern life (for women) in Pressburg at the turn of the century. They rode bicycles, played tennis and were quite self-assured in their conduct, as was clear by their willingness to voice their own opinions in public. In the immediate vicinity of the emperor, such behaviour would not have been possible. An archduchess bicycling through the city parks was, for the emperor, beyond the pale.

But it was on the young archdukes more than anyone else that Francis Joseph trained his strictest gaze. He had his staff report to him on all their successes and failures in the military, on the people they kept company with. His deepest disapproval was reserved for those who slipped out in the dark of night to consort with their comrades or mistresses. The policemen on night duty had to note down every time of exit and entry of these persons. The notations were presented to the emperor every morning, and they were read with great interest. He often inquired in surprisingly well informed ways of the young officers themselves as to just what had drawn them to leave the palace in the dead of night and return in the wee hours, causing great embarrassment. They learned through hard experience that there was only one answer which the emperor would approve: headaches had forced them to take a nocturnal stroll.[156] As the emperor received this answer more and more often, he soon stopped his questioning, but observed the young archdukes even more assiduously.

The emperor saw his family only on Sunday evenings at family dinner, at which every family member who was in the city was compelled to appear. Only illness or official responsibilities were acceptable reasons for absence, and even then, written excuses had to be submitted to the Lord Chancellor well ahead of time. If the emperor suspected unwillingness or some ploy behind the explanation, he sent his own personal doctor to find out the truth. The emperor had zero tolerance for dissimulation and dishonesty of any kind.

If the imperial family was alone, as was the case at the Sunday evening dinners, their relations were relaxed and lively. "*The conversation at table was quite peppery. Afterwards, too, when we had withdrawn into little groups – one might call them 'groups of like minded' – in this or that corner of the room. With no constraints, we chatted about anything and everything. The emperor was an avid listener and often piped up with a defense of someone or a point of view which he would express ardently. We heard lots of interesting tales about the 'good old days' when neither the railways nor the telegraphs raised the hackles of the people.*"[157] These memories stem from one of those young archdukes who had been ostracized from the family, who certainly had little reason to portray the family in a positive light.

That the family life of the emperor was tedious and boring is claimed only by the people who were invited to official dinners. For these, the imperial family was stoically silent, utterly restrained, performing purely representational functions with their legendary sense of duty. Family members deferred to the highest ranking person at table; one told no private stories; and one never, ever uttered personal opinions. The family also made efforts to conceal their candid intimacy when court employees were present, including court ladies and the Lord Chancellor himself. The Habsburgers were intensely aware of their being under scrutiny from their earliest moments on earth. Every careless word or act might leak to the outer world. And the brash candour with which Crown Prince Rudolph let his opinions on day-to-day politics be known led to harsh criticism from his own family. His reckless, free-wheeling speech with people outside the family was notorious far and wide, including the fact that his views often differed radically from those of his family elders. He made himself vulnerable through this behaviour, but he exposed himself again and again with his lighthearted palaver, making it easy for others to manipulate him.

The emotional tone of family repartee was formal, but warm hearted. One always addressed the emperor as 'Majesty' in company; when alone the familiar 'Du' form was admissible, but 'Majesty' as the form of direct address remained. Even the emperor's own children spoke to him as 'Majesty' unless they were alone, when 'Papa' was sufficient.

Apart from the Sunday dinners, not even family members who lived inside the palace of Vienna got to see him. True, they had the right to consult him at any time, which meant that they alone did not have to clear a visit with the Lord Chancellor beforehand, but could simply appear before the doorman and ask to be admitted; but next to no one dared to take advantage of this privilege. Even the emperor's brothers first asked permission of the Lord Chancellor. Only Francis Joseph's mother, wife and children took advantage of this privilege, and then, only in urgent situations.

The emperor's own contact with his family was limited to written notes and correspondence, and to being together on the hunt. When family members were called up for mandatory appearances at ceremonies, receptions, visits of foreign rulers or balls, the Office of the Exchequer sent out circulars to all the archdukes and archduchesses with the details of time, place and appropriate dress. Their appearance was taken for granted; if it was not possible, written arrangements and excuses had to be undertaken through the Office of the Exchequer.

The family was completely in the control of the emperor. Every contact with the outer world had to be reported to him. As regarded invitations to the palace, he was more lenient. Some family members regularly invited over friends from aristocratic circles, quite inofficially. Otherwise, the dukes dined alone with their own small court. For any invitation outside the palace or participation at a public event, prior permission had to be obtained from the emperor by submitting a written request to the Lord Chancellor, who showed it personally to the emperor. A notation of Prince Hohenlohe to the emperor dating from 1870 is an example of this. He asks whether Archduke Ludwig and family might be permitted to appear at a children's ball. The curt answer in red by the emperor: "*Can go to the ball.*" The official answer of the emperor was then written out on court stationery and handed to the archduke.[158] Most family members spent their evenings with siblings and relatives, if they did not utilise their private boxes at the Burgtheater or Opera House (the only public events at which they were permitted to appear without prior approval from the emperor).

The emperor not only supervised the appearances and visits of his family, he also watched over the company they kept with eagle eyes. Each archduke had his own chancellor, who answered all official queries to the archduke; a secretary, who assumed the burdens of written correspondence; and personal valets. The archduchesses had court ladies and servants. Children had their own nannies. The closer one was to the throne, the larger the personal household was. In selecting the personal chancellor for an archduke, the emperor did not exercise criteria of agreeableness or personal wishes, but only of which aristocrats at court he chose to distinguish by such an appointment. Most of the selected persons submitted to the honour of being a personal chancellor, even though the task was not always agreeable.

Sometimes even the emperor himself had to admit that two people simply could not get along with each other. Archduke Otto, father of the last emperor, was 'liberated' from his personal chancellor Montenuovo when Francis Joseph appointed him as imperial Lord Chancellor. Otto was a highly likeable fellow who did not take formal etiquette very seriously. He was simply mowed down by the over-dominant Montenuovo, who lacked any sensitivity to the character nuances of his master. Since both Archduke Otto and Montenuovo requested to be relieved of one another, Francis Joseph saw the point, and fulfilled the request.

The heir to the throne, Franz Ferdinand, was the only one who dared to demand the appointment of his own chosen individuals, if he deemed necessary through pure obstinacy. The rest of the family submitted to their fate. Most lived in utter harmony and satisfaction with their respective chamberlains and chancellors, sometimes the relationships even grew into intimate friendships which lasted many years. Only the rich, independent family members such as Archdukes Albrecht and Friedrich selected their staff utterly independently, but in most cases also paid them from their own purse.

In such a large family as the Habsburgs, there were ongoing differences of opinion. Francis Joseph, as *pater familias*, always mediated: *"To his credit it must be said that he invariably listened impartially to both sides, questioned them exhaustively and made his decision only after long, deep consideration. He was relentless in making sure that his ruling was respected minor disputes annoyed him above all other things. When his patience was exhausted, he was capable of exploding like a clap of thunder. But soon thereafter, his blue skies became visible and, accompanied by a bit of grumbling, he calmed down again."* [159]

No one outside of Empress Elisabeth exercised personal influence on the emperor. In fact, most of the family members did not even come in the physical vicinity of the emperor except at family dinners, and the emperor strictly forbade any and all interference by family members in his affairs. *"It was nearly impossible to get to him directly; he himself wished to know well ahead of time about everything and everyone with whom he would be confronted over the course of the day ... any attempts by us archdukes to mediate in individual issues were seen – and rejected – as overstepping the bounds of our authority."* [160]

When archdukes wished to effect certain things with the emperor, they usually attempted it via the Lord Chancellor, which in turn explains his enormous power at court. Good relations with the Lord Chancellor guaranteed that matters of personal importance would be presented to the emperor. All of Francis Joseph's Lord Chancellors were exceedingly careful to prevent any manipulation of their office, their person and their services, but nonetheless could not simply brush off pressing matters of the archdukes. A strategy of first sifting the quality of the atmosphere before presenting a request to the Chancellor was often pursued. The son of Chancellor Hohenlohe reported to his father an unusual conversation he had with Franz Ferdinand, heir to the throne: *"I recently spent the whole afternoon with His Majesty Franz on a walk, he was very friendly, and asked ten times when you were coming to see him. On the same day, Marie Thérese* (Ferdinand's stepmother) *was with Mudding* (Marie Hohenlohe's nickname) *which led me to the not unjustified conclusion that the whole family wants something from you. After all, they do not dispense that kind of graciousness for no reason."* [161] And a few days later, when Franz Ferdinand still did not yet have an appointment with the Chancellor, *"I go for a walk with His Majesty Franz nearly every day and he smothers me with graciousness, it is downright eerie!"* [162]

As a rule, such attempts to cut through the decision making process were to little avail, the emperor kept his family at sufficient distance from power and influence, permitting no interference whatever. His relatives remained under his adamant and unrelenting control. It is evident that even members of imperial families born to wealth and the highest rung of the social ladder must have led lives markedly less free than many an aristocrat or normal citizen.

XI
Scandals at Court

Even in Francis Joseph's day, there was high demand for news from the royal and imperial court, particularly for stories coming from the personal spheres at the highest levels. Due to the iron-clad censure, free wheeling political reporting was disbarred, it was not even permitted for personalities from the imperial family to be the subject of public discussion. Reports from or about the court were on the borderline of what was allowed, just barely permissible when the court itself released public announcements regarding appointments of privy councillors or court ladies, listings of audiences and data pertaining to official journeys to the newspapers. These reports were previously approved by high court offices, sometimes combed through by the Office of the Exchequer line by line.

The court maintained brassbound borders of separation between itself and the outer world. Even official correspondence between the imperial court and the ministries of state government could only be passed on to the hands of the Foreign Ministry, which was at the same time the Ministry of the Imperial Dynasty, for the simple reason that any and all close contact had to be avoided. The dignity of the House of Habsburg was to be maintained at all times through this demonstration of aloofness. The court, in its policies and in all details regarding its inhabitants, simply could not be the subject of open, public debate.

From the very day Francis Joseph was crowned in 1848, the reading public of the vast array of Austrian newspapers – who had well entrenched and proficient habits of knowing how to 'read between the lines' – showed great interest in the emperor. He was young, handsome and unmarried. Every visit to a foreign country, every invitation to the court of Vienna might harbour untold implications. The fact that Archduchess Sophie arranged for the first meeting of the emperor with the woman he was later to marry, Elisabeth, in Ischl of all places was due to the fact that the court had gathered ample experience of rumours quickly accumulating in speed and potency in Vienna. Every invitation of a lovely countess to visit court which was not in the context of a ball gave rise to wild speculations and gossip.

The first scandal and the first imperial thunderstorm arrived in the opening year of Francis Joseph's reign when suddenly and inexplicably, a great amount of reporting about life at court could be read in the newspapers. Whoever was leaking all these stories to the press had to come from the palace – that much was clear at a glance – in all probability from the Office of the Exchequer. Visits of esteemed personalities which were not intended to become public; information of intimate private dance festivities which Archduchess Sophie organised for her son to permit him a bit of ordinary fun during Carneval season just like any other 18-year old, and to which a series of lovely countesses were invited, who subsequently could read their names in the newspaper (which in turn stirred the jealousy of the families who had not received an invitation); reports about chamber music concerts and private dinners; without warning, all of this could be delectibly read about in the newspapers.

Besides the young emperor's antipathy to being associated with private pleasures in the public eye (as sparse as such pleasures might be), the court under no circumstances had any desire to encourage gossip about the reviewing of potential brides for the monarch. What raised imperial hackles still further were the exaggerations and inventions which were added, to spice up the newspaper articles.

Francis Joseph had his Chancellor write a stern lecture which was then read to each and every employee at court. Every staff director had to sign a paper that he had urged its importance on the members of his department. "*Public newspapers have for some time now published articles about the imperial court in which either consciously or unconsciously statements or acts of the highest persons at court are doctored or downright invented out of wholecloth. Among these erroneous reports are also information which could come only from persons employed at court. This displeases His Majesty to the utmost.*"[163] All court employees were instructed about their oath of secrecy and warned in the severest terms.

For Lord Chancellor Liechtenstein it was important to find out how the informational flow from court to the newspapers worked. Since most of the leaked information had been handed on orally, the court was powerless. But the instructions to court guards to report anything unusual led to success. One attentive guard was able to catch a staff member *in flagrante* as he furtively handed some notes to a passerby. It turned out that the passerby was a reporter for the local paper which had been publishing such court stories. In the course of the disciplinary proceedings against the servant which subsequently followed, the Office of the Exchequer found out just how the information transfer had functioned in the past. The servant had written everything he had uncovered onto tiny slips of paper and deposited them at secret drops, where they were later picked up by the journalist. During the interrogation, the servant confessed that he had received 100 guilders annually – more than a third of his court salary – for these indiscretions. Thus, it was a lucrative supplementary income.[164]

The problem of court news appearing in public newspapers was something the court never learned to get under control. No prohibition can be found as often in the court archives as the one forbidding any contact with newspapers. No warnings or admonishments were proclaimed as unflaggingly. At least once every five years, the entire staff at court was sworn to secrecy anew, but it never stopped the flow of information to the newspapers.

Daily politics seldom reached the hallowed halls of court. After parliamentarianism had been introduced, political debate took place there, where it belonged, in the Imperial Council ('Reichsrat'). But now and again, politically involved citizens who were irritated about one or another aspect of daily politics made their opinions felt at court as well. Such was the case in 1871, when Emperor Francis Joseph abandoned his agreement with the Czech opposition in the last moment.

Four years earlier, the Czechs, one of the most loyal nationalities in the Habsburg empire, had been ignored in the settlement with Hungary which had transformed Austria into a Double Monarchy. The Czech population of Bohemia was deeply offended by this and incensed that the ancient crown rights of Bohemia had not been confirmed in the emperor's new coronation as King of Bohemia. The most loyal crownland of the empire had not risen like the Hungarians during the Revolution of 1848 and its population felt they deserved special prerogatives far more than the Hungarians.

Bohemia decided on a course of passive resistance. It refused to send any parliamentary representatives to the Imperial Council, thus throwing a monkey wrench into the works of the monarchy. Emperor Francis Joseph decided in 1871 to attempt a settlement with Bohemia. He released an official proclamation: "*... in view of the unshakeable loyalty which the population of Bohemia has shown the throne at all times, we are happy to recognize the rights and prerogatives of this kingdom and willing to reinforce these rights by taking the coronation oath anew.*"[165]

The Czechs were delerious with joy. Finally, Bohemia would have its old rights and privileges confirmed. Yet the Bohemian settlement, which seemed poised to be fulfilled, was destined to never come about. The German and Hungarian politicians demanded additional alterations in the negotiated results, since the 'Fundamental Articles', as the settlement was called, were incompatible with the Constitution of 1867, which articulated special privileges for German and Hungarian citizens, to the implied disadvantage of Slavic populations.

In Bohemia, the mood of the people swung an about-face. In the eyes of the population, the emperor had broken his word, even if he had stuck to the strict legal terms of the Constitution. In the collective grief and rage against the policies of Vienna and Budapest, objectivity disintegrated. All segments of Czech society regressed into a nationwide emotionality. A framed copy of the non-implemented imperial proclamation of the settlement, the so-called 'September Re-write', hung on the walls of every household, every restaurant, every newsstand in Prague, thus ridiculing the 'validity' of imperial promises in demonstrative fashion. On orders from Vienna, the police force of Prague had to immediately remove all these posters, whose only purpose was to mock imperial authority. This did not impede the Czechs from immediately posting new ones, of course.[166]

Czech media mogul Jan Stanislav Skrejsovsky, one of Bohemia's wealthiest men, who behind the scenes had worked hard for a settlement of Bohemia and whose newspapers had great influence on the people, printed the imperial Re-Write in large quantities as posters. He then had the rascally idea of printing the imperial promise in a different form, namely, "*in small, pocket-like format on fine, thin, brownish-coloured paper, the kind which was used by aris-*

tocrats and the very wealthy for their most intimate sanitary business, usually sold in rolls of several hundred sheets and labelled 'WC paper'. It was nailed on walls wherever the emperor was expected to pass by on foot and would see it."[167]

In this way, Skrejsovsky, a well known cynic, elected to express the 'true value' of the imperial paper. His 'imperial toilet paper' was a runaway success, it was printed in immense quantities and distributed while the police tried desperately to remove it wherever it popped up. The WC paper was even sent to the court itself, where the court post office was astonished to see what had arrived and sent on the packet to the cabinet chancellery. Emperor Francis Joseph initially found the waggish joke rather amusing and tried to demonstrate indifference at the obvious provocation. He let it be known that he "*was highly pleased at this special attention.*"[168]

Skrejsovsky's joke took on a dynamic of its own, however, as critics of imperial policy began to use the paper for its originally intended purpose and sent it subsequently to the emperor. In this version, not the promise was printed, but the subsequent Re-Write which annulled the agreement between monarch and Czech political representatives. When samples of these 'utilised' specimens arrived via post at the cabinet chancellery of the emperor, his amusement met an abrupt end. His chancellery turned to the police in Prague for 'dutiful assistance' in ferreting out the source of this unacceptable behaviour and locating the '*perpetrator of this boyish prank*' – of course, without success.[169] The court, past master that it was in ordering and filing all paperwork, placed the toilet paper (which still today bears evidence of its having been 'used for private purposes') along with other written documents into the archives. They bear witness even today of the rage of the Czechs over the coronation of Francis Joseph as King of the Bohemians that was never meant to be.

Awkward occurrences and embarrassments arrived at court not only from external sources, there were also internal affairs which were inappropriate to the Apostolic Emperor. Prime Minister Eduard Taaffe, a friend from the emperor's youth, employed a veritable army of snoops and spies whose only job was to uncover and bring any and all stories antipathetic to the dynasty or its policies to his ears. He even placed such persons at court, with orders to keep their ears to the ground for offenses and insults to the emperor. The court snoop was not able to deliver any material, since the emperor was so popular with and highly respected by his employees. However, the court spy did supply one piece of information which showed how much went on at court of which no one had an inkling: "*A few years ago, a palace captain Montoje* (*Montoyer) *took in two nieces who were buxom beauties, daughters of the convicted and bankrupt butcher Max Wös, and as wicked tongues would have it, he treated them as if they were his wives. With the help of friends in high places, he even managed to wrangle the older of the nieces a position of employment at court as Keeper of the Silver. Yesterday evening, a supplier named Unterwalder showed me a photograph he said he had acquired from a city procuress for 10 florins. I was astonished to see the court Keeper of the Silver pictured on it!*"[170]

Prime Minister Taaffe did not file this information in his archives, but quietly squirreled it away in his own private records. It popped up only many years after his death.

At about the turn of the century, the younger members of the imperial family entered the limelight of scandal, weakening the standing of the dynasty in the public eye. The desire for individually concocted lifestyles and marriage based on romantic affection rather than imperial decision stood in stark conflict with the family laws of the Habsburgs, and with the strained concepts of duty of Francis Joseph in particular, which he demanded from every member of his family.

One of the greatest worries of the emperor was Archduke Leopold Ferdinand, first born son of Grand Duke Ferdinand IV, the last Habsburg ruler of Tuscany. Since the unification of Italy, he had lived with his large family in Austria. His '*wayward youngling*'[171], as the emperor dubbed him, had already brought his family a number of embarrassments. Leopold Ferdinand was a rather unusual character. He was a firebrand who loved nothing better than to undermine rules and regulations and then gloat over the chaos which he had unleashed all by himself. A typical incident occurred on a round-the-world voyage of Franz Ferdinand, heir to the throne, on which Leopold accompanied him. Leopold Ferdinand – quite contrary to the explicit instructions of the emperor – always sought out the company of the lowermost staff, wherever he was.

On the ship voyage, he instigated the ship's crew to rebel against their officers. When the commander questioned him, he insulted him in front of the entire crew and even threatened that he might commit suicide. Franz Ferdinand was witness to the whole performance and wanted to discharge his cousin dishonourably from the army without recourse, but first attempted to put a lid on the affair. Franz Ferdinand entreated Archduke Albrecht, the doyen of the imperial household following the emperor himself, that *"even the mere appearance of a fissure in the family had to be avoided."* [172]

Emperor Francis Joseph, too, had always shied away from the ultimate consequences of his family or staff's bad behaviour. He decided to give one last chance to the black sheep of the family. Even when Leopold Ferdinand started an affair with a former prostitute who was well known to the authorities not only as a streetwalker but as a seditious anarchist as well, he tolerated the liason to start with, cursing silently to himself. But when the affair became public, the emperor demanded that Leopold put an end to the embarrassing relationship. The archduke was forced to promise in writing to terminate the affair. Initially, he complied, ending the relationship and settling a large sum of money on his mistress. But a few days after his 'letter of intent', Archduke Leopold let the emperor know that a permanent separation from his mistress was not feasible, after all.

The next move of Archduke Leopold was the one which sealed his fate as member of the Habsburg family. He fled to Switzerland with his sister, the married Crown Princess of Saxony, who had betrayed her husband with her language teacher. This scurrilous gang of four – Archduke Leopold with his former prostitute mistress and the Crown Princess of Saxony with her language teacher – then communicated to the courts of Vienna and Dresden that they would not even consider returning to the fold. The news of this escape descended in Vienna like a bombshell. Even before the emperor was able to complete an act of family ostracism and exclusion, the archduke sent a quitclaim memorandum to the court of Vienna. He resigned from the position and rank of archduke and would henceforth live as simple citizen Leopold Wölfling far from his family and the court. Yet this was not the end, the affair would keep tensions high for months still to come. For Wölfling may have withdrawn from the imperial dynasty but did not have any desire to dispense with the money which he believed he had coming to him. Every archduke had a right to an apanage and a fixed percentage of the imperial family fund, the private assets of the Habsburgs. Wölfling hired a lawyer, who inquired of Foreign Minister Goluchowski how the archduke was expected to live without means, such a situation would be in crass contrast to the dignity of the imperial dynasty. The Foreign Minister replied, probably before having conferred with the emperor, that the archduke had not given a tinker's dam for the dignity of the imperial dynasty to date and the only money he could hope for was from his father's inheritance, since personal inheritance claims were not affected by exclusion from the official imperial family.

Wölfling refused to give up. With the help of his clever lawyer, he tried to press legal action in public litigation to force the courts to confirm the separation of birth rights and honourable privileges of a member of the imperial dynasty. Wölfling's lawyer argued that his client might relinquish certain honourable privileges by withdrawing from the official house of Habsburg, e.g. as an officer, but not his rights by birth, i.e. his percentual claim to the Habsburg financial assets. With his hard-headed tenacity, Leopold Wölfling forced the Supreme Court to make a ruling confirming that Archduke might lose his honourable privileges, but not his inheritance or his livelihood.[173] To seek justice or redress in a normal lawsuit of *Emperor vs. Wölfling* in order to obtain such livelihood and inheritance was now possible. Count Cziraky, Lord Marshal and legal representative of the emperor, shrank in horror at the thought of a public lawsuit against the emperor, since it would force him to reveal the secret family statutes. He pleaded for an out-of-court settlement. The family would have to support Leopold financially. The emperor demanded that the Grand Duke pay for his son's livelihood, the perils of a court case were simply too great. Following a generous settlement, Leopold Wölfling relinquished his claim to file suit. He wed his mistress, became a Swiss citizen, got divorced, and thereafter frequented the milieu of the red-light district in Munich. After the First World War, he returned to Vienna where, after a few experiments as an actor, he opened and ran a general store in the town of Kaisermühlen.[174]

Leopold's sister, Crown Princess of Saxony, also managed to keep the courts in Vienna and Dresden on tenterhooks. She briefly considered returning to her husband. But he would have none of it, especially after details of several other affairs of hers became known. He demanded a divorce. In case the divorce was deemed to have been caused by the wife, the husband could demand that she give up his family name. The court at Vienna, however, had no desire that this archduchess convicted of having caused a divorce receive back the name of Luise of Austria-Tuscany, even if it was her right. After long, drawn out negotiations, and doubtless upon demand of her father, who thereby stepped on the emperor's toes, Louise ultimately took the name Montignoso. She had a few more affairs, and later married an Italian pianist, Enrico Toselli, in 1907.

Cout Béla Cziraky, in his function as Lord Marshal, was operating on the cusp of a new age. At the affair of Leopold Wölfling, alarm bells went off at court. For the first time in history, a family member had provoked a very public dispute and attempted to seek justice through the civil courts of justice against the express decisions of the head of the Habsburg family. The helplessness of both the court and the public agencies became evident in this affair. In full public view, private family matters could be implemented or challenged, depending on whether the conditions were based in civil law. From the very outset, the Lord Marshal maintained the sensible view that in such cases, only out-of-court settlements were acceptable. Every public discussion, every court case to decide the civil law's validity of a family claim meant igniting a dynamic which had to end in the Habsburg family statutes forfeiting all validity with regard to their family rules.[175]

Yet also from the point of view of the dynasty, the scandals inside the imperial family which were paraded to public view in the final years of the monarchy were highly damaging to the prestige of the imperial family. When one considers the efforts Francis Joseph had made ever since his succession to the throne in the year 1848, a full fifty years earlier, to prevent all public discussions about the court; how even in the middle of the previous century, each and every tidbit of unauthorised information published in newspapers about the inner life at court was pursued and investigated, even if it was no more than the menu of a court dinner; how the imperial principle that the court must never, ever be the subject of public discussion was sacrosanct since time immemorial and would be so for all time; then it was easy to imagine the shock and rage at court over the scandals of family members. The family had become exposed, down to its most vulnerable core, to an extent that it could no longer demand restraint from the public without provoking open mockery. Prime Minister Count Franz Thun articulated what many people must have been thinking, with regard to the Habsburg scandals at the turn of the century: "*It is actually a terrible tragedy, to see how the highest ranks of society are voluntarily doing the work of the revolutionists for them.*"[176]

Even the Lord Chancellor was destined to become the butt of public discussions in Vienna. After Rudolf Liechtenstein had been appointed first man at court, he meddled to achieve positions and benefits for the children and sons-in-law of his favourite sister, Marie Kinsky, particularly for the later-born offspring who could not count on receiving any money from home. He managed to get them positions at court by intervening with the emperor. Prince Liechtenstein's patronage and pull were avidly discussed in Viennese society. His niece Franciska Kinsky had married Alfred Montenuovo, who then also had to be provided for. Liechtenstein didn't just manage to wrangle a position for his nephew at court, he created a brand new position to accommodate him. The new position of Deputy Lord Chancellor was created in his first year in office, and immediately filled by Alfred Montenuovo. A new position was also created for his nephew Ferdinand Kinsky: he was appointed to the newly established position of First Master of the Stables, directly subordinate to his uncle Rudolf, since Liechtenstein continued to hold onto the position of Master of the Stables, even though he had been appointed as Lord Chancellor. August Bellegarde, a son-in-law of Princess Kinsky, was named Master of the Kitchen, even though court society knew that he didn't have the slightest idea about culinary matters.

Court society was up in arms. Such obvious nepotism had never occurred before, most of all actually creating new positions for favoured individuals in need of a job. It incensed many aristocrats that the only obvious point in such positions was to provide for Rudolf Liechtenstein's nephews. Count Adalbert 'Montschi' Sternberg, infamous for his biting verses, composed a couplet which was often recited in the salons of Vienna: "*Go ring the bell at Freyung 4, to see how you might make a score!*" (Freyung no. 4 was the address of Palais Kinsky.) The folk singers engaged to perform this little song by Sternberg proceeded to sing it not only in the designated salon, but also in public – and it promptly became a hit. This was too much for the emperor, who resolved to intervene. He was undone by laughter over court business and ordered the police to take the texts from the folk singers.[177] The court had not been the centerpiece of public discussions like this for many, many years. Securing positions had long been a practice; and the court had made a habit of recruiting from its own ranks, since the confidence which was so necessary seemed to be more loyally secured. But that the whole city was guffawing about rampant nepotism at court was something which had never happened before. Whether put on display with poetic doggerel or not, enough was enough. The emperor never permitted another new position to be created at court as long as he lived, and no high positions were ever again filled by close relatives.

XII
Politics and the Court

There exists no more enduring or more deeply rooted prejudice about the court than that Emperor Francis Joseph was conservative, downright reactionary and the plaything of a coterie of court advisors whose arch-conservative values he perpetrated. For that reason, it is no less than astonishing that scientific research leads to precisely the opposite conclusion. Neither were men who came from the politically conservative forces of court in the majority among the emperor's political advisors – on the contrary, there is hardly one to be found who did not serve the interests of the Constitution (such was the way the rather liberal members of the Constitutional Party were described); nor – and this is the point which matters above all else – did the emperor ever let himself be influenced by anyone.

Francis Joseph was considered to be utterly immune to influence. Even his most intimate advisors learned very quickly that the emperor rejected nothing more vehemently than unsolicited opinions. Even those whose job it was to advise and provide information and opinions to the emperor had to be highly prudent not to overstep their very well defined borders of responsibility. The emperor went so far as to spurn – and very sharply at that – the opinions of members of the government who uttered opinions on matters which were not their specific purview. One baleful glance from the emperor and the advisor was put in his place, rendered speechless. Even men who were personally favoured by the emperor had not the slightest possibility of influencing his political decisions or even expressing opinions on subjects beyond the boundaries of their office.

Prince Rudolf Liechtenstein, one of Francis Joseph's favourites, both as a personal friend of his youth, a highly likeable personality and a personally selected Chancellor of the Exchequer, once made the grave error of stretching the definition of his office. He told his nephew and designated successor, Prince Montenuovo, that he had once, "*upon the urgent request of highly placed friends, drawn His Majesty's attention to a certain dignitary who had made certain accomplishments in public service and longed for an award of personal distinction. The emperor listened to him quietly and then replied drily: 'First tell me why this matter is of concern to you.' Never again did I dare to raise an issue which was none of my business."*[178]

The fact that even such a treasured friend as Liechtenstein, upon uttering such an innocuous request as this, was brusquely put in his place shows just how careful Francis Joseph was in disallowing, purely as a matter of principle, any and all external efforts to influence him. And if even such harmless requests were summarily repulsed, it is easy to extrapolate how he reacted to requests from other people, with regard to other issues.

Even as an 18-year old, the emperor permitted no one to counsel him. This trait drove his former adjutant, Count Grünne, the fatherly friend whom he even entrusted with management of his private finances and the military chancellery, to utter despair. Grünne would have been happy to make his influence felt on a number of matters pertaining to the court and to public issues, and was (incorrectly) believed to be one of the 'court whisperers' who manipulated the emperor. In fact, he had not the slightest chance of doing so. For example, the arch-conservative Grünne argued fiercely against the introduction of a Concordat, a kind of super committee which would regulate and ensure the influence of the church in secular affairs. But he was able to do this only behind the scenes, since the emperor was not in the slightest interested in Grünne's opinion. As director of the military chancellery, he was not allowed to even have an opinion on such an issue. Grünne was probably the bravest man ever to serve in the immediate surroundings of the emperor and was the only one courageous enough to utter an unsolicited opinion to the emperor. But before long, he, too, realized that Francis Joseph did not even acknowledge such voiced opinions, much less give them any credence, and usually brushed them off like so much detritus. Grünne told a friend that he was treated like a *'raven on the mantlepiece'* by the emperor, since he talked down the imperial policies so often.[179] As time went on, Grünne became desperate and started placing foreign newspapers in the emperor's field of vision as a way of making him aware of the harsh criticism of imperial policies in other countries.[180] Later on, Grünne changed his approach, having finally realized how sceptical the emperor was toward any political advice which was being proffered. One time, when, together with his friend Kempen, Minister of Police, he wished to rail against Ministers Buol and Bach to the emperor, he held his tongue with iron discipline, knowing full well to what degree the emperor despised Grünne's interference in political affairs. The Minister of Police noted in his diary: "*At 1:00 I was with Count Grünne. He put away a note of discredit regarding ministers Buol and Bach and refuses to give it to the emperor, in an effort to avoid the appearance of mixing into the emperor's affairs.*"[181]

After the disastrous battle of Solferino, Grünne was removed from his position as adjutant and director of the military chancellery and appointed to the position of Master of the Stables. By then, Emperor Francis Joseph had become more immune to political advice than before. No one was ever again permitted to be in Grünne's position, of being able to express personal opinions to the emperor, despite the fact that such opinions were never countenanced anyway, to say nothing of being acted on.

The emperor became more and more sensitive on the subject of his persuasibility. Any attempt to even talk politics enraged the monarch, who stood more than ever on the inviolability of each office's closely defined areas of authority.

Some people had served the emperor in political matters for many years, and believed they had a right to make a political statement now and then. But they were horrified at the monarch's response. Governor Kielmannsegg: "*The emperor hated it when members of the government or court ministers aired their views on politics. Even Prince Adolph Auersperg, who was Prime Minister for many years, when he was making a speech of thanks for a new post he had been given as Director of Accounting, felt called upon to make a few political remarks. Francis Joseph let him know in no uncertain terms that he was no longer authorised to give political advice.*"[182] The emperor sometimes even cut off discussions in mid-stream when someone expressed personal opinions on political matters.[183]

And to complete the issue of interference, Francis Joseph was also not open to flattery. Those who believed they could weasel their way into his good graces through complimentary remarks were disillusioned just as swiftly. As time went on, no one even tried it anymore, as the newphew of the emperor wrote later on: "*Since the Emperor despised eloquent speakers and deflated them with remarks such as 'Come, come, it can't be all that bad,' people soon desisted in delivering such polemics."*[184]

Thus, since it can be proven that the emperor made his decisions alone, independent and uninfluenced, where did the legend of the 'court coterie' and the conspiratorial groupings who whispered their sinister opinions in the ear of the emperor stem from? It has long been a fixed attitude of the Francis Joseph historical record that the court advisors were arch-conservative, often clerically influenced. Those aristocrats whom the emperor appointed to the top positions at court were in actual fact of a completely different political persuasion. All the uppermost court officials – and any 'court coterie' must have come from those ranks – were politically on the side of the 'Constitutionalists', in other words, diametrically opposed to the other large party in parliament, that of the 'Feudal Conservatives'. That means, the emperor was surrounded by men who were may have shared his conservative personal values and his loyalty to the dynasty, but were just the opposite of politically conservative. Francis Joseph was surrounded by anti-clerical, mildly liberal officials whose only problem was that the emperor didn't want to hear their political opinions, did not even take cognizance of them.

Even the very first advisors of the young Francis Joseph, his adjutant, Count Grünne, who indisputably enjoyed great personal influence, and the Lord Chancellor, Franz Liechtenstein, stood in recognized opposition to the politics of the emperor, one of them openly, the other secretly. Adjutant Grünne, director of the military chancellery, and Lord Chancellor Liechtenstein opposed the political course of young Francis Joseph. Both were anti-clerical, rejected the idea of a Concordat, since they felt that excessive church influence was damaging to the state, and utterly disagreed with the neo-absolutist economic policies of the court. Liechtenstein's friends knew this. *"He spoke freely about many administrative dead-ends, he bemoaned the helplessness of the parliament which was not able to control the machinery of state and went ballistic on the subject of the Concordat ..."*[185] *"He regretted the deal which sold the railways to a French company, but most of all the deal which established the Concordat, even called Archbishop Cardinal Prince Schwarzenberg an ass."*[186] Grünne, too, *"was astonished that the emperor, who guarded his own rights so carefully, permitted himself to be paralyzed by the Concordat.*"[187] In his first period of administration, all the emperor's trusted counselors were deeply sceptical of the official government, but they had no way of making their influence felt.

After the military campaign in Italy was lost in 1859, which ultimately brought about the end of neo-absolutism, the victory march of parliamentarism in Austria was launched. The emperor, whether he wanted to or not, had to make great concessions to wide sectors of society in the political selection processes. With the introduction of the Constitution in 1867, Austria became a constitutional monarchy. As of that moment, the emperor had to share his powers with elected popular representatives (who of course did not represent the whole population). The most significant consequence of introducing parliamentary elections was that the emperor had to relinquish his sole control over the finances of the state. He appointed and dissolved governments, but as of now, any and all new laws had to be passed by the parliament, together with the *Herrenhaus*, i.e. House of Lords. All that he was able to retain was the right of veto. Foreign affairs and the command of the military abided in the hands of the emperor, as did the awarding of orders and distinctions and raising of individuals to the nobility.

Francis Joseph adhered strictly to the provisions of the Constitution his whole life long. He could no longer pass laws himself, but persisted in wishing those laws be approved before they took effect. What could he do to bypass the House of Representatives and effect laws which he viewed to be important for the empire? The historical records have to this day not acknowledged how brilliant Francis Joseph was as a tactician in this respect, as of his middle years. A lack of evidence or subjectively interpreted sources have misled historians for many years, blinding them to his ingenious skills of diplomacy to get his way. The emperor knew whom he had to convince, what strings to pull, what levers to lift, to steer the parliamentary processes. The *Herrenhaus*, equivalent of the House of Lords, the second chamber of parliament which had to sign all legal bills, consisted of aristocrats and a few appointed dignitaries. If the emperor was nervous that a parliamentary vote might result in an undesirable resolution, he would send his uppermost court officials, who each had one vote in the Herrenhaus (but who rarely appeared, since the emperor did not wish them to form the subject of daily conversation in the city) to demonstrably cast their vote for a specific legal resolution – in a public, roll-call vote, as were all such votes in the empire. Thus, every aristocrat knew just what the emperor wanted and what he expected of their loyal conduct.

The first clear demonstration of the imperial voting approach occurred a year after the Constitution was introduced. The highly disputed marriage laws, which meant that the Concordat of 1855 would be rendered pointless, were on the agenda. The dissolution of the Concordat was one of the conditions of the liberal party for their agreement to the Hungarian Settlement and the emperor was determined to keep his word. The result of the vote was uncertain, especially how the House of Lords would vote, since the aristocrats rejected the liberal marriage laws. Suddenly, when it was time to vote, Lord Chancellor Konstantin Hohenlohe appeared. He voted for the passing of the marriage laws. This signal was immediately understood by all the aristocrats present. If the Chancellor of the Exchequer publicly approved the marriage laws, it could only mean the emperor approved them, too. The voting continued and brought about Francis Joseph's desired end, the Lords having 'got the message'.[188]

What becomes clear with fastidiously applied historical research is that not the court advisors manipulated the emperor, but that the emperor took advantage of his court advisors and officials to make his own wishes visible and make sure that they were carried out. In 1879, the emperor even managed to have a new party established. Once again, he used his Lord Chancellor to this end. The liberals had been defeated and Count Taaffe, friend of the emperor's youth, had been appointed Prime Minister. Taaffe depended on the support of the conservatives, but for the reforms he advocated, he required a large majority in parliament. The emperor knew that all the opponents of the new Prime Minister (who sat in the House of Lords) were simply waiting for an opportunity to push Taaffe over a cliff, together with his reform plans. What the new Prime Minister needed, but did not have, was a party which could supply him a majority vote when he required one. In this situation, the emperor became active behind the scenes. Officially, his intervention was prohibited, so he had to find other ways to exercise his influence. Lord Chancellor Hohenlohe was used to this purpose once again. He communicated discreetly to his aristocratic friend that he would like the gentlemen who were loyal to the emperor to form a small, distinguished, mildly conservative, state-supporting party with the aim of furthering orderly, continuous and effective statehood.[189] Fundamental political principles, e.g. the constitutional organisation of the monarchy, Bohemian statehood and the relations between church and state, should not form part of this party's agenda. Decisions which had to be made to effect the daily business of statecraft and which would transcend party lines were to be its backbone. As a result of this imperial wish, an important segment of the aristocracy formed a "party of the political center", whose members functioned solely to carry out the wishes of the emperor and the imperial governments. In other words, Francis Joseph's brainstorm worked. The middle-of-the-road party would be the decisive factor in future votes of the Taaffe era, and would support the imperial standpoints in all votes from now on.

It was clear that Emperor Francis Joseph knew precisely how to use his upper ranks of officials for his purposes. They were his tools, not his manipulators. Thus, to claim he was pushed around by them is far off the mark. Governor Kielmansegg was right on target when he said, "*... everything you might have heard about a court coterie, or even a secret conspiratorial group, who bent the ear of the emperor and exercised uncontrolled influence on government business is pure poppycock.*"[190]

One of the additional advantages he enjoyed with regard to the court and the upper rank of officials was his putatively conservative-clerical leanings. But here, too, as soon as one looks more closely, the opposite proves to be the case. No one single person of the highest officials at court in all the years of his reign and not one single person who purportedly exerted great personal influence over Francis Joseph came from the clergy. All high court officials were practicing Catholics like the emperor himself, but by no stretch of the imagination were they clerical. Quite the contrary, they utterly rejected the efforts of the clergy to exert more influence at court, were even attacked by them. Count Grünne got rid of all clerical influences at court in the early years of the monarchy and continued to view the circle around the emperor's mother as dangerous. Liechtenstein, too, was highly critical of the Concordat.

Chancellor of the Exchequer Hohenlohe was subjected to especially virulent attacks by the clergy. Not only his vote in the House of Lords was held against him, but Hohenlohe's family was also sharply criticised. On the occasion of his delegation as imperial representative to the 25-year Jubilee of Pope Pius IX to Rome in 1871, the Roman correspondent of the Viennese paper *Vaterland* wrote: "*The emperor clearly wishes the Holy Father all the best and thus sends him a personally written letter of congratulations; but Prince Hohenlohe is not a person to stir much confidence, for it is well known at the Vatican how he voted against the Concordat and for the marriage and school laws in the House of Lords, thus leading a number of members of the House to believe that he was voting in accordance with the emperor's wishes. The brother of the ambassador, Prince Clodwig, as Prime Minister of Bavaria, has made a sorry name for himself through his war against the Vatican Consilium, while Cardinal Hohenlohe, the third brother, who made the now excommunicated Professor Friedrich his theologian and is still close friends with him, has been compromised to no small degree.*"[191] The fact that even one of Hohenlohe's adjutants at one of the ceremonial occasions boasted of a large sized medal he wore, on which was engraved 'Friend of God, Enemy of Priests', as was widely reported in the clergy press, did not exactly ease the clergy's profound distrust of Hohenlohe.[192]

Even Chancellor of the Exchequer Rudolf Liechtenstein, the penultimate highest dignitary of the court in Vienna, was anything other than clergy-friendly. The German ambassador, who swiftly wrote to his master Emperor Wilhelm II everything he could relate about the court in Vienna, reported that Liechtenstein was "*a free thinker and deeply antithetical to the Jesuits, even though he does not reveal it to everyone.*"[193]

The last Lord Chancellor, Prince Alfred Montenuovo, was nothing short of a guarantor to the public that the clerical movement which had gained strength in the imperial family at the turn of the century, supported mainly by the successor to the throne Franz Ferdinand and the emperor's daughter Marie Valerie, did not stand a chance of gaining a foothold in court decisions. For, as the heir to the throne tried more and more to exercise influence at court, those very conservative and clergy-oriented advisors who had been rendered powerless in the background saw that their chance might finally be coming, and tried to increase their influence on the aging emperor. The critical public, the chiefs of the civil service and large parts of the enlightened aristocracy were afraid that the old emperor might succumb to such attempts; but their fears were unfounded, since the conservative endeavors failed, as Montenuovo smashed each and every attempt by any member of the imperial family to place members of the clergy in important positions at court. The price for this effective and deliberate resistance was high, of course: the heir to the throne hated Montenuovo until his dying day.

The most significant political demonstration at court took place in 1906/1907. The quality of parliament had reached an all-time low as of the notorious 'Badeni Crisis' in 1897. The language ordinances of Prime Minister Badeni, who desired two official languages, Czech and German, not only led to demonstrations in Vienna and Prague, it also turned the House of Representatives into a three-ring circus. German-national representatives attacked Slavic representatives. Screams and shouting duels between Germans and Czechs, even fisticuffs, were regular occurrences. The rows of ministers were stormed, the manuscripts of the stenographers were torn to shreds, pandemonium reigned. As the obstructions reached their zenith with the attack on the presidential office and the ministers, the Prime Minister decided to cut off the parliamentary revolts with violence. After the Badeni crisis, most of the quickly changing administrations had to work under the terms of a 'state of emergency', the notorious Paragraph 14.

The citizens' parties had over the course of ten years worked to demolish parliament and had worn away at each other uninterruptedly, making all constructive parliamentary work impossible. With the years, a competitor to this wing was born, which had been kept from representation in parliament to date by voting reforms: the labour party, a mass movement which could no longer be ignored.

And then something happened which surprised both the parties themselves and the general public: the emperor expressed a desire to admit the socialists into parliament. He commissioned Prime Minister Beck to prepare a bill which would extend voting rights to every male citizen 24 years and older. The minimum taxation which one had to pay in order to participate in the elections was suspended.

The emperor perceived the socialists to be a catalyst towards orderly parliamentary work. With such a powerful new player in the arena, the undisciplined and much too self-assured citizens' parties would have to make mighty efforts to show that they were up to the task. With representatives of this mass movement as competitors, the emperor hoped, the parties would have to worry about their own survival and would return to constructive parliamentary work.

The emperor wanted everyone to know about his hope to have the voting laws accepted without opposition. It was his unshakeable wish that general voting laws be finally passed. For the vote in the House of Lords, the emperor sent every available dignitary at court. When even the famous dandy, Prince Ferdinand Kinsky, Lord of the Stables, who had rarely been seen in parliament for years, being interested only in horses and hunting, also showed up for the vote and voted for the approval of the voting laws, along with all the other court officials, all of Vienna laughed that the emperor had even mobilised the stables to have voting reform passed.

In January 1907, the new voting bills were signed into law by the emperor. Subsequently, an election campaign the likes of which had never before been seen in Austria was unrolled. One trend became immediately clear. Politics had become a mass phenomenon. The socialists brought nearly the largest faction into parliament. After years of obstruction, both a positive working climate and a patriotic attitude celebrated a re-entry into the new parliament.

His whole life long, Francis Joseph forbade intrusions of anyone who did not possess the appointed authority over a particular field of business. Yet during the First World War, in the last year of his life, he was destined to witness how a Lord Chancellor pushed his way into political terrain, although unsolicited and undesired. Alfred Montenuovo dared what until then had been unthinkable. He abandoned his strictly defined field of authority at court. He wished to bring about a change of government, to get rid of the reigning Prime Minister, Count Stürgkh, who had been running parliament since 1914 under the terms of the state of emergency, and replace him with Ernst Koerber.

Montenuovo's motive for this coup was his concern about the constitutionality of the government, at least as it was perceived by the general public, whose dissatisfaction was growing by leaps and

The emperor at the annual opening of Parliament in the Hofburg

bounds. At the same time, he wanted to improve the food supply in the Austrian part of the realm, which was suffering from food shortages to an increasing degree. In the interest of maintaining the peace, Prime Minister Stürgkh defended the so-called 'policy of agricultural enrichment' advocated by the Hungarian representatives. The shortcomings and rising prices in Austrian territory stirred Montenuovo's opposition, as well as that of the House of Lords. One conspiracy in the House of Lords, about which Montenuovo was well informed, was a failure; and the final attempt to send Montenuovo to personally advise the emperor also fell on its face. Francis Joseph held fast to his Prime Minister. What is remarkable was that this was the one and only endeavor by a Lord Chancellor to change the government of the emperor. It confirms once again that Francis Joseph made his political decisions alone and independently until the day he died, unhampered in the slightest by his closest advisors.

XIII
Crisis – The Times Change

Just before the turn of the century, the court stumbled into a grave crisis of administration. At the same time, a generational fissure tore a hole in the imperial family and led to immense conflicts both in the art of statehood and in ceremonial matters. Lord Chancellor Konstantin Hohenlohe had held the reins of court administration tightly for more than 25 years. At the beginning of the 1890s, he turned seriously ill with heart disease. He tried by means of long, restorative sojourns at the well known spas of Karlsbad and Marienbad, as well as through ever higher dosages of digitalis (the only heart medicine known to the nineteenth century) to get control of his cardiac situation and be able to continue to perform the duties of his office. But by 1895 he was so ill that he could no longer do so (his normal working day was between 15 and 18 hours long).

In the last years of his life, Hohenlohe tried for that reason to include and introduce his successor, Prince Rudolf Liechtenstein, more and more in the daily activities which faced him. It had been a kind of unspoken agreement that Liechtenstein would be the next Chancellor. He was a friend of the emperor and of the Chancellor alike. He was loyal, had an amenable personality and possessed – essential for a Lord Chancellor – an impeccable family tree. As member of a princely house, he would be accepted without qualms as Chancellor, just as Hohenlohe had been. This *de facto* appointment, not yet formally effected but well known all the same down the entire ladder of court employees, was an act of pure friendship on the part of the emperor.

'Rudi', as he was fondly nicknamed by the emperor and his wife, had already performed countless services as friend of the family. He was a pillar of support to them after the death of the crown prince, was often sent on delicate family missions and lived utterly for his monarch. Yet apart from his personal loyalty to the emperor and his wife, there were no other bonds tying him to court, neither hope of advancement nor power. His main motive was financial. Although he came from a wealthy side branch of

Konstantin Hohenlohe in later years

the family, Liechtenstein was the second born son, and thus had no claims to the huge family inheritance.[194] He lived from a small apanage granted him by his brother, whose behaviour had become bizarre and unpredictible following an accident in which he suffered head injuries. This brother had been urged by their father to relinquish his right of inheritance and permit Rudolf to take over the leading position of the family, but he had refused to do so, on the contrary kept his younger brother on a very short leash. Everyone knew that Rudolf Liechtenstein had to live on a very small purse. Due to his modest ways and kind personality, he was pitied by many, yet highly respected for his ability to make do on little means without complaint. Empress Elisabeth's court lady once said, referring to how Liechtenstein was perceived by the court employees: "*He lived very simply in his house in Pardubitz, complete with tattered wallpaper. And yet he had acquired, if I might phrase it this way, a certain philosophical tuxedo, that is, he pretended utter sufficiency and satisfaction, explaining that he had no greater needs than these. Thus did he win the approbation of one and all through this contentedness."*[195]

The emperor knew well of Liechtenstein's poor financial standing. He wanted to provide his friend with a certain degree of security, initially giving him the position of Master of the Stables, which at least earned him a salary of about 6,000 guilders. At the same time, he began to groom him for the position of Hohenlohe's successor. Liechtenstein was close friends with Hohenlohe, he often was a visitor at his home. There was not the least bit of jealousy visible on the part of Hohenlohe; on the contrary, Hohenlohe tried to draw Liechtenstein increasingly into the work spheres of the Lord Chancellor. But Liechtenstein had a certain antipathy to the enormous work load of a Chancellor, he simply was not interested in all the subjects which required his attention.

Rudolf Liechtenstein may well have been one of the most likeable and loyal men in the circle of the emperor, but one thing he definitely was not: a good manager. Unlike Hohenlohe, he did not even possess a minimum degree of interest in the administrative processes of the court. He thought his role as Lord Chancellor would be the way it had been a century earlier, as the director of a staff, utterly immune from all work and aloof from small tasks. His friendship with the industrious, over-correct director of the Office of the Exchequer simply failed to make a mark, it left no impression on him. Liechtenstein counted on the top officials in Hohenlohe's staff to carry out the day-to-day business and continued to devote himself to the one and only business which interested him: running the imperial stables.

In February 1896, Prince Hohenlohe died. For 30 years, he had served the emperor with loyalty and competence as Lord Chancellor. The German ambassador Eulenburg wrote as an appendix to the obituary in his diary: *"A heavy blow for Emperor Francis Joseph, whose friend he remained through all the hard and sad times of his reign."*[196] Hohenlohe's funeral was held in Vienna four days after his death. His burial was a grand diplomatic occasion. Konstantin Hohenlohe's brother, the Chancellor of Germany, Chlodwig Hohenlohe-Schillingsfürst, came to the graveside and Emperor Wilhelm II sent his ambassador. Messages of condolence arrived from all the artist and writer circles. The protocol of the funeral celebrations was published in the *Wiener Zeitung*, since the burial of an imperial Lord Chancellor of the Exchequer was a solemn ceremonial event.[197]

Konstantin Hohenlohe was the most important of all the emperor's Lord Chancellors. With his death, the burgeoning florescence of court life under Francis Joseph came to an end. As soon as Hohenlohe resigned, due to his illness, it became immediately evident to what degree he had held the reins of court life so tightly for more than 30 years. He alone had guaranteed that the court remained functional, down to the smallest detail; that it was imbued with a sense of economy; and that excesses and corruption were prevented. His successor Liechtenstein was popular, but it was soon apparent that he would not be able to step in the giant footsteps of his precedessor. Even his closest friends admitted: "*As Lord Chancellor, he was simply not in his element. He thought too generously for this office. It was a matter of utter indifference to him whether Prince X preceded Prince Y in court ceremonial entries, or whether court etiquete was adhered to or not. In this respect, he was the precise opposite of Prince Hohenlohe.*"[198]

The death of Hohenlohe ushered in a profound crisis at court, one which showed to what extent the personality of Hohenlohe had until then guaranteed that waste, shoddy economy and corruption could not take hold. The new Chancellor, Prince Liechtenstein, depended completely on the officials of his precedessor. Since he had taken ill, the actually running of the daily business of the court had been taken over by the bourgeois officials who had been raised in the Office of the Exchequer. More independent than they had ever been before, they managed and supervised the lower civil servants of Hohenlohe, numbering no more than ten, and all the departments in ways they imagined their deceased employer would have desired them to do. On occasion, when they perceived the need, they took harsh measures on their own responsibility, covered by their new Chancellor, hated by the noble dignitaries who despised the bourgeois citizens who presumed to control and them and order them about.

At the top of this ladder of officials was Counselor Franz Wetschl, dubbed 'Scrooge'. Wetschl had suspected for some time that the Household Utilities Office and the Court Kitchen were not conducting their affairs properly and economically. The accounts were too imprecise, the costs were exploding. Wetschl sent the court controller more and more often to Count Heinrich Wolkenstein, Master of the Kitchen, whom he suspected no longer had his office and his employees under control. In the Office of Household Utilities, immense irregularities had been uncovered in purchasing and accounting. On the purchase invoices, the discrepancies were altogether obvious: the expenditures remained equally high, but the amounts of expensive foodstuffs were lower than ever, making subsequent purchases necessary in order to fill the gaps and prevent shortage.

A check-up of the receipts and bills of lading showed that in the recent period the very same amounts of meat and vegetables had been delivered as always, invariably signed for by the head chef, who had to take deliveries in receipt personally in order to check the quality of the merchandise and produce, as well as the quantity. Theft in grand style was thereby excluded, since only the head chef and his trusted staff were permitted into the pantry and storerooms full of very expensive foods. It was watched over so well that when chefs required expensive ingredients for their preparations, they had to sign for everything they fetched from the storerooms. It was nearly impossible for servants or unauthorised persons to enter the locked and supervised pantries and storerooms to pilfer anything.

After intensive investigations and observations, it turned out that the head chef himself was the criminal, having filched various foodstuffs over a long period of time, together with the meat supplier and certain employees of the kitchen. They separated large amounts of meat, let the court pay the full amount, although it took far less in receipt. Since the head chef took the produce and meats personally into his hands, no one was in a position to notice that less was being delivered than was being paid for. The system was airtight, since the labourers in the pantry were in on the affair. The not-delivered-but-paid-for food was simply sold by the chef and his suppliers, bringing them a sizeable additional income. Those who were in on the secret were kept docile by small amounts of hush money.

Also the other invoices showed enormous discrepancies, once they had been adequately studied. What was most obvious of all was that the officals overseeing the work of the Master of the Kitchen had carried out their oversight in very negligent fashion, and that this had led to the excesses and theft.

The head chef and his accomplices were sent into retirement at once. Efforts were made to keep the matter from becoming public. The court decided not to call in the police, nor were the accused dismissed dishonourably. The chef received his full pension and was simply let go, without any noticeable consequences.[199] His accomplices from the pantry and storerooms who were able to prove that the theft was not a result of their own initiative were not dismissed, but rather transferred to Schönbrunn Palace and to other activities. A new team to manage the imperial foodstuff and pantry storerooms was assembled from servants in other sectors, thus dispersing all old groupings.[200]

When this corruption affair became known in the Office of the Exchequer, the directors were shocked to the core. If it was possible that such things could happen literally right in front of their eyes, then there was doubtless a grave lack of leadership in the office of the Master of the Kitchen which supervised the kitchen and the storerooms. Wetschl took harsh measures against the kitchen office. Over the head of Count Wolkenstein, he not only had every single activity of the court kitchen controlled; he also retired Wolkenstein's officials who had observed not an iota of this business. He then redirected the whole business of the Chancellor to the court supervisory office, thus exposing the Master of the Kitchen to everyone in all clarity.[201] The position of Count Wolkenstein, who personally had nothing whatsoever to do with the corruption in the kitchen, became untenable. Although the harsh actions had all been cleared with the Lord Chancellor, all Wolkenstein's authority in the kitchen department had been destroyed. He resigned. The emperor did not let him go, but reassigned him to another office and even gave him a pay raise. Francis Joseph knew that Wolkenstein was not guilty, but simply sorely overtaxed; he wished to spare him the fate of defamation, libel and slander. However, just a few weeks after Wolkenstein was appointed to the office of Master of the Hunt, the news broke: the former Master of the Kitchen had committed suicide. The reasons were multifold. Wolkenstein did not feel capable of fulfilling the responsibilities of his new office; moreover, the shame which had covered him in his old office weighed deeply on his inner peace.

On top of everything else, he had financial problems. For a high official at court to commit suicide was awkward in the extreme for the Apostolic Court. But the reporting on the affair was surprisingly discreet. It was as if the court had bent over backwards to keep the reasons for the suicide secret and the background veiled in discretion.

The consequence of the grievous corruption in the Household Utilities at court was that all departments were subjected to a thoroughgoing investigation. The annual balance sheets had to be submitted without delay; for each and every transaction, the name of the official approving and signing for it had to be crystal clear, thus ensuring clarity and accountability for every step.[202] The accounts and bookkeeping were examined with a fine tooth comb. No further financial problem areas were detected, but it came to light that in general, a rather lax attitude for dealing with court money was prevalent in every department. For example, equipment and objects were removed at the discretion of officials as soon as they were no longer in good condition, which simply meant that they were transferred to that official's private residence.[203]

In many departments, officials treated court property in such cavalier fashion that Counselor Wetschl had to issue a sharp admonishment. During the inventory of the imperial laundry chamber, which now also had to keep precise records, it became apparent that the employees treated the laundry so recklessly that many pieces were returned to court torn or irreparably soiled. Counselor Wetschl wrote a sharply worded warning to all departments at court and said that whenever anything left court, the name of the commissioned recipient had to be noted, regardless for what task, so that he/she could be charged for any damages which were incurred.[204]

Wetschl made this general investigation the occasion of reducing court expenditures, which had risen drastically over the previous decade. Over the following three years, Wetschl took a series of steps to cut costs. Apart from the usual departments guilty of habitual overspending, Wetschl proceeded with radical force against other departments as well, going much too far in the minds of most employees, cutting even minor costs which made life difficult and had little effect. For example, with immediate effect at court dinners, only one bottle of champagne per person was made ready and cooled, until at one dinner for the German Emperor, where a great deal of alcohol was consumed, there were no back-up supplies at hand and a bottle of warm champagne had to be whisked upstairs from the wine cellar. The court left an impression of penny-pinching niggardliness on its guests, unwilling even to grant the German Emperor a second bottle of champagne. The fact that Wetschl did not hesitate to sell the leftovers from this court dinner – *"a chicken drumstick for 60 heller"* – only increased the mockery level, and didn't improve court finances a whit. Even the burned-down candles from the rooms of their guests (no guest was ever given half-used candles) now had to be turned in and have a value set for them. Until now, the servants and lackeys had simply taken them home for their own use.[205]

One cost-cutting measure which was the cause of widespread mirth was the programme to reduce the number of cats prowling about the inner courtyards, which were maintained by the kitchen staff in order to keep down the numbers of mice. Wetschl thought that the leftovers given to the cats was unreasonably expensive and simply had the cats removed. Within the shortest time, the court was invaded by armies of mice, thriving on the sudden lack of natural predators. This mouse plague became a subject of city-wide amusement, and Wetschl's cost-cutting agenda along with it. At a court concert, for which the entire court society was assembled in their finest festive array, one of these mice caused a stir. One of the court ladies felt something scurrying around beneath the petticoats of her gown, and sprang up in alarm in the middle of the concert, interrupting the music and causing a groan of frustration to ripple through the audience, with knowing laughter interspersed among the cries of complaint. The Ceremonial Master was standing next to the emperor and could not figure out the reason for the uproar until the mouse itself appeared without warning right in front of the emperor's seat, staring up at His Imperial Majesty. The Ceremonial Master chased away the evildoer with an arrogant gesture, and peace was restored. The Viennese adored relating this incident and decided to weave a poetic story around it which could be spread about town with ease and merriment. The closing stanza of their verse ran:

"At a concert, one gent spoke a jeer
To a lady in a brief musical pause:
For all this, my honourable dear,
Counselor Wetschl alone is the cause.
With ease, a small mouse found its way
Into the palace interior grand;
As cost-cutting now rules the day
Imperial cats have all now been banned."[206]

There were problems not only in the Household Utilities. Even in the General Direction of the court theaters, which were in the authority of the Office of the Exchequer, embarrassing incidents were becoming the norm. Among the general directors, stage directors and actors there were, as a rule, running disputes and a high degree of over-sensitive complaining with regard to who was receiving preferential treatment, being promoted unjustifiably, etc. Towards the end of the 1890s, these quarrels and jealousies intensified to such a degree that the overall respect of the theaters began to suffer. Criticism of patronage and personal pulling-of-strings attained a new zenith, and letters attacking the arbitrary and personally oriented policies of the general direction poured into the Lord Chancellor's mailbox daily. The court always defended the General Director, Counselor Eduard von Wlassack, a protegé of Chancellor Hohenlohe. But one private incident stoked the fires of discontent mightily. The general director, in the course of an argument in his office with an opera singer named Sommer, injured him with some brass knuckles. This was such a grave violation that it led to court proceedings.[207] Wlassack was kept in his position nonetheless.

Not only administrative departments etched lines of worry and stress across the imperial forehead, his family also played a major role in his burdens. Around the turn of the century, the number of morganatic marriages increased in alarming proportions among the Habsburgs. One reason for this was that the overweening desire for individual, personal happiness was triumphing over all feelings of duty to the dynasty. But another was the simple pragmatic fact that the number of potential marriage candidates was decreasing so rapidly, since the number of noble reigning houses (the

Counselor Franz Wetschl, Chancellery Director at the Department of the Exchequer, in his office

only adequate source of marriage partners for a Habsburg) was going down so rapidly. This, in turn, led to more and more Habsburgs simply leaving the fold of the family. The granddaughters of the emperor were among them, of course, but the more worrisome source of these class departures were the male Habsburgs.

The large number of class-violating marriages placed the emperor and his court in a dilemma. Should he simply accept this as a trend of the time and take no umbrage at the development? That was tantamount to admitting that the extraordinary status and mystical rank of the dynasty which played such a paramount role in ceremonials had all been a sham, a ruse, and would have to be given up. The more the claim to special status became diluted, the more the age-old traditions at court became a butt of criticism. Francis Joseph saw the danger which lurked in tolerance and any relaxation of the family laws, all deviations from which were inevitable consequences of the search for personal happiness and self-fulfillment. The House of Habsburg and the court would have to cope with ever-increasing criticism. As soon as the high claims to exclusivity and untouchable status could no longer be fulfilled, those claims would first be questioned, then challenged.

To many, Emperor Francis Joseph seemed far too unbending in his approach to this matter. He demanded that every member of the imperial family without exception stick to the guidelines as set down for ages past and not be permitted to wed without the approval of the emperor; and that all those who wed without such approval be disbarred from the family and all concomitant privileges. The emperor nevertheless made one exception: the female family members were treated with leniency. They were, upon such non-approved marriages, permitted to retain the title 'Imperial Highness'. But the male nephews and great-nephews who violated the codex were dealt with harshly. It was a black hole in the emperor's mentality that he simply could not comprehend the quest for personal happiness above and beyond the laws of the dynasty. He himself was the personification of duty, a master of self-discipline who never abused the privileges of his position for personal advantage. He gave up every iota of his private life for the benefit and furtherance of the dynasty. He lived for nothing but the preservation of the monarchy.

In view of this strict interpretation, those archdukes who decided on marriages for their own personal purposes suffered severely tarnished reputations at court. For the highest dignitaries at court, such yearnings were no more than negligence of duty, and rendered them unworthy of the imperial family. Their criticism was not long in coming. Lord Chancellor Liechtenstein's poisonous commentary on yet another class-violating marriage in the imperial family – this time it was Archduke Ferdinand, the youngest brother of Franz Ferdinand, heir to the throne, who wished to marry a bourgeois woman – was picturesque: "*Another uninspiring wedding has to be dealt with, but fortunately without any interference from me. This time round, one promoted the goat to be the gardener* (*Franz Ferdinand also had married a bourgeois woman and was now supposed to talk his brother out of it) *and it would probably not be a bad idea if one were to ask the goat to gobble up the whole garden, since nothing is growing in it but weeds … I couldn't care less who marries whom, since the perils of the future will not be any greater because of Franz Ferdinand's having married a mid-*

dle class woman. At worst, it might deliver a few more drunkenly conceived kids into the world, which would do it no great harm."[208]

Such caustic words from one of the emperor's most loyal representatives make clear what faultlines had been opened by this issue. And these fissures of discontent were destined to yawn only wider between the court dignitaries and the approaching generations. Fifty years earlier, such biting remarks against members of the imperial family would have been unimaginable. The aristocrats would not even have dared to commit such things to writing in their most secret diaries. But the refusal of many young archdukes to maintain the dignity of their family position led to unseen loyalty conflicts with court society. That the nobility lined up so unflinchingly behind their monarch can also be attributed to the fact that Francis Joseph led the way by an unparalleled power of example. Thus, it was hard to show tolerance towards the young people who simply dropped out of their responsibilty. The unconditional fidelity of the noble class was not so much being sworn to anachronistic dynastic laws, but to a person who commanded their utmost respect.

XIV
The Final Years

Just before the turn of the century, a shattering personal crisis shook the emperor's life. Empress Elisabeth, who in spite of all her flamboyant extravagances remained the great love of Francis Joseph's life, was murdered in 1898. His only son was dead. His daughters had married far from Vienna. His beloved grandchildren were seen only on high holidays. His sole personal contact, the one person who at least for brief intervals managed to lift him from the gloom of daily burdens, was an actress at the Burgtheater, Katharina Schratt, referred to simply as the 'gracious lady', the emperor's 'dear, good' friend. But this one and only friendship sought and maintained by an emperor who generally maintained great distance from human beings, on the one hand so that he could not be manipulated or taken advantage of, and on the other, because he had difficulties being intimate with anyone, threatened to founder at this juncture.

For as long as Elisabeth lived, the friendship between the emperor and the actress was tolerated and approved and was able to blossom. Following the empress's death, Katharina Schratt's position became untenable at court. Thus, the emperor was in danger of losing the sole human being whose acquaintance he treasured. His daughter, Marie Valerie, cut off all contact with the actress. She did not wish to be the patroness of a platonic friendship between emperor and an actress. Katharina Schratt herself believed that the whole court was conspiring against her and desired for that reason to terminate the relationship. She feared that she herself might get into irreparable difficulties without the requisite back-up support from the imperial family, a fear which was quite understandable amidst the conditions of the time.

Katharina Schratt's retreat was a matter of great satisfaction to many people at court, and viewed with malicious rancour by some. Her friendship with the monarch had been a thorn in their sides. Anxiety that the general public would lower their opinion of the emperor or that the actress would take shameless advantage of her nearness to him; yet also pure and simple jealousy that such a simple person could enjoy such a degree of confidence of an emperor, all led to a wave of antipathy rising against Katharina Schratt. As long as Elisabeth lived, it was held at bay. After she died, however, Schratt no longer had any backing. She began to loosen her ties to the emperor, went on long journeys, more or less abandoning an old and lonely Francis Joseph.

It was in this situation that Lord Chancellor Liechtenstein, who had been the top man at court since 1896, went into action. Rudolf Liechtenstein was certainly not the emperor's most illustrious Chancellor, he was simply too disinterested in court management and court ceremonies. However he was doubtless the Chancellor who was most deeply attached to the person of the emperor. Liechtenstein said about himself that *"he liked simply being near the emperor, not for reasons of patriotism, but out of human attraction."*[209] Whereas his predecessor Hohenlohe saw himself as the foremost official of a monarch whose private life was out of bounds for him, and who absolutely rejected Francis Joseph's friendship with Katharina Schratt, Liechtenstein had a far more relaxed relationship with his employer. He was the only one who attempted to iron out the differences between Francis Joseph and Schratt, particularly after he saw how much the emperor suffered at the loss of her companionship. He felt deeply sorry for his master, as he wrote to the deceased empress's friend: *"His Majesty is desperate and will have a tough time shouldering this utter lack of joy and good cheer ... I dread the coming of winter ... to lose the one and only diversion in his desolate life."*[210]

Liechtenstein wasn't fooled for a minute by the strictly disciplined daily work schedule of his master, nor did he shy away from questioning the emperor's valets about their personal impressions of their old lord, and reported: *"Externally, nothing is visible; and the outside world believes him to be in good spirits. But if you ask his chamber valets, you hear something much different."*[211] Liechtenstein resolved to act, still feeling an inner sense of duty to the deceased empress to provide the emperor with a modicum of social life. If Francis Joseph needed a little friendly chatter over coffee and cakes each day in the 'gracious lady's' living room, as compensation for the lonely life he led, then those in his vicinity should do everything in their power to make it possible.

Chancellor Prince Rudolf Liechtenstein

The bizarre situation arose that Prince Liechtenstein became a mediator between the emperor, the emperor's daughter and an actress. Daughter Marie Valerie wrote in her diary that Rudolf Liechtenstein had written her a letter asking how much "*she had done to spare her father the repeated agitations to which he was being subjected in the Schratt issue ... so he is on Papa's side, out of sympathy for him ...*"[212] He pleaded, negotiated with the imperial daughter, begged Katharina Schratt to relent and resume contact with her father again, and kept his employer informed of his progress. Francis Joseph wrote to Katharina Schratt: "*Prince Liechtenstein came to see me yesterday ... and brought me some tidings which were a relief to my ears.*"[213]

Liechtenstein was finally able to get the aggrieved actress to re-institute the daily conversations over coffee and cake. In order to clearly demonstrate to the outside world just how 'officially recognized' her position as 'friend of the emperor' was, and also to prevent her from changing her mind, Chancellor Liechtenstein, the pre-eminent representative of the Austrian aristocracy, visited the actress's villa in the city district of Hietzing often and highly visibly. He knew he was the link between the emperor and the actress. He also desired to fend off in good time the actress's notorious moments of crisis when she would withdraw from the lonely emperor and go on long, drawn out journeys.[214] Liechtenstein publicly defended the emperor's friendship with Schratt. He even went so far as to call those who thought ill of it *"people with superficial, shallow vision. Each sees life the way he is able to ..."*[215]

Chancellor of the Exchequer Liechtenstein was in name and title the First Lord. But Prince Alfred Montenuovo, Liechtenstein's married nephew and distant relative of the emperor, had in fact been managing court affairs since 1898. Montenuovo was the 'Second Lord Chancellor', a position which had never before existed at the court of Vienna, the creation of which served only the convenience of Liechtenstein and the patronage of Montenuovo.[216] The actual work of administration was accomplished by Montenuovo, while Liechtenstein merely presided over affairs as a kind of Olympian patron. One never saw him at work in the Office of the Exchequer, the way one always had seen Hohenlohe, only Montenuovo – who held all the threads of court affairs in his hands – could be observed at work there.

Alfred Montenuovo, Second Lord at court until Liechtenstein's death in 1908, and as of that moment First Lord at court, was the most despised dignitary the court had ever known, yet with a fascinating discrepancy. Only the imperial family and the aristocracy condemned him, the officials and servants treasured his highly correct working style and the protective hand he held over their heads (whenever external complaints or interference disturbed daily affairs, he invariably took the side of the court employees). Alfred Montenuovo's problem in dealing with the aristocracy had its roots in his own background, which made a precisely defined status in the court hierarchy a dicey business. For Montenuovo was, on the one hand, through his grandmother Archduchess Marie Louise, herself daughter of Emperor Franz and Napoleon's second wife, a direct blood relative of Emperor Francis Joseph, to be specific, his great nephew. Yet on the other, Montenuovo had the ineradicable shortcoming in the eyes of court society of being an illegitimate offspring. Marie Louise, married quite young to Napoleon

Emperor Francis Joseph's last Chancellor, Prince Alfred Montenuovo

for reasons of statehood, was granted the Duchy of Parma by the Congress of Vienna after Napoleon was banned to St. Helena. Separated from her son, who remained under supervision of the court in Vienna, Marie Louise felt herself to be too young to play the role of grieving widow. She disported herself with one of the military attachés assigned to her, the portly Count Adam Neipperg. Evil-minded gossipmongers said the spiritual father was Metternich himself who astutely assigned the stately Neipperg to the side of the duchess, whose attraction to men was well known even at the court of Vienna, in hopes that a love affair would make her more pliable politically. Marie Louise, however, succumbed to Neipperg's charms a little too quickly, thus placing her imperial father in a prickly dilemma. She bore Neipperg two children while her legal husband simmered on the isle of St. Helena (he didn't die until 1821). The children were given the name Montenuovo, the italianised form of Neippberg. When Alfred's father was raised to the nobility in 1864, so was his family.

Thus, the Montenuovo family occupied an odd, indefinable position in the court hierarchy. Neither were the Montenuovos on a par with the Habsburgs and the aristocrats, nor did they wish to stoop to be seen as co-equals with the aristocracy, since real Habsburg blood ran in their veins. A not small number of subsequent condemnations of Alfred Montenuovo by the aristocracy were based in the fact that he was never a part of the complexly intertwined aristocratic network of relatives. But his most implacable enemy was, of all people, the future emperor, heir to the throne, Franz Ferdinand, who hated Montenuovo's guts for cooly smothering every attempt of the heir to gain a certain say in court business. Franz Ferdinand also hated Montenuovo because he held him responsible for the suffering his own bourgeois wife went through at court, day in and day out, under the strict etiquette of daily court life. The animosity between them was well known to the court, and to the general public as well, even though it was a war fought by proxy. Behind the scenes, it was in fact Emperor Francis Joseph himself who wished to keep his unloved nephew at arm's length from daily court business. As of the moment of Franz Ferdinand's morganatic marriage, which itself was launched in an act of spite against the monarch, Francis Joseph wanted nothing more to do with him.

The roots of the difficult relationship between Franz Ferdinand and the officials at the court of his uncle were to be found in the clumsy and rough-hewn manners at court during the grave tuberculosis illness of the successor. While Franz Ferdinand fought his illness with enormous fortitude and discipline far from the capital, the policymakers in Vienna were grooming his brother, Archduke Otto, as the next successor to the throne. Otto was granted an expanded court retinue, the highly representational Augarten Palace as his residence, which had been unoccupied since the death of Konstantin Hohenlohe, and was smothered with attractive representational duties, which created the impression to the general public that Franz Ferdinand had been cut off completely. Franz Ferdinand had to put up with the fact that the Viennese already numbered him among the deceased. "*I am physically, but most of all morally, a broken man.*"[217] wrote the gravely ill successor to a friend.

Yet Franz Ferdinand possessed will power of tempered steel. He surprised not a few people when he returned to Vienna in restored health. His illness and the grievances which grew from the circumstances surrounding the conflict only spurred Franz Ferdinand's fighting spirit, infused with a sense of injustice. Barely returned to court, he began to put his private affairs in order and aggressively play his cards to obtain power at court. In order to marry his beloved Bohemian countess, Sophie Chotek, he was even willing to embark upon a confrontation course with the emperor. He was not willing to forego his plans to marry her, he said; nor to relinquish his claims to the throne. He demanded both. No efforts at persuasion, no imperial threats, could change his mind. Franz Ferdinand's refusal to stick to the marital guidelines of the Habsburg family plunged the emperor into constitutional problems and the court into ceremonial complications. His relationship with his uncle was all but destroyed by his spiteful marriage. A morganatic wedding of the next emperor of Austria was not just a personal matter in the eyes of Francis Joseph, it raised fundamental questions about the future of the dynasty. Even the emperor's daughter, Marie Valerie, who had always been highly critical of the family marriage laws, said this marriage was: *"the only thing that was lacking to make the survival of Austria and the dynasty absolutely doomed."*[218]

Emperor Francis Joseph, after a long series of arguments and disputes on the subject, managed to come to terms with this marriage which was so far out of keeping with his personal views; but at the same time, he forced Franz Ferdinand to bear the full consequences of his move. His wife Sophie was not to be considered a member of the imperial family; she came, hierarchically speaking, after the youngest unmarried archduchess in rank and was thus not permitted to enter at the side of her husband in official ceremonies. It was understandable that Franz Ferdinand broke his promise, and repeatedly attempted to obtain a special dispensation for his wife and secure her a better position in the rankings at court, since she suffered greatly under this stubbornly prejudicial treatment. But court ritual permitted no leeway in the matter.

To the general public as well, the unusual situation of the successor and his bourgeois wife gave rise to many a discussion. The citizens began to pose the question of whether the special status accorded the imperial dynasty and a court society replete with privileges were not in themselves anachronistic in a modern world. It was precisely this question about the necessity of a dynasty being raised above all other people in rights and privileges, an issue unleashed by the difficulties of public appearances of a skewed wedding relationship, which the emperor had so fervently wished to avoid through the strict adherence to court etiquette. If the dynasty demonstrated, for all the world to see, that it could not even uphold the standards it had devised for itself, public dispute, which could prove to be anathema to the future of the dynasty, would not be long in coming.

Lord Chancellor Montenuovo has often been accused of desiring to offend and aggrieve Franz Ferdinand by wielding the weapon of court ceremonial etiquette against his wife. However, such accusations can only be made by those utterly unfamiliar with the court hierarchy and its necessities. The ceremonial could not be bent out of shape by its guardians. Power and power's legitimation depended on the maintenance of the rules. The purpose of the famously strict Viennese court ceremonials was, superficially, to heighten the glamour and glory of the dynasty; yet thereby, to perpetrate the social order and the institutionalization of a well defined hierarchy. If that system which brought the dynasty a mystic status extending far beyond its immediate vicinity were to be hollowed out from inside, its entire reason for existence would be shown to be absurd.

Franz Ferdinand also placed high demands on those immediately around him. His manners were far from gracious, downright rude, in fact. He had the feeling that others were conspiring against him, and consequently countenanced only downright obsequious behaviour. Lord Chancellor Montenuovo, for his part, refused to supply the kind of behaviour which Franz Ferdinand claimed to be his due. Montenuovo saw his sole responsibility as owed the emperor. Thus, relations between Franz Ferdinand and Montenuovo, who was almost the only one without any fear of the heir to the throne and who continued to act with eminent imperturbability towards him (which enraged Franz Ferdinand) worsened from year to year.

The successor was, on the one hand, embittered about the implacable and consequential ways of court ceremonies. Yet he also suffered at the distance the emperor maintained between them. Francis Joseph kept his successor far removed from any and all political tasks and decision making. In spite of their differences, Franz Ferdinand did indeed show ardent obedience in his manner to the emperor, but the emperor remained aloof and kept all contact to a minimum. The successor burned with ambition to play a part in state affairs. He was however condemned to remain utterly passive; in order to balance his feelings of helplessness, he tried to ratchet up his influence in the areas of family and court conduct. Through this attempt to compensate his statecraft powerlessness, however, he got into the hair of Montenuovo and the emperor's most loyal employees. And they cruelly fended off every such endeavor. What disturbed these officials most of all was how Franz Ferdinand, while Francis Joseph was still alive, tried to influence affairs which were the sole province of the ruler. That was something Montenuovo and his team were not willing to accept. They repudiated Franz Ferdinand's efforts to a man. The nephew saw this, felt it, and it only intensified his hatred of them all, and of his uncle.

Franz Ferdinand cultivated a great interest in the family fund containing the emperor's private wealth. He bombarded the fund managers and the Office of the Exchequer with criticism that a variety of family members had been accorded unjustified extra allocations. At the same time, he claimed for himself a privileged financial treatment from the family fund, which was clearly against the rules set up for the fund, since it was designed to serve all the members of the family according to the percentage they were allotted. Franz Ferdinand tried again and again to wrangle special payments for himself, based on his position as heir to the throne, which objectively speaking, was understandable. His three children, since they were born of a morganatic marriage, had no claim whatsoever to later provisions from the family fund and Franz Ferdinand wished to secure their future now, while he was alive. History was to prove this a very prudent move. His attempts resulted in a sharp rejection of his claim, both by his uncle and by the officials at court.

Over the course of time, Franz Ferdinand took on a role of virtual financial oversight at court which even included the emperor and his family. The fact that Montenuovo, who was devoted to Francis Joseph, was profoundly opposed to this activity, can surprise no one. Montenuovo's response to one of the many written communications of Franz Ferdinand, when he sent a complaint to the Director of the Office of the Exchequer that he had not been informed about certain happenings at court, was illustrative. "*The archduke should not be upset about not being informed. The highest of all family statutes recognizes only one head of the family.*"[219]

Franz Ferdinand also bemoaned the lack of deference and obedience shown to him by the officials of his uncle. The heir to the throne, however, was himself guilty of placing those officials in conflict of duty by issuing direct orders to them without first having them cleared with the Lord Chancellor. The officials were often astonished at the exaggerated requests and demands coming from Franz Ferdinand, e.g. when he demanded that a taxi driver be criminally charged for having blocked the archduke's rented car in the entrance to court. These were sensitivities which had never existed in the emperor himself.[220] But most of all, the court officials suffered from the eratic, emotional, at times hysterical, outbursts of the heir to the throne in the course of which he regularly berated the court employees beyond all reasonable measure. Such moody, arbitrary conduct was something the court employees were in no way accustomed to. The old emperor was always an inordinately kind and lenient employer. The older he got, the more Francis Joseph was viewed with awe by all those who worked for him.

The officials, therefore, were completely on the emperor's side. Franz Ferdinand was deeply aggrieved by the knowledge of just who was emperor; that that person was the recipient of infinite respect and devotion; it deepened his hatred for all the dignitaries and officials of his uncle still further. Certain highly placed officials in the Office of the Exchequer knew well that their career would abruptly end when the aged emperor passed away, and this made their behaviour towards the heir even bolder. Franz Ferdinand was known to carry grudges long and far in time, they knew they could depend on not a whit of understanding for their difficult position trying to balance present and future monarchs. Based on that awareness, they tended to support their true employer, Lord Chancellor Montenuovo, to an even more extreme degree, even daring to show themselves distant and unwilling to respond to Franz Ferdinand's special requests. Franz Ferdinand's personal doctor reported about the self-assured manner of the high ranking officials, who blocked Franz Ferdinand's requests as a matter of course: "*Wetschl* (*Director of the Office of the Exchequer) *once told me with amazing candour: 'The archduke is not a person of any* *importance to us.'"*[221] Franz Ferdinand had only cynical commentaries for these high officials and ministers of his uncle. He once confided to someone close to him that he had devised a motto for how to deal with them: "*Blessed are the poor in spirit, for they shall inherit the heavens.*"[222]

In 1909, when Montenuovo formally became the First Lord at court following the death of his uncle, Rudolf Liechtenstein, a rumour was initiated that the new Chancellor was trying to barricade the emperor from the outer world in order to expand his own position of power. Although it is not true that Montenuovo attempted to enlarge his own power base in such a way, there is indeed an interesting correlation between this rumour and the marked change in Francis Joseph's behaviour. As of the year 1909, the personal circle around the nearly 80-year old monarch became noticeably smaller. His last confidant of earlier days, 'Rudi' Liechtenstein, was dead, and with his passing the position of Katharina Schratt – the last personal contact of the emperor from outside the walls of court – again became more difficult, since Montenuovo would not countenance taking over his uncle's role as patron-protector of this friendship. The emperor became more and more lonely, which in turn intensified the importance of his immediate and most intimate circle, comprising his only regularly seen human contacts. This meant, above all else, the Lord Chancellor.

On top of this, the emperor's health took a turn for the worse that year, which inspired his immediate circle of advisors to fear the end was near. The crowds at the next court ball were larger than ever, since everyone, as one aristocrat reported, wanted to have one last "*look at our wonderful, old emperor.*"[223] After his recovery, again demonstrating what an iron constitution he had, Montenuovo began to press the emperor to take better care of himself and to voluntarily cut down his own work load. His contacts with the cabinet heads, ministers and appointed authorities were reduced for health reasons. In the last years of the emperor's life, those long, drawn out political conversations of an earlier epoch took place only very sporadically. Francis Joseph's contact with the outer world was reduced to written communications, the number of personal audiences diminished further and further until they almost disappeared. Montenuovo became the only human link

The old emperor at his desk –
a picture like an emblem of his life

between the head of state and his ministers. The fact that this led the staff to anxious overreaction and exclusive concentration on what would and what would not benefit the health of their master, completely ignoring the absolute necessity of regular consultations with ministers, was condemned in no uncertain terms by the aristocracy. "*The emperor appears to be in good health, but will now retire for his season of hibernation to Schönbrunn Palace, where Krezl* (*his personal doctor) *will hover over him as if his patient were a rare orchid.*"[224]

The general public judged this situation of protecting the emperor from every manner of confrontation, even if it did serve the interests of his health, negatively, as a form of spiteful isolation. "*Not only every breath of fresh air, also every fresh political breeze is removed from his vicinity by the Lord Chancellor, his military advisors and his doctors. More and more, the life of this epoch is going straight past our emperor, as if it were nothing but a faint rustle in the wind.*"[225]

While the emperor visibly became older and older, and withdrew increasingly from the external world, and the heir to the throne had now been waiting 25 years to realize his own political goals, a tsunami was brewing not far from the monarchy of which no one had the slightest anticipatory inkling. The Great War which for years everyone had feared was coming, was triggered by the murder of Franz Ferdinand and his wife. As the details about the assassination became known and preparations for the funeral were made, the gossip which set in was destined in future days to bring great discredit to the court in Vienna and to Lord Chancellor Montenuovo. The preparations for the journey on which the heir to the throne would be murdered were so ill-conceived and shoddily executed that a misfortune was practically preordained. The population murmured that out of nothing but pure personal animosity, the Lord Chancellor would surely now give the heir a meagre and paltry funeral on top of everything else, at which the stooping down to his bourgeois wife would be given inordinate emphasis. Regardless of such malicious accusations, a close examination of the evidence disproves them.

In spite of later memoirs claiming the opposite, the Chancellor, first of all, had nothing whatever to do with the preparations for the Bosnian journey, which admittedly bore the signs of unforgivable negligence. The programme and agenda of military trips lay completely in the hands of the military, not of the Exchequer. Franz Ferdinand's own military chancellery and the territorial leaders alone were responsible for it. Their miscalculations of the political situation led them to make utterly inadequate provisions for security. The safety measures in the Bosnian capital were actually reduced on the express request of the national government in order not to alarm or annoy the population (which was assessed as being flawlessly loyal to their imperial visitor) by excessive military presence. It was a fatal decision. The entrance of the archduke into Sarajevo on Vidovdan, the Serbian national holiday, was approved, despite many urgent warnings against that date.

The preparations for the funeral in Vienna began with a certain sense of relief. Just before the corpse arrived in Vienna, Franz Ferdinand's last will and testament became public, in which he expressed the wish to be buried in Artstetten. Through this request, the murdered heir to the throne spared the emperor a delicate, not unperilous task. For, the archduchess could never have been interred in the Tomb of the Cappuchins, the *Kappuzinergruft*. This was not because even in death she should be further humiliated as not measuring up to the required class standing for such a tomb, but because an interrment there would have implied that the class rules were being suspended, which would become a legal precedence case having a bearing on the future. The class equality laws on which the succession to the Habsburg throne rested would no longer be applicable, could no longer be defended or justified. That, in turn, would have ramifications on claims of family members who had left the family fold, relinquished their responsibilities or crossed the same borders and married below their class. It was also necessary to protect the future emperor, Karl, whose regency should not be overly burdened even before he took the throne. The rule of the next emperor, who had always adhered to the family laws, should not be launched with a hollowing out of the very laws he had respected and followed.

Now that the inheritance and family laws, insofar as they applied to the selection of a place of burial for the murdered couple, had become academic, Francis Joseph proclaimed that Sophie should receive all due family honours in the funeral and mourning ceremonies as they were foreseen in tradition and protocol for members of the Habsburg family. This was an extremely generous interpretation of the dynastic guidelines. The stories in the newspapers, to the effect that the funeral ceremonies had been drastically reduced, corresponding to the lesser social status of the murdered archduchess, were just as false as the reports in later history books that the successor to the throne had been denied the funeral to which he was entitled because he had violated class rules in his marriage. Neither was the morganatic character of his marriage underscored, nor were the funeral ceremonies in any way reduced or diluted. On the contrary, the ceremonies and the guidelines which determined them were laid out in particularly generous fashion, far more elaborate than protocol required.

Emperor Francis Joseph actually raised the funeral and the obsequies to the 3rd rank in stature, which in a strict interpretation of the guidelines only the son of an emperor was entitled to. Funeral rites of the 1st and 2nd rank in stature were only permissible for the monarch and his wife. For the wife of the successor to the throne, inofficial court mourning was proclaimed, the same as applied to members of the imperial family. This was the one and only signal of Sophie's class inequality, and even this step was invisible to all observers, being referred to only in written communiquès. The criticism which persists still today that her coffin was placed lower than that of her husband in order to demonstrate the unequal status of the couple is false; both coffins in the court chapel were perfectly adjacent to one another, atop a catafalque draped in golden cloth. The fact that the coffin of the archduchess was smaller and less pompous cannot be attributed to any court decision. The coffins were selected by Franz Ferdinand's own personal chancellor. And it is uttlerly unthinkable that this man, who was so utterly devoted to his master, would have done anything with a mind to belittle the status of Franz Ferdinand's wife. The funeral items placed on the coffin of the archduchess – a pair of white gloves and a fan – were also not Montenuovo's nasty reference to her previous status as a court lady, as some contemporaries claimed; they were the customary props of a female funeral which were allotted to all Habsburg women as an insignia. Even the modest funeral wreath was not a malicious act of court officials, but had a completely different background. In order to provide more room for bystanders, only the children's wreaths were distributed in the tomb; all the other floral offerings were spread out in the Redoutensaal of the court.[226] The bevy of criticism and insidious interpretations still being perpetrated in the historical literature of today about intentionally degraded ceremonial aspects will simply not stand up to examination of the sources and background materials of Habsburg tradition.

The funeral of the murdered couple was, however, utterly abused by the opinion-makers and the press of the day in order to stoke negative attitudes towards the unpopular Lord Chancellor, completely ignoring the long history of funeral rites of the Habsburg family. The massive criticism of Montenuovo might, at the same time, be seen as the only legitimate way of criticizing what the public perceived as a long outdated and anachronistic institution, namely, the court and its attendant society. Any other form of criticism of the privileges of the dynasty would have been subjected to the strictures of the court censor. Beneath the smoke screen of public mourning, court critics made bold to go further than they ever had done before. Even in the immediate family of Franz Ferdinand's wife there was consternation and concern at the extent of public criticism of the court. Sophie's brother-in-law, Count Jaroslav Thun, guardian of the now orphaned children, was astonished at the harshness of the criticism and went so far as to defend Montenuovo. *"Everyone is ranting and railing against the poor fellow, the loyal servant of the emperor, who is simply sticking nervously to the rules of ceremony without any deviations or inspirations. He isn't particularly bright, but he is honest and competent."* [227]

What remains is the question of which aspects of this tragic political murder did not come to light in the imposing funeral which was so far removed from all court rules and guidelines and traditions. After all, Franz Ferdinand had been murdered in the fulfillment of his duties as heir to the throne and official representative of the House of Austria. As General Inspector of the entire military weight of Austria, he was entitled to an honourable military funeral. It was highly irregular to prohibit the presence of foreign heads of state at the funeral; worse, it was a grave political error. If the political aspects of the tragedy had been placed in the foreground, i.e. the assassination by an anarchist of a future head of state, a funeral replete with other European heads of state would have sent a powerful signal to the rest of the world. In the agitatated, nearly hysterical pre-war atmosphere which prevailed throughout Europe at the time, the last card – the harmonious appearance of all European leaders together – was not played, it was simply neglected.

Even the exceedingly brief public viewing of the lying-in-state, for which only four hours were allotted, can to this day not be properly explained. The people of Vienna had been permitted to whisper silent farewells to Crown Prince Rudolf and Archduke Albrecht until well into the night. The small numbers of people filing by Franz Ferdinand's coffin were viewed by many as an insult. Particularly the aristocrats condemned the hastily arranged court funeral ceremonies and felt that their class had been intentionally shut out of the official mourning. They went out of their way to form a private funeral march to the Westbahnhof train station, from where the coffins were to be transported to Artstetten. This procession of nobility was written up in almost all the newspapers as a piquant criticism of court and its officials on the part of the aristocracy. The participants themselves claimed that it was no protest against court bureaucracy, on the contrary, it stemmed from a profound need to demonstrate deep personal grief. One special jab in the direction of Montenuovo was not lacking, however: influential personalities at court had seen to it that not even in face of the majesty of death could ancient and picayune details of court ceremonial be rendered their appropriate, i.e. secondary status. This was an unjustified criticism of Montenuovo; it merely reflected his arm's length treatment of – and often cynical detachment from – the aristocracy.

What followed was something the court had expected least of all. In the Labourer's Newspaper, of all places, the mouthpiece of the socialists, came a spirited defense of the imperial court and an equally spirited reproach of the aristocracy. "*The extremely wealthy gentlemen ... put on a great show of bravado against Prince Montenuovo, but precious little against Count Stürkgh* (*the Prime Minister, who had not convened parliament for more than a half-year) ... *If the aristocrats had been serious in their mourning, they would have forced a session in the House of Lords, the only true place for a genuine show of grief, a far more fitting locale than Hotel Sacher* (*where the aristocrats had assembled)." What followed in the same newspaper was something all court officials would have countersigned. "*And thus, the following contrast is drawn for our entertainment: those who are currently so incensed that the sanctified ceremonials were heeded down to the last detail are the same ones who usually kowtow and beg that precisely those details be respected and paraded, and woe to those who smirk at them! In all other situations, their 'ceremonial' is the highest, holiest thing they know, higher than the etiquette at the court of Spain! And now they are bitching that it was adhered to!*"[228]

Emperor Francis Joseph placed himself behind his Lord Chancellor for all to see. To calm the waves of criticism swiftly rising against Montenuovo, the emperor wrote a handwritten note of personal thanks and approval of the services Montenuovo performed for the funeral ceremonies. The emperor thereby assumed the full responsibility for the way in which the mourning and official ceremonies had been conducted, a rare gesture, through which the monarch demonstrated something the critics were unaware of: the Lord Chancellor had in this instance, as always, carried out the wishes of his master.

The outbreak of war in 1914 did not significantly change the life of the emperor or the habits of court, except that the monarch met with the military chiefs more often. Francis Joseph continued to work from early morning until nine o'clock in the evening. The strenuous dinners were suspended at the beginning of the war. His immediate circle pressed him to withdraw to Schönbrunn Palace in the last two years of his life. The apartments there had been newly renovated and specifically tailored to the needs of the emperor in his old age. Above all else, his apartment in Schönbrunn was much brighter than the one at the Hofburg, was easier to heat and had far better air quality than in the center of town. His daily walks would now be a greater pleasure than his quarters in the heart of the 1st district. He merely had to walk out the door of Schönbrunn Palace and was immediately surrounded by greenery. He could also avoid coach rides – or automobile rides – entirely, something surely welcome to an 86-year old man.

Physically, Emperor Francis Joseph remained in fine fettle, in full possession of his powers of mind, until the very end. The effects of his advanced age were evident only in certain ways. However, his 17-hour working days did begin to become difficult for him. In autumn of the year 1916, the emperor began to weaken visibly. His personal doctor's recommendation to engage nurses to take care of his daily needs was brusquely rejected with the words, "*My three servants have long attended to a healthy emperor, they can very well attend to a sick one.*"[229] His Lord Chancellor, his daughter Valerie, and most of all his loyal valet Eugen Ketterl pressed him to take regular naps. His circle watched over him, did their best to take care of him; every visitor was asked to be brief and not tire the monarch needlessly. They were informed of a special bell which had been installed on the underside of the desk and which could be rung if urgent assistance were needed. Even though his strength was waning rapidly, the emperor still got up at 3:30 every morning, sat down at his desk and began to work. More and more often, he had to take a break in the middle of his working day and snooze in his armchair, something which had been unthinkable in earlier days. More and more often, his adjutants – who had set up mirrors in the foyer so that the emperor would literally never be out of their sight – noticed that he had sunk his head onto his desk in pure exhaustion, usually only for a few minutes, until he regained his strength and then contined with his paperwork.

On 21 November 1916, Emperor Francis Joseph died at nine o'clock in the evening. Even on his very last day, he worked, albeit only intermittently. Before his valet brought him to bed, he issued his final order of the day, as he always had, to awake him punctually the next morning at 3:30 am. At his death, not only the emperor's daughter, the next emperor and his wife were present, but also those who made up his innermost personal circle: his Lord Chancellor, his adjutants and his valets.

When the doctor confirmed the death of the emperor, lackeys ran across the courtyard to inform the palace captain that their master was dead. The many people who had been waiting in front of Schönbrunn Palace, hoping for news about the ailing emperor, were the first to hear of his passing. The Lord Chancellor informed the heads of state, but even before the official proclamation could be issued, the news had spread through court like wildfire: the father of all the employees at court was gone. After 68 years of rule, every single servant and official had served under this man. And only a few rare old retired servants could dimly remember that once upon a time there had been another emperor.

XV
The End of the Imperial Court

After the death of Francis Joseph, his last Lord Chancellor and employees of the Department of Ceremonies began with their final services to the emperor. They set about designing and implementing funeral celebrations in accordance with the highest rank in status which imperial ceremonial guidelines recognized: the famous Burial Class I, to which only crowned emperors were entitled. The last true imperial burial had taken place in 1835, for Emperor Franz I (II). The immediate predecessor of Francis Joseph, namely Emperor Ferdinand, had died in Prague and was simply interred in the Cappuchine Tomb. It had been carried out with a certain pomp, but on a decidedly more modest level.

Francis Joseph had reigned for 68 years, so there were no longer living officials who could remember the details of ceremonial guidelines for Burial Class I. The Department of Ceremonies had worked for centuries with a mixture of fixed rules for ceremonial events and certain finely drawn divergencies which corresponded to the respective situation at hand. Many of these finely drawn lines had been handed down orally over the generations, but the last imperial burial was simply too long past to have any ceremonial specialists at hand with helpful suggestions. Lord Chancellor of the Exchequer Montenuovo pulled out the records from the funeral of 1835 and studied the protocols in order to devise an appropriate ceremony for Francis Joseph's final path. But Montenuovo no longer held the reins in his hand, the new emperor Karl had his own ideas. He wished to walk behind the coffin himself, not only with Empress Zita, but with the little Crown Prince Otto as well.

On 30 November 1916, on a sunny autumn day, Francis Joseph set out on his last journey. The streets which the funeral procession would pass through were jammed with crowds, every window was occupied with onlookers. Almost the entire population of Vienna had been born while this man was reigning, and now they wished to bid him a final farewell. The body of the emperor was drawn through the outer courtyard in its magnificant black solemn coach, drawn by eight horses, and in a wide arc over the quay to St. Stephan's Cathedral. Countless wagons filled with wreaths as well as wagons with the highest dignitaries of state preceded the funeral coach, behind it came the imperial family. Behind them followed the official delegations, the guards and the court employees. The Prince Archbishop of Vienna was in charge of the funeral mass. From St. Stephan's Cathedral, the funeral pageant proceeded on foot to the Cappuchine Tomb. Behind the coffin walked Emperor Karl and Empress Zita, between them the heir to the throne in white clothes and blonde locks. The pictures of the little boy, the only bright spot in this pompous, dark-coloured procession, imprinted themselves on the collective consciousness of the population. No modern PR expert could have devised a better, a more effective presentation. Behind the coffin of the emperor who was a personification of the endurance and quality of imperial ideals, whose end was feared by many and was downright inconceivable to most, the future of the empire followed in train, light-hearted, bright-spirited and untroubled: the little Crown Prince, whom many perceived as a positive symbol of the future.

At the gates of the Tomb of the Cappuchines, Lord Chancellor Montenuovo requested admittance of Pater Guardian for his master. After the Cappuchine monks had granted admittance and taken possession of the coffin, placed the emperor between his wife and his son and the nearest family members and said their farewells to him, the monks closed up the tomb. Emperor Francis Joseph had reached his ultimate resting place, he lay among his forebears as the longest reigning monarch of the entire, long Habsburg history.

After the burial, life at court continued in customary ways. There was a new emperor who now guaranteed the rights of the court employees. At the top of the court there were, of course, a few changes to be made. Tradition had it that the period of service of the upper rank of court officials ended with the death of their employer. Each new emperor had his own list of confidantes who would manage the court in his desired ways. Lord Chancellor Montenuovo cleared his desk. He retired to private life, since he was too old for war service. Alfred Montenuovo died in Vienna in September 1927 at the age of 78. He left no memoirs behind, had never given interviews to the press or tried in any way to capitalize on his knowledge and experience at court. The publishers had to go without a priceless source of information who lived and worked at the elbow of Emperor Francis Joseph. Prince Montenuovo maintained his silence until the end; he even had most of his correspondence and personal documents burned upon his death.

The new Lord Chancellor under Emperor Karl was the oldest son of the former Lord Chancellor Konstantin Hohenlohe: Konrad Hohenlohe, a candid, modern, highly critical spirit who already had a remarkable career behind him. He had been Prime Minister, Governor of Triest and was known to the general public as the *Red Prince* because he was not in the slightest loath to take up contact with the socialists. He was considered to be an enlightened aristocrat. His appointment was a sign for a new start, although he was not truly able to set new accents.

At the coronation of Emperor Karl, the war had already raged for two long years. The shortage of food supplies had reached the court itself. There was still food to be had, but the sumptuous court kitchen of Francis Joseph's day was long past. The new emperor himself had only modest personal needs, he ate simple meals, cheap wines and enjoyed meat only seldom. The court employees still had the security of employment, of sufficient firewood for the winter and at least of elementary provisions of food for themselves and their families. But the court had gone through a sea change. All the young, strong men were away at war, the old and wounded formed the majority of those left behind at court.

The changed style of leadership at court under Emperor Karl was less noticeable in administration – something for which the new emperor had little acumen – than in the loosening of restrictions for audiences and visits. The way Emperor Karl dealt with his ministers and confidantes was completely different from his predecessor. Gentlemen – and all of them without exception, at that – were invited to be seated in the presence of the emperor. Their conversations not seldom went on for several hours, something unimaginable under Francis Joseph. Karl inspired candid conversation and encouraged his vis-à-vis to articulate independent opinions. The organised agenda of appointments for audiences soon lost all meaning, since each appointment went on for much longer than was scheduled. Important talks with the emperor took as long as was necessary, became the going attitude. Karl was much more open than Francis Joseph had ever been, but that in turn made him far more vulnerable. After all, the old emperor had maintained a strict distance between himself and all his advisors precisely because he did not wish to let anyone believe that he could be influenced. Personal contact was much easier with the new emperor and not a few of those who visited him believed that they might well be able to influence the young monarch.

During the last two years of the monarchy, daily life at court went on much as it had before, with the one distinction that everything seemed simpler, more tranquil. There were no pompous court festivities, there was no entertainment. In autumn 1918, the war was lost for Austria and its allies; thereupon the internal dissolution of the Danube monarchy began. On 11 November 1918, Emperor Karl gave up all claim to state government, but did not abdicate. On the same evening, he departed from court in the direction of Eckartsau. He would never return to Vienna.

On 12 November the Republic of German Austria was proclaimed. The young republic immediately laid claim to the court. The German-Austrian state notary was made administrator of the court, one month later the control was transferred to the State Seals Office. At the beginning of 1919, the entire court was placed under the authority of the 'uppermost authority of court affairs', Section Chief Baron von Beck-Mannagetta. The four traditional departments of court were kept, but their names changed. The Office of the Exchequer, Office of the Chamberlain, Office of the Marshal and Office of the Stables became Departments I – IV. Nothing was supposed to remind anyone of the old regime. Department III, the Office of the Marshal, was liquidated in May 1919, the legal office of the imperial family being no longer needed. The remaining departments remained in existence and functioned under the direction of the uppermost administrator.[230]

It was the job of the Court Administrator to liquidate the imperial court as soon as possible, but at the same time to make sure that the former possessions and properties of court brought as much profit as possible to the young republic, which sorely needed as much income as it could muster. To begin with, there were large scale plans of what might be earned by turning the court properties to cash, but the uppermost administrator soon faced the selfsame problems that the Lord Chancellor had once had. Most of the court assets could only be preserved for future generations by investing a great deal of money in their maintenance. And from the possessions themselves, there was very little money to be earned. Maintaining the buildings and art collections had always cost far more than it earned. The government had a few notions about how to generate revenues from Schönbrunn Palace. However, they were all rejected by the Palace Administrator, since they would require sacrificing cultural assets for a short-term financial profit. One of the initial ideas was to lease the rights to Schönbrunn park to filmmakers. The palace administrative office was adamantly against this. Not only were 200-year old trees supposed to be cut down by studios for purposes of filmmaking, they also intended to close off most parts of the park from the public. This was rejected for the reason that the park was indispensable for the children of the nearby districts. The main argument of the palace administrative office was that in case the filmmaking company went bankrupt and investors were granted access to palace assets in the court proceedings, it could lead to the relinquishing of imperial property for the sake of a film company.[231]

The profit-making potential of former court assets and properties remained a pipe dream. Even the actual distribution, i.e. which ministry would receive which properties, dragged on for years. Only the treatment of the question of the private wealth of the Habsburg family was able to be settled without delay. Since Emperor Karl refused to make a statement of relinquishment of assets, National Chancellor Dr. Karl Renner laid state claim to the family fund which had always been the prerogative of the head of the imperial family. All assets went into the fund to pay for the damages and injuries of the war wounded. The family was even dispossessed of the small private account of the former ruler, those parts which he had personally inherited and which bore no relation to his former rights as ruler. This was effected in a manner starkly contrasting with the treatment of family members who officially relinquished their membership to the House of Habsburg; they were permitted to retain their assets and properties.

The palace administrator also had another delicate problem to tackle: the many former court employees who either had to be sent back to their home countries or taken care of in Austria. Among the files of liquidation are some pre-printed notes which provide information about the first group examined and dealt with by the administration. Among the questions to be answered, such as 'name' and 'profession' was also a question regarding nationality, which was mandatory for each employee to answer. For many, the answer they filled in was 'Czech', adjoined by a scribbled note 'to be returned to homeland'. People who had served under the emperor were suddenly considered to be foreigners and were put under pressure to return to their homelands. Although the court itself was always supra-national, the former staff members were now sub-divided into Austrians and Czechs.

The remainder of the staff members, many hundreds of them, had to be taken care of in Austria. But the administrator had one problem which was nearly insoluable: most of the court employees could no longer be employed. Those officials who had enjoyed a high level of education could at least be transferred to national ministries, but there was hardly any need for them. The court officers and servants, on the other hand, had next to no chance of finding employment. Even those who had solid training in some craft or other could not find any work, given the extremely adverse economic conditions. Only two professional groups enjoyed a certain demand: chauffeurs, who were immediately engaged by private families or aristocrats; and cooks, who also found positions either in private homes or in exclusive restaurants which were happy to boast that they employed one or two former 'royal and imperial' chefs.

All the other former employees of court were left to hope that the new state would take care of them as the emperor always had. The administrator had an immensely difficult task. The only ones who could be given new work found it by themselves; for the others, those for whom there were no chances on the labour market whatsoever, the hundreds of people who, whatever their performance at court, knew they would always have work and gainful employment, were part of the imperial household establishment with a long list of rights, there was no chance. For all of the servants, porters, coachmen, doormen, guardians, laundresses and cleaning crew, there simply was no alternative to working at court.

The liquidation office of the palace administrator attempted to entice the former court employees to relinquish their claim to their work contracts. But even the simplest servants knew such a move could only be to their disadvantage. After all, since 1914 they had enjoyed the privileges of tenure, just as national employees had. For the palace administrator, that meant no less than that the state would have to take every official and every servant of court into its employ. Completely aside from that, every apartment in the Hofburg and in the other palaces was occupied with former court employees and retired officials, which meant that there was not even the possibility of renting the imperial properties to generate revenues.

For Francis Joseph's employees, the collapse of the monarchy meant much more than a new beginning in the service of the state. Working at court had not only brought them security; a certain, modest career ladder was also a part of the syndrome. Every few years, one advanced to the next rank in status; loyalty and a life of service were honoured in regular fashion; and one's children were also assured of a position some day. The countless forms of social assistance which court and emperor guaranteed were now gone. There were no supportive payments of any kind, no emperor with private purse in emergencies to whom one could turn with a personal petition. With immediate effect, for example, only those court apartments were supplied with firewood whose occupants had pre-paid the delivery. Whoever was not in a position to do that had to throw himself on the mercy of the state, and received a bit of firewood only in hardship situations.[232] The days when such donations were always assured were over. The former court employees who had elected not to take an apartment in the palace, or for whom there was no apartment free, and had instead received quarterly payments as assistance, were the biggest losers of all. They were no longer able to keep their own apartments. When it became known that peace negotiations were being conducted, the value of the currency crashed, inflation skyrocketed to 100% monthly. The sparse salaries and pensions were no longer enough to live on.

By the end of 1921, the liquidation of the court was completed. The former court assets and properties had been distributed. The National Ministry of Education was granted the theaters and art collections; the Ministry for Agriculture and Forests was granted the horse breeding farms and the Spanish Riding School; the Ministry of Commerce and Public Buildings received all buildings, all horses and the fleet of vehicles, together with the Wagenburg and the Chamber of Saddlery and the Armoury. The Ministry of Social Management received the Court Pharmacy.[233] When the court was finally dissolved, the Office of Administration was dissolved at the same time.

The period before the First World War in retrospect came to be called the "*Chicken-in-the-Pot Era*", partly in fondness, partly in pure irony. For all those in any way attached to the court, it was a period of absolute security. The monarchy promised them a place of work, social security, an array of social services and a net of support mechanisms, which as of 1914 were even immortalised in writing through the rights of 'service tenure'. Court officials and court servants thereby became un-fireable. And everyone believed that nothing could disturb or derange that security. Even if the graying emperor, Francis Joseph, were to pass away one day, his successor would surely continue the age-old traditions of the imperial patriarchs. The court would always remain the last bastion of a longstanding tradition of taking care of those who served it.

But the "*Chicken-in-the-Pot Era*" abruptly ended with the First World War. For four years, those at court were granted a certain period of grace, were able to enjoy the final interval, since everyone knew that sooner or later the war would come to an end. And even if the court in the years following did not have as much largesse to distribute as it had had under Francis Joseph, at least the old alliance of ruler and household would surely endure. Following the end of the monarchy, it quickly became clear to all those who persisted in this illusion that more than a governmental form was coming to an end. For them, their world and their life were being disbanded. Apart from their respective fields of work and their varying performances at their jobs, their home, their meals and their safety had been inextricably enmeshed with this governmental form. It was their salvation and their anchor of final resort, which would always lend them a helping hand when needed. Most of all, the old emperor was the embodiment of that guarantee. Until the very end, that was how the employees viewed him: the patriarch of last resort, always there to help them.

Acknowledgements

There are many who must be thanked after a work such as this. To begin with, all those who generously opened up their private archives to the author.

I extend a debt of thanks to the head of the house of Wittelsbach, Duke Francis of Bavaria, for permitting me to utilise the secret house archives. I thank Dr. Gerhard Immler, Director of the secret house archives for his counsel and help in my search for interesting sources. The correspondence between Arch Duchess Sophie and her brother King Ludwig I. of Bavaria brought fascinating insights into court life from the point of view of the ruling family.

The most important private archives for research in court and society life under Emperor Francis Joseph were provided by the family archives of Prince Hohenlohe-Schillingsfürst in Vienna. Their owner Karl Hohenlohe not only opened for the first time the entire inventory for research purposes, but also made available rich sources of illustration for utilisation in this book. Above all else, the legacy of Lord Chancellor Prince Konstantin Hohenlohe-Schillingsfürst and his sons, Prime Minister Konrad Hohenlohe-Schillingsfürst and Gottfried Hohenlohe-Schillingsfürst, Austrian ambassador in Berlin, made views of Emperor Francis Joseph's court from the innermost circles of power possible.

Hans Hoyos, owner of the family and official archives of Count Hoyos in Horn, is extended a debt of thanks for permission to look through the estate materials of Count Heinrich Hoyos, aide-de-camp of Emperor Francis Joseph. His wide ranging correspondence contains fascinating observations and views of the court of the aging emperor.

Mrs. Elisabeth Hiller made available the handwritten memoirs of her great-grandfather, Franz Ritter von Srbik, thereby facilitating a deeper examination of the lives of the top officials at the court of Vienna under Emperor Francis Joseph, for which there are next to no private sources.

Mrs. Dr. Ingrid Haslinger generously permitted me to use many pictures from her personal collection for purposes of this book, as well as her own evaluation and research of the dining culture at court and the court kitchen.

Mrs. Gabrielle Lobjeyr made available pictures from her own private archives for this book, for which I am most grateful.

I also extend a debt of thanks to the representatives of the State Archives for their help in my search for comprehensive materials and sources of substance.

Mrs. Irmgard Pangerl, consultant for the Archives at the Viennese Court and State Archives was a constant support at the archives, as was Dr. Thomas Cernusak, an able and willing contact.

Apart from that, I would like to thank all those who provided personal talks, clues, information and explanations in working out the thematic complex of "Emperor Francis Joseph and his Court".

Professor Dr. Lothar Höbelt is acknowledged not only for many clues and interesting sources at the Czech Archives, but also for his patience in dealing with the many questions which arose, as well as requests for more precise details about the inner-political history of the era. In addition, thanks are also due to him for the scientific editing of my manuscript.

To Prof. Dr. Milan Hlavacka, Professor at the History Institute of the Czech Republic at the Charles University in Prague, a debt of thanks for tips and inspirations in my search for source materials which cover and newly illuminate the relations of Francis Joseph to former Emperor Ferdinand I. in Prague, a subject still not sufficiently clarified to this day. I also thank my highly estimable colleage Dr. Lubos Velik, Assistant at the Intitute for Czech History at the Charles University in Prague for permission to use his own research results on the Bohemian Settlement in this book.

Ms. Elfriede Iby, directress of the Scientific Department of the Schönbrunn Society, gave me valuable information on the living and residential situation of the court employees. Her colleague Mr. Michael Wohlfart helped in locating the old plans of Schönbrunn.

Wolfgang Beer made possible many insights into the plans of the court apartments and gave me valuable tips about the furnishings and appointments of these dwellings in the era of Emperor Francis Joseph.

The Director of the Military Museum of Vienna, Dr. Christian Ortner, made a valuable contribution to the better understanding of the position of the military personnel at court in Francis Joseph's era.

Dr. Karl Megner, specialist for the history of civil servants in the Austrian monarchy, not only made avaliable special research material to me, but even gave many special, thought provoking suggestions about dealing with the various individual positions of court officials in the overall complex.

Dr. Mario Döberl, expert in court matters and contributor to an FWF project researching the Imperial Office of the Stables under the direction of Dr. Monica Kurzel-Runtscheiner, directress of the Wagenburg at the Kunsthistorisches Museum, was a well versed and important contact, providing research materials and clarifying many uncertainties.

I was also able to solve certain problematic items through the help of Silvia Hölbl and Martin Kreutz, both of them well versed in the thematic complex of court and court society through their dissertations, with whom regular scholastic conversations and clarifying talks were of enormous help.

Mrs. Caroline Haug de Monchy provided a connection to several important private archives, for which I thank her.

Finally, I wish to thank all those who made it possible that the research results were not reserved solely for historians but also could be made accessible to a wider public: my publisher, Dr. Herbert Fleissner, and the publishing director Dr. Brigitte Sinhuber-Harenberg, who not only embraced the theme with warmth and enthusiasm, but also helped me to find the essential forum for these research materials on the history of the imperial monarchy.

Bibliography

State Archives in Austria

Haus-, Hof- und Staatarchiv Wien

- OMeA = Bestand Obersthofmeisteramt
- OKäA = Bestand Oberstkämmereramt
- OStA = Bestand Oberststallmeisteramt
- HWA = Bestand Hofwirtschaftsamt
- HÄL = Bestand Hofärarische Liquidationsakten

Wiener Stadt- und Landesbibliothek – Handschriftensammlung: Nachlass Heinrich Friedjung

- Friedjung, Interview Festetics = Wiener Stadtbibliothek/ Collection of hand-written documents, estate of Heinrich Friedjung – Interview with Gräfin Marie Festetics on 27. and 28. May 1909 in Campiglio
- Friedjung, Interview Fürstenberg = Wiener Stadtbibliothek/ Collection of hand-written documents, estate of Heinrich Friedjung – Handwritten summary of an interview with Therese Landgräfin Fürstenberg in February 1908

State Archives in Germany

- Geh.HA = Bayrisches Hauptstaatsarchiv, Abt. III – Secret private archives, estate of King König Ludwig I. 89/2/XII – correspondence of Archduchess Sophie

State Archives in the Czech Republic

NA Prag = Staatliches Nationalarchiv Prag

- FA Metternich = Familienarchiv Metternich, estate of Richard Metternich (Richardiana), correspondence
- Polizeidirektion Prag = secret correspondence/Kanzleischreiben K.14 Z.6/1872

ML Brünn = Mährisches Landesarchiv Brünn

- FA Liechtenstein Mährisch Krumau = Archives of Moravia Brünn, Family archives of Liechtenstein, estate of Rudolf Liechtenstein

SRA Leitmeritz, Tetschen = Staatliches Regionalarchiv Leitmeritz, Außenstelle Tetschen

- FA Thun = Family archives of Thun, estate of Jaroslav Thun, diary

Private archives

ÖFAFH Wien = Österreichisches Familienarchiv der Fürsten Hohenlohe-Schillingsfürst in Wien

- Estate of Konstantin Hohenlohe-Schillingsfürst, correspondence
- Estate of Gottfried Hohenlohe-Schillingsfürst, correspondence

- Estate of Marie Hohenlohe-Schillingsfürst, correspondence

GFAH Horn = Gräfliches Familienarchiv Hoyos in Horn

- Estate of Heinrich Hoyos, correspondence

FA Hiller = Familienarchiv Elisabeth Hiller

- Estate of Franz von Srbik, dictated memoirs

Printed Source Materials

Beust, Erinnerungen = Friedrich-Ferdinand Graf von Beust, Aus drei Viertel Jahrhunderten. Erinnerungen und Aufzeichnungen, Stuttgart 1887

Bittner, Archiv = L. Bittner, Inventare des Wiener Haus-, Hof und Staatsarchiv, V., Vienna 1937

Eulenburg, Erlebnisse = Eulenburg-Hertefeld Philip Fürst zu, Erlebnisse an deutschen und fremden Höfen, Band 2, Leipzig 1934

Fellner, Redlich = Fritz Fellner, Schicksalsjahre Österreichs 1908–1919. Das politische Tagebuch Josef Redlichs, Graz/Cologne 1953/1954

Hamann, Briefe = Brigitte Hamann, Meine liebe, gute Freundin. Die Briefe Kaiser Franz Josephs an Katharina Schratt; aus dem Besitz der Österreichischen Nationalbibliothek, Vienna 1992

Mayr, Tagebuch Kempen = Mayr, Josef Karl (Hg), Das Tagebuch des Polizeiministers Kempen von 1848–1859, Vienna 1931

Nostitz, Briefe = Nostitz-Rieneck Georg, Briefe Kaiser Franz Josephs an Kaiserin Elisabeth, 1859–1898, Band 1, Vienna 1966

Skedl, Nachlass = Skedl, Arthur, Der politische Nachlaß des Grafen Eduard Taaffe, Vienna 1922

Tornau, Tagebuch = F. F. Tornau, Ein Russe im k. u. k. Wien. Das Wiener Tagebuch des Barons F. F, Tornau (Hg: Gennadi E. Kagan), Vienna 2002

Hof- und Staats-Handbuch des Kaiserthumes Österreich für die Jahre 1847–1848, 1856–1860, 1866, 1868, 1874, 1876–1882, 1884–1916 (The years 1849–1852, 1855, 1861–1865, 1897, 1869–1873, 1875 were not published)

Literature

Bettelheim, Marie Hohenlohe = Bettelheim Anton, Marie Fürstin zu Hohenlohe-Schillingsfürst (= Neue Österreichische Biographie 1815–1918, Biographien, 4. Band), Vienna 1927

Böhmer, Faber = Peter Böhmer, Ronald Faber, Die Erben des Kaisers. Wem gehört das Habsburgvermögen, Vienna 2004

Corti-Sokol, Kaiser = Egon Ceasar Conte Corti, Hans Sokol, Der alte Kaiser, Vienna 1955

Eisenmenger, Erzherzog = Victor Eisenmenger, Erzherzog Franz Ferdinand. Seinem Andenken gewidmet von seinem Leibarzt, Vienna 1930

Fugger, Glanz = Fugger Fürstin Nora, Im Glanz der Kaiserzeit, 2. Auflage, Vienna 1980
Haslinger, Tafel = Ingrid Haslinger, Tafeln wie ein Kaiser. Franz Joseph und die kulinarische Welt des Wiener Hofes, Vienna 1999
Ketterl = Eugen Ketterl, Der alte Kaiser wie ihn nur einer sah. Der wahrheitsgetreue Bericht des Leibkammerdieners Kaiser Franz Joseph I., Vienna 1929
Kletecka, Kunstförderung = Thomas Kletecka, Staatliche Kunstförderung zu Beginn der franzisko-josephinischen Epoche. In: Jenseits und diesseits der Leitha. Elekronische Festschrift für Eva Somagyi zum 70. Geburtstag, Herausgeber: Imre Res-Szabo Daniel, Budapest 2007
Luedin, Leibgarden = Maja Luedin, Die Leibgarden am Wiener Hof, Phil. Diss., Vienna 1965
Megner, Beamte = Karl Megner, Beamte. Wirtschafts- und sozialgeschichtliche Aspekte des k. k. Beamtentums, 2. unveränderte Auflage, Vienna 1986
Redwitz, Hofchronik = Marie Redwitz, Hofchronik 1888–1921, Munich 1924
Rust Reichskanzler = Rust Hermann, Reichskanzler Fürst Clodwig zu Hohenlohe-Schillingsfürst und seine Brüder Herzog von Ratibor, Cardinal Hohenlohe und Prinz Konstantin Hohenlohe, Dusseldorf 1897
Sandgruber, Konsumverbrauch = Roman Sandgruber, Konsumgüterverbrauch, Lebensstandard und Alltagskultur im Österreich des 18. und 19. Jahrhunderts, Habil. Univ. Wien, Vienna 1980, S. 471–475
Silber, Montenuovo = Silber Margit, Obersthofmeister Fürst Alfred Montenuovo, phil. Diss, Wien 1991
Sokop = Brigitte Sokop, Jene Gräfin Larisch, Vienna 1985
Stekl, Aristokratie = Hannes Stekl, Österreichs Aristokratie im Vormärz. Herrschaftsstil und Lebensformen der Fürstenhäuser Liechtenstein und Schwarzenberg, Vienna 1973
Vasili, la Société = Comte Paul Vasili, La Société de Vienne. Augmenté de Lettre Inédites, Paris 1885
Velek, Staatsrecht = Lubos Velek, Böhmisches Staatsrecht auf „Weichem Papier“, In: Zeitschrift für Geschichte und Kultur der böhmischen Länder, Band 47, Heft 1, Munich 2006/2007
Winkelhofer, Hofbeamte = Martina Winkelhofer, Die obersten Hofbeamten unter Kaiser Franz Joseph, Dipl., Vienna 2005
Wölfling, Habsburger = Leopold Wölfling, Habsburger unter sich. Freimütige Aufzeichnungen eines ehemaligen Erzherzogs, Vienna 1921
Zolger = Ivan Zolger, Der Hofstaat des Hauses Oesterreich, Freiburg i. Br. 1917

Footnotes

I A Day in the Life of the Old Emperor

1 Ketterl, Der alte Kaiser, 24–25
2 GFAH Horn Fach 393 Karton 59 – NL Heinrich Hoyos, Aide-de-camp 1908–1916, correspondence, Ischl, 29. 6. 1908
3 Friedjung, Interview Festetics
4 Redwitz, Hofchronik, 79
5 GFAH Horn, correspondence, Ischl, 29. 6. 1908
6 Fugger, Kaiserzeit, 164
7 Zolger, Hofstaat, 91–104; and Luedin, Leibgarden, 69–70
8 Ketterl, Der alte Kaiser, 28
9 GFAH Horn, Fach 393, Karton 59 – NL Heinrich Hoyos, Korr. 26. 6. 1908
10 GFAH Horn, Fach 393, Karton 59 – NL Heinrich Hoyos, Korr. 26. 6. 1908
11 Haslinger, Tafeln, 33

II Taking the Reins: A Young Emperor at an Old Court

12 ÖFAFH Wien, NL Marie Hohenlohe, Karton III, Letter to Marietta Coudenhove, 29. 1. 1913 Friedstein
13 OMeA r121/6/1849
14 OMeA r121/6/1849
15 OMeA r1/16/1842
16 Friedjung, Interview Fürstenberg
17 OMeA r121/12/1849
18 OMeA r121/12/1849
19 OMeA r1/23/1849 and Cabinet Chancellery -Index a-l / 627 /849
20 OMeA r14/3/201851/1871
21 OMeA r121/12 ex 1849
22 Geh. HA Archduchess Sophie 21. 5. 1854
23 OMeA r121/12 ex 49
24 I thank Prof. Milan Hlavačka, Prof. of Bohemian history at the Charles University in Prague for the information.
25 Viennese City Library, letter Karl Graf Grünnes, 6.9.1849
26 Tornau, Tagebuch, 46
27 Winkelhofer, Hofbeamte, 29–31
28 OMeA r8/4/1849
29 OMeA SR 204 Status I 1850–1873/1867
30 OMeA r8/3/1849
31 OMeA SR 373/4

III The Structures at Court

32 See Hof- und Staats-Handbuch des Kaiserthumes Österreich für die Jahre 1847–1848, 1856–1860, 1866, 1868, 1874, 1876–1882, 1884–1916 (The years 1849–1852, 1855, 1861–1865, 1897, 1869–1873, 1875 were not published)
33 See HVZ des HHStA, Bittner and OMeA Rubrikenweiser im HHSTA
34 OMeA r1/15/1865 and r1/1851
35 OMeA SR 163/31
36 OMeA SR 163/54
37 HWA r23/1896
38 HWA r23/1896
39 OMeA Ah.Schreiben 11. 9. 1910 Z. 10815 1910
40 OMeA SR 163/60
41 OMeA SR 163/50
42 (RGBl 1895/113)
43 OMeA r14/7 1858

IV Life and Work at Court

44 OMeA r289/1/1851
45 Sandgruber, Konsumgüterverbrauch, 471–475
46 Neue freie Presse 1871, Nr. 155 vom 6. 6. 1871
47 Megner, Beamte, 154
48 OMeA r121/1839–1875
49 OMeA SR 163/31
50 OMeA SR 163/31
51 OMeA r289/1851
52 OMeA r1/10 1852
53 OMeA SR 163/47
54 Kabinettskanzei-Index a-l/1849/627
55 OMeA r18/1848
56 OMeA r41/1850
57 OMeA r342/1816
58 OMeA r3/4/1849
59 OMeA r121 and 14/1873
60 OMeA r271/1905
61 Information from Burghauptmann Hofrat DI Beer
62 OMeA r28/11 1861
63 OMeA r68/11 1848
64 OMeA r25/88 1850
65 OMeA SR 163 Nr. 28
66 OMeA r53 1853

67 OMeA r8/12 1898
68 OMeA r128/a/6 1853
69 OMeA SR 119

V **Court Society. Glamour and Representation**
70 Stekl, Aristokratie, 127–129
71 Zolger, Hofstaat, 143
72 Zolger, Hofstaat, 141
73 Zolger, Hofstaat, 141
74 Zolger, Hofstaat, 146–150
75 Zolger, Hofstaat, 144–145
76 Stekl, Adel und Bürgertum, 16 and Bruckmüller, Sozialgeschichte, 329
77 Kielmansegg, Kaiserhaus, 50
78 Kielmansegg, Kaiserhaus, 51
79 Kielmansegg, Kaiserhaus, 50
80 OMeA NL Hohenlohe Notiz Nr. 92 Jän 86 Franz Joseph to Konstantin Hohenlohe
81 OMeA NL Hohenlohe Notiz Nr. 95 Franz Joseph to Konstantin Hohenlohe Feb. 86
82 Fugger, Kaiserzeit, 94
83 Fugger, Kaiserzeit, 94–95
84 Fugger, Kaiserzeit, 96
85 OFAFH, Karton 3 Konstantin Hohenlohe I, Korr. Gottfried Hohenlohe, vom 25. 1. 1891, St. Petersburg
86 Fugger, Kaiserzeit, 183
87 Kielmansegg, Kaiserhaus, 26–27
88 Ceremonial protocols of the 1880s
89 Fugger, Kaiserzeit, 184
90 Information from Dr. Lubos Velik, Charles University, Prague, who found the same complaints in countless unpublished diaries by ball visitors.
91 OMeA NL Hohenlohe, Notiz vom 8. 3. 1888 Franz Joseph to Konstantin Hohenlohe
92 Fugger, Kaiserzeit, 77

VI **The Fateful Years: 1866/1867**
93 Vasili, la Société, 56–57
94 Bettelheim, Marie Hohenlohe, 58–76
95 OMeA r97/1 2427/1865
96 OMeA r121/14, 9/1866

97 Rust, Reichskanzler, 913–931
98 OMeA r121/7/1866 Ah. Schreiben vom 5. 8. 1866
99 OStA Karton 156 Zl 518/ex 1870, unfol.
100 OStA, B, Karton 144, Zl. 631/ex 1866, unfol.
101 OStA, B, Karton 144, Zl. 631/ex 1866, unfol.
102 OMeA r121/7 1866
103 Nostitz, letters, Franz Joseph to Elisabeth of 10. 8. 1866, Schönbrunn
104 OMeA r121/9/ 1866
105 OMeA r121/1/ 1867
106 OMeA r121/1 2586, 26321867
107 Bettelheim, Marie Hohenlohe, 75
108 Friedjung, Festetics Interview 27. and 28. 5. 1909
109 OMeA SR 398 vom 23. 8. 1883

VII The Golden Years

110 FA Hiller, Estate of Heinrich von Srbik, dictated memoirs
111 OMeA r121/1/1869
112 OMeA r25/ 1869
113 OMeA r121/1/c/1872
114 OMeA r121/1875
115 OMeA r121/1/1872
116 OMeA r25/1873 and OMeA r25/1874
117 OMeA r25/1875
118 Information from Dr. Mario Döberl. For details, see FWF Wagenburg project directed by Dr. Monika Kurzel-Runtscheiner. Notes on imperial kindergarten, also at OMeA SR 163 ad 1217
119 OMeA SR 163 Zahl 1536
120 OMeA r125/37/1887
121 OMeA SR 163
122 OMeA SR 163 Zahl 10.562
123 OMeA SR 163 Zahl 23 and OMeA SR 163 Ad 1217
124 OMeA SR 163
125 OMeA SR 163
126 HWA r76/18 96
127 Haslinger, Tafeln, 25
128 OMeA SR 163/28 Nr. 4912
129 OMeA SR 163 Zahl 23
130 GFAH, Fach 393 Karton 59 Estate Heinrich hoyos, aide-de-camp 1908–1916 to his wife, Schönbrunn 10. 7. 1909
131 OMeA r1/E/11 1881

VIII The Court Finances

132 Zolger, Hofstaat, 245
133 Bittner, Band V, 346
134 OMeA r2/1849–1866 and r 121/1866
135 Statistisches Zentralamt Umrechnungswert 1850–1860
1 Gulden = 15 Euro
136 OMeA r2/1849–1866
137 OMeA r2/13/1852
138 Zolger, Hofstaat 250–253
139 OMeA SR 163/54
140 Zolger, Hofstaat, 260–270
141 Böhmer, Faber, Habsburgvermögen, 22
142 Sokop, Larisch, 335
143 Böhmer, Faber, Habsburgvermögen, 11–16

IX Art and Culture at the Court

144 Kletecka, Kunstförderung 33–49
145 Winkelhofer, Hofbeamte, 33
146 Wiener Zeitung vom 25. 12. 1873
147 OKäA 1875/76, Heft 4, 546 ex 1876
148 OKäA 1875/76, Heft 4, 546 ex 1876
149 OMeA r19/A726/1905
150 Silber, Montenuovo, 107
151 Fremdenblatt vom 20. 5. 1911
152 OMeA r19/A/24/1898
153 OMeA r19/A/24/1898
154 Silber, Montenuovo, 171

X The 'Private Life' of the Imperial Family

155 Wölfling, Habsburger, 114
156 Wolfling, Habsburger, 121
157 Wölfling, Habsburger, 115
158 OMeA SR 398 Nachlass Hohenlohe Constantin,
Notiz vom 5. 1. 1870 an den Kaiser
159 Wölfling, Habsburger, 113
160 Wölfling, Habsburger, 155
161 ÖFAFH Wien, Karton 3 – Konstantin Hohenlohe I
Letter of Gottfried Hohenlohe from 27. 1. 1894, Vienna
162 ÖFAFH Vienna, Karton 3 – Konstantin Hohenlohe I
Letter of Gottfried Hohenlohe from 27. 1. 1894, Vienna

XI Scandals at Court

163 OMeA r1/17/1849 and r1/7/1852
164 OMeA SR 373/4
165 Dictated to Bohemia on 15. 9. 1871 (morning edition)
166 Velek, Staatsrecht, 103–118
167 Velek, Staatsrecht, 112
168 Velek, Staatsrecht, 116
169 NA Policejni reditelstvi v praze-tajne, K.14 Z.6/1872 vom 22. 2. 1872
170 Skedl, Estate, Confident Breitenfeld an Eduard Taaffe am 8. 11. 1886
171 Nostitz, Briefe, Franz Joseph vom 3. 2. 1894
172 Silber, Montenuovo, 400
173 Silber, Montenuovo, 525 Ministerium des k. u. k. Hauses, „Einzelne Abhandlungen" Karton 14, Referat Departement 1. bei Silber 525
174 Silber, 404–418
175 Silber, 419
176 Silber, Montenuovo 433 NL Aehrenthal, Karton 4, Franz Graf Thun an Alois Lexa von Aehrenthal vom 2. 2. 1903
177 Goldinger, Kielmansegg, 145

XII Politics and the Court

178 Kielmansegg, Kaiserhaus, 32
179 Mayr, Diary Kempen, 326, of 16. 4. 1854
180 Mayr, Diary Kempen, 380, of 1.12. 1855
181 Mayr, Diary Kempen, 364, of 15. 5. 1855
182 Kielmansegg, Kaiserhaus, 31
183 Kielmansegg, Kaiserhaus, 31
184 Wölfling, Habsburger, 159
185 Mayr, Diary Kempen, 404, of 11. 7. 1856
186 Mayr, Diary Kempen, 374, of 13. 10. 1855
187 Mayr, Diary Kempen, 374, of 18. 10. 1855
188 Beust, Erinnerungen, 325
189 NA Prag, FA Metternich (Richardiana), Karton 6 Correspondence, letter of Ferdinand Trauttmannstorff to Richard Metternich from 3.1.1878
190 Kielmansegg, Kaiserhaus, 32
191 Rust, Reichskanzler, 926
192 Rust, Reichskanzler, 928
193 Eulenburg, Erlebnisse, 231

XIII Crisis – The Times Change

194 ML Brünn, FA Liechtenstein Mährisch Kromau: G 409, Karton 16 +17 Estate Rudolf Liechtenstein
195 Friedjung, Festetics Interview 27. und 28. 5. 1909
196 Eulenburg, Erlebnisse 100, Tagebuchnotiz vom 14. 2. 1896
197 Wiener Zeitung vom 17. 2. 1896
198 Friedjung, Festetics Interview 27. und 28. 5. 1909
199 HWA 69 /1896
200 HWA 69 /1896
201 Silber, Montenuovo, 590
202 HWA 24 /86
203 OMeA r1/1/1893
204 HWA r76 /1896
205 Eisenmenger, Erzherzog, 147–148
206 Fugger, Kaiserzeit, 203–205
207 Silber, Montenuovo, 60
208 ÖFAFH Vienna, Karton 10 Gottfried Hohenlohe II, Correspondence Rudolf Liechtenstein, letter from 6.3.1903

XIV The Final Years

209 ÖFAFH Wien, Karton 10 Gottfried Hohenlohe II, Korrespondenz Rudolf Liechtenstein, letter of 23. 10. 1893
210 Corti-Sokol, Kaiser, 264, Rudolf Liechtenstein to Ida Ferenczy, Archiv Farkas/Felsöbabád, printed without date
211 Corti-Sokol, Kaiser, 264, Rudolf Liechtenstein an Ida Ferenczy, Archiv Farkas/Felsöbabád, printed without date
212 Hamann, Briefe, 453
213 Hamann, Briefe, 24. 2. 1899, Schönbrunn
214 Fugger, Kaiserzeit, 402
215 Corti-Sokol, Kaiser, 264, Rudolf Liechtenstein an Ida Ferenczy, Archiv Farkas/Felsöbabád, printed without date
216 OMeA r121/1898
217 Fugger, Kaiserzeit, 311
218 Silber, Montenuovo, 609, diary Marie Valerie of 29. 6. 1900
219 Silber, Montenuovo, 522, HHSTA Estate Schiessl, Konvolut 2, handwritten letter of Montenuovo to Schiessl from 26. 7. 1911
220 Silber, Montenuovo, 626, Vienna war archives, NL B/800/85, OMeA vom 16. 11. 1912
221 Eisenmenger, Erzherzog, 150
222 Silber, Montenuovo, 653, Estate Ferdinand, II, Faszikel 8a, Franz Ferdinand an Beck vom 8. 8. 1896
223 ÖFAFH Vienna, Karton Wien, Karton Marie Hohenlohe II, Brief an Marietta Coudenhove vom 15. 1. 1910, Friedstein

224 SRA Leitmeritz, Tetschen, FA Thun, diary of Jaroslav Thun, Entry from 11. 9. 1919
225 Fellner, Redlich, 444
226 Silber, Montenuovo, 772–801
227 SRA Leitmeritz, Tetschen, FA Thun, Tagebuch Jaroslav Thun, Entry from 3. 7. 1914
228 Arbeiterzeitung vom 5. 7. 1914
229 Ketterl, Der alte Kaiser, 173

XV **The End of the Imperial Court**
230 Bittner, archives, 368
231 HÄL, Karton 25, correspondence of 9. 8. 1921
232 HÄL, Karton 25, proclamation Oct. 1919
233 Bittner, archives, 369

Illustrations

Austrian National Library: pp. 211, 213
All other illustrations are from private collections.

Index

L

M

T

V

W

Z